BEHIND BROTHEL DOORS

BEHIND BROTHEL DOORS

The Business of Prostitution in Kansas,
Nebraska, and Oklahoma (1860–1940)

JAN MACKELL COLLINS

TWODOT®

ESSEX, CONNECTICUT
HELENA, MONTANA

A · TWODOT® · BOOK

An imprint of Globe Pequot, the trade division of
The Rowman & Littlefield Publishing Group, Inc.
4501 Forbes Blvd., Ste. 200
Lanham, MD 20706
www.rowman.com

Copyright © 2023 by Jan MacKell Collins

British Library Cataloguing in Publication Information available

Library of Congress Cataloging-in-Publication Data
Names: Collins, Jan MacKell, 1962– author.
Title: Behind brothel doors : the business of prostitution in Kansas, Nebraska, and Oklahoma
(1860–1940) / Jan MacKell Collins.
Description: Essex, Connecticut ; Helena, Montana : TwoDot, [2022] | Includes bibliographical
references and index.
Identifiers: LCCN 2022024963 (print) | LCCN 2022024964 (ebook) | ISBN 9781493066155
(paperback) | ISBN 9781493066162 (epub)
Subjects: LCSH: Prostitutes—Kansas—History. | Prostitution—Kansas—History. | Prostitutes—
Nebraska—History. | Prostitution—Nebraska—History. | Prostitutes—Oklahoma—History. |
Prostitution—Oklahoma—History. | Women—Great Plains—Social conditions.
Classification: LCC HQ117 .C58 2022 (print) | LCC HQ117 (ebook) | DDC
306.7420973—dc23
LC record available at https://lccn.loc.gov/2022024963
LC ebook record available at https://lccn.loc.gov/2022024964

Contents

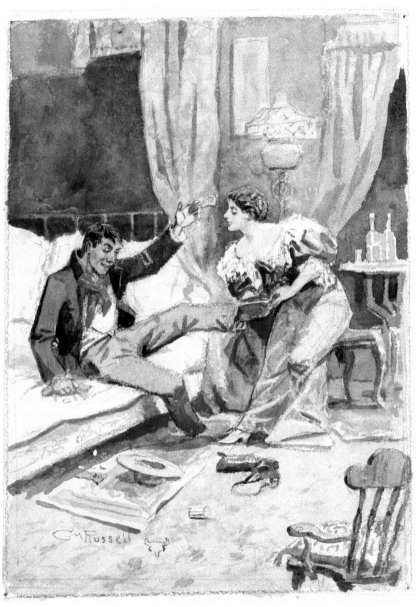

Charles M. Russell (1864–1926), *Just a Little Pleasure* ca. 1898. Transparent and opaque watercolor, and graphite on paper; 13½ x 10⅝ in. Amon Carter Museum of American Art, Fort Worth, Texas, Amon G. Carter Collection 1961.285.

ACKNOWLEDGMENTS

WHEN YOU WRITE ABOUT ONE SUBJECT FOR A LONG TIME, IT WILL INEV-
itably evolve into a big, pleasant mess of notes, documents, and books.
Tidbits of information get scribbled on your hand if paper isn't available,
or cocktail napkins or the backs of grocery receipts that all get filed one
day into a filing cabinet or your computer. Writing down who told you
what is a chore, but integral to recording how and where you found that
tiny piece of information. At this point, having written for many years
about the prostitution industry as it was known during the 1800s and
early 1900s, my library quite literally runneth over. But it is important to
me to recognize the many important people who have helped me along
and championed my efforts. That being said, I would like to thank those
who assisted me on this latest journey to document, explore, and explain
the illustrious history of prostitution in America, as well as the ladies who
made it so colorful.

Back in 2005, when I was working as the director of the Cripple
Creek District Museum in Colorado, amateur historian and researcher
Rod Cook happened into the gift shop for a visit. He told me about
Maggie Wood, a prominent madam of Kansas, and followed up by
sending me his booklet, *George and Maggie and the Red Light Saloon*. At
the time, I did not know if I would ever get around to writing about the
prostitution history of Kansas, but now that I have, Mr. Cook's book has
proved invaluable to discovering the workings of the industry in Caldwell
and other places. Thank you, Mr. Cook, for your insight and for documenting the life of Miss Maggie. Also in Colorado, I am indebted to the
Pikes Peak Library District in Colorado Springs, which I have worked
with for many years. Their extensive archives provided the final clues
to what became of Maggie Wood. Findagrave.com volunteer Pamela

Rasfield was very kind in assisting me in finding out what happened to Maggie and where she is buried, as well as members of her family.

In 2016, I was invited to give a presentation about prostitution along the Santa Fe Trail at Fort Larned National Historic Site in Kansas. While there, I was able to take an underground tour in nearby Ellinwood where brothels once flourished. I would like to thank the good people of Ellinwood who took me on the tour, as well as Chris McCord of the elegantly appointed Wolf Hotel for feeding me lots of interesting information about the town's early days. A nod also goes to George Elmore, chief ranger at Fort Larned, for pulling up important census information for me just minutes before I began my program.

Others who remain close to me regarding my writings include Professor Jay Moynahan, whose spirited research of wayward women throughout the west has resulted in quite a few collectible books on the subject. It seems there is always something, if only an interesting tidbit, in Jay's books and I am indebted to him for his support of my work. Likewise, my friend Terri Stierhoff is always buying my books for her family and friends, and constantly shares my history posts on social media. I want to thank Terri, as well as the hundreds of supporters I have online who cheer me up, cheer me on, and make me feel like the research I share is important. Cheers also to the many librarians and museum docents across the Great Plains whom I have reached out to in search of some bit of information I need. They have always come through.

On my home front, my sweet husband, Corey, has tirelessly put up with me researching and writing in our various homes for many years, and even in our motorhome as we travel around the west. Corey is well versed in what I go through while completing a book, and keeps a fine stock of wine on hand for me at the end of the day. On that note, I also want to give loving thanks to my in-laws, Freddie and Galynda Swoape, for allowing me to disappear for days at a time as I finished my manuscript while camping in their front yard.

Last, my thanks go to my publisher, Rowman & Littlefield, and those I have worked with there: Erin Turner, Kristin Mellitt, Alyssa Messenger, Alden Perkins, Jacqueline Plante, Lynn Zelem, and most of all Sarah Parke, who exhibits much patience with me and gives me room to make my manuscripts the best they can be.

INTRODUCTION

THIS TOME BEGINS BY STATING AN IMPORTANT FACT: WESTERN HISTORY has often glossed over the subject of historical prostitution. Only a prized few writers got it right when it came to recognizing the world's oldest profession for what it was, and why women participated in it. "They are not much better understood today than a hundred years ago," noted author Elliott West, and he was correct. West actually made that statement about how the business of prostitution "can be understood only as part of western life" just over forty years ago.[1] This was in the wake of writers who preferred to poke fun at prostitutes instead of exploring why the prostitution industry was an important facet of American history. A case in point is the title of Cy Martin's *Whiskey and Wild Women: An Amusing Account of the Saloons and Bawds of the Old West*. What was so "amusing" about women selling their bodies as about the only way to make as much money as men in the old west? Other writers have better remembered soiled doves of the past. Ronald Dean Miller's *Shady Ladies of the West*, for instance, gives specific details on the lives of western madams including Mattie Silks—the famed Denver madam who got her start in Abilene, Kansas. Unlike other historians of his time, Miller successfully illustrated how the prostitution industry heavily influenced the development of the west.

Working in the sex trade was not easy by any means, although it could be lucrative. One time, in Oklahoma, three school teachers in a rural part of the state were shocked to learn that prostitutes made as much in one evening of work as they made in one month, and decided to switch jobs. But women who chose this line of profession were plagued by a host of difficult and delicate emotional, financial, and health issues. In public, they were often an unwelcome sight at the shops, restaurants,

theaters, and churches they yearned to visit. At risk were their relation-
ships with their families, who often shunned them and even refused to
claim their bodies if they died. They were in constant danger of violence
by their customers, madams, and pimps, contracting venereal illnesses,
pregnancy, and addiction to alcohol or drugs. But compared to the
drudgery of becoming a housewife, bearing and raising children, and
never having their own money or freedom, prostitution was a viable way
to maintain independence while making money, possibly lots of it.

As much as they made good money, the ladies also had expenses in
the way of pricey clothing, toiletries, birth control, medicine, rent to landlords or madams, business licenses, monthly fees and fines, and, if they
owned their own property, exorbitant property taxes. One of the worst
maladies that could befall a prostitute was pregnancy, which would put
her out of work for a time and leave her with an infant to care for. When
Congress passed the Comstock Act in 1873, an "Act of the Suppression of Trade in, and Circulation of, Obscene Literature and Articles of
Immoral Use," information about contraception and abortion was made
illegal. While women could still access information about such things via
a friend, neighbor, or other means, the subject remained largely forbidden
and the information unreliable. Few frontier doctors were skilled, willing,
or even allowed by law to perform abortions. Within the red-light district
might be a woman who knew how to perform abortions, but such an
operation came with great risk of infection or a botched procedure that
could result in dire injury or death. Such back-alley "grannies" were only
sometimes held responsible if their patients died. By 1900 the procedure
was a felony in every state.

The caste system of prostitution was often a difficult ladder to climb.
Many women chose prostitution after fleeing their homes due to abuse,
the loss of a husband, or a desire to begin their lives anew on their own
terms. Those who did not have enough money to remain independent
out in the world often began their careers as dance hall girls or crib girls
who worked above or behind a saloon, or in small one- or two-room
apartments. Only by saving their money or finding a wealthy paramour
in their circles could these young ladies move forward and eventually find
work in a brothel. That, however, often required such important skills as

Birth Control Methods of the Wild West

- condoms (which were exceedingly rare)
- diaphragms (made with aluminum buttons, globs of Vaseline, half an orange hollowed out, or large coins or sponges with a thread tied to them)
- douching (sometimes with a "weak solution of white vitriol")
- the "French Passaire" (a cervical cap)
- spermicide (made with alum, rainwater, sulphate of iron or zinc, and applied to the sponge, if one was available)
- withdrawal[2]

knowing how to dance, how to play cards, and how to engage in eloquent conversation. In the higher end houses, the ladies needed additional skills such as singing or playing an instrument or reciting poetry, and knowing enough about the business matters at hand to carry on a lucid discussion with their customers. Only the very lucky ladies were able to open their own fashionable parlor houses where, as madams, they could choose whether or not to sleep with men for money. Some madams became wealthy enough to purchase more than one house, and either hire other madams to run them, or rent to other women for a cut of their profits.

The Great Plains states of Kansas, Nebraska, and Oklahoma have some of the most interesting histories of women in the sex trade. All three states were the scene of numerous trails going west, from the Santa Fe and various cattle trails crossing Kansas to the Overland and Oregon trails through Nebraska, to the cattle trails and one of the earliest trails, the California Road, which traversed across Oklahoma during the California Gold Rush of 1848. Wayward women would eventually utilize these early roads as a means of reaching the far-away west and making money. It was a time when prostitution was more acceptable to the men who outnumbered women in these primitive places. Later, during the Victorian era when more women came west, the presence of prostitution was recognized as a "necessary evil." University scholar Anna Marie Munns submits that this attitude "was based on the notion that the sexual needs of men could not be controlled, and prostitution helped mitigate any issues that would arise from men's repressed sexuality."[3]

Compared to the early mining camps of the west proper, the prostitution era in the Great Plains really didn't take hold until about 1867 when cattle drives began winding their way through Kansas and Nebraska. From May to September each year, towns sometimes quadrupled in population as cowboys brought sizable herds of cattle to these places to ship them off to larger cities. Like the cowboys, shady ladies were predominantly transient in nature. Some of them had outstayed their welcome in eastern cities and were in need of a fresh start, while others were working their way further west to a new frontier. For these reasons, many prostitutes working in the Great Plains tended to stay on the move, taking cool advantage of the thousands of cowboys riding through during the summer months and sometimes working out of mobile "cat wagons." Come fall, the women moved on to whatever profitable winter quarters they could find.[4]

By the 1870s, when much of the Great Plains and the west were being settled proper, a healthy handful of harlots were putting roots down in the larger cities. But respectable women were mostly against the saloons, gambling houses, and harlots who not only took their husband's earnings but also introduced dangerous social diseases. In one instance in 1872, four angry wives attacked a wayward woman known as Mrs. Neiswender who lived outside of Topeka, Kansas. Believing that their husbands "were led into devious ways through her attraction," the women "tarred, feathered, turpentined, and red peppered" Mrs. Neiswender. In reporting the brutal attack, the *Wichita City Eagle* gave a little editorial, leading to speculation that the paper thought Mrs. Neiswender got what she deserved.[5] Some twenty years later, attitudes were more sympathetic toward prostitutes. In December of 1893, the *Pond Creek Tribune* in Oklahoma announced that a police matron of Topeka, Mrs. Thorpe, had invited at least twenty prostitutes to a home-cooked Thanksgiving dinner so they would "have something to be thankful for." Commissioner Yount commented that "This dinner will do more good than a great many prayers."[6]

Even Nebraska's Josie Washburn, who worked as both a prostitute and madam during her career, claimed that the women she knew came from all walks of life, also that their parents were to blame for the red-light road they chose. Josie submitted that had parents "known that a certain condition existed at a certain time," with their daughters, they would have worked to change it. Instead, she lectured, it was the parents' duty "to make themselves familiar with the conditions which make the downfall of their daughters a possibility." In other words, education about the red-light life was key to keeping young teens safe from it. But as cities began grappling with the "social evil," Josie wisely concluded that prostitution would never "be overcome or abolished" but, instead, should "be tolerated, and possibly regulated." Wherever there was someone willing to buy sex, there surely would be someone willing to provide it. Clearly, Josie recognized the hypocrisy in government vs. the prostitution industry: the fines gained by municipal courts from fallen women were liberally distributed among the churches and schools, the same institutions who condemned prostitution and did little to help women working as prostitutes. And although men were free to "propose, suggest, hire and tempt the women in all ways," they were rarely held accountable for the damage inflicted on the fairer sex.[7]

Not surprisingly, the men who occupied chairs on various city councils, the police department, and the courts also did little to assist the very women who fed their city coffers, all while degrading prostitutes to a great degree. Enter the Woman's Christian Temperance Union (WCTU), founded in Ohio in 1874 to champion women's causes as well as other issues of the day. Not until 1879, however, was founding president Annie Wittenmyer challenged by another WCTU leader, Frances Willard, to approach the issues generated by men imbibing in alcohol. Willard successfully took over as president and began leading temperance movements all over the country that also focused on closing down houses of prostitution. Many cities simply raised the fines and fees already in place, with good results. In just over a year during 1884–1885, Dodge City took in $1,675 in fines from its red-light ladies, some of whom hardly made enough money to pay them.

Monetary Matters

Average prostitute's income, late 1800s:

- saloon and crib girls: $0.25 to $1 per customer
- common brothel girls: $2 per customer or $15 for overnight stays
- parlor house girls: $15 per customer or $35 for overnight stays

Average prostitute's expenses, late 1800s:

- fee to crib landlords: $18 per week
- fee to common brothels: $5 to $15 per day
- fee to madams: half of their income, plus evening wear and toiletries charged to the madam's account.[8]

Especially after Frances Willard's death in 1898, the WCTU began focusing almost exclusively on prohibition of alcohol. Prostitution remained a secondary focus as one of the accompanying evils. But it would be over ten years before legislators would finally pass the first official "Red Light Abatement" law in 1909, parts of which were eventually copied over to the law books of Nebraska in 1911. Still, brothels continued to flourish in the Great Plains states. They ranged from fine parlor houses "equipped with expensive furniture and furnishings including the finest of upholstered chairs, well-done paintings and costly rugs, while others were hovels of repulsive squalor."[9]

The fight against prostitution continued well into the twentieth century as various cities did what they could to abolish the industry. In Ellinwood, Kansas, during the 1920s, some of the underground tunnels harboring illegal businesses were filled in as the city paved their streets with brick. The effort was sometimes an exercise in futility; when the upscale Wolf Hotel was built during the 1920s, another tunnel system appeared beneath it. Other underground businesses, meanwhile, closed in the 1930s when coal, which was kept in the basements, was replaced by natural gas.[10] In larger cities like North Platte, Nebraska, the Prohibition

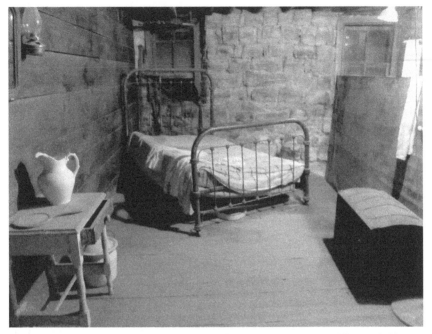

An underground brothel has been recreated in the tunnels below Ellinwood, Kansas. AUTHOR'S PHOTO

era only served as a means for underworld leaders to quietly gain control of the illegal liquor, gambling, and prostitution business anyway. Albert Hastings, who gained much notoriety for "his control of the North Platte underworld," was able to manage such illicit businesses for nearly twenty years.[11]

Like Kansas and Nebraska, Oklahoma also saw its share of underground tunnels where women of the night remained in business as late as the 1940s. The famed "Tulsa tunnels" where prostitutes could be found are still well known in Oklahoma City, and at least one tunnel was connected to a bar in Guthrie. There were likely many more. When illegal prostitution as it was known in the old west finally ceased in the 1950s or so, much of its history was lost as those who knew about it moved away, died, or declined to talk about it much. One exception was Adriana Deerhoff, whose father built what is known as the Dick Building in Ellinwood in 1887. Tunnels underneath the structure included saloons and barbershops but also a working girl or two. Adriana remembered her father telling her firmly, "Good girls aren't allowed underground in Ellinwood." In an effort to save the tunnels under the city that were being destroyed by revitalization efforts in 1970, Adriana successfully nominated the Dick Building to the National Register of Historic Places. Meanwhile, the tunnels under the Wolf Hotel were home to Ellinwood's public library for a time, and today's tours include the quaint and cozy Underground Saloon, which keeps the memories of the city's shady past alive.[12]

In 2016, the Society for Historical Archaeology's annual conference in Washington, DC, included several seminars regarding "historical and archaeological research on brothels, saloons, and prostitution," which "has helped to create a more inclusive view of past societies."[13] The sessions sought to further recognize the contributions of the prostitution industry to the growth of America and the west, as well as to broaden the scope of people in the industry, including male brothel owners and the women who worked for them. At last, worthy scholars are taking time to locate, assess, and dig around sites of prominent red-light districts and brothels as a means to better understand the prostitution industry of the past. Hand in hand with such efforts are the historians who research, document, and interpret the lives of the bawdy women who lived, worked, and died in the west as well as the Great Plains. And that is what this book is all about.

CHAPTER ONE

Concubines of Kansas

THEY SAY THAT THE TERM FOR A NEIGHBORHOOD OF PROSTITUTES, THE "red light district," originated in Kansas when railroad men left their red lanterns sitting on the porch of their favorite shady ladies while they did business inside. Whether or not that is true remains up for debate, but the prostitution industry was thriving long before the Union Pacific Railroad completed a border-to-border line of tracks across the state in 1867. Kansas's earliest prostitution actually dates to the early 1850s when the Santa Fe Trail snaked through the territory, bringing settlers to the raw west. Several outposts along the trail were available to the weary traveler, and often offered women whose favors could be purchased. In 1853, Santa Fe Trail traveler James Mead noted that "every trading or hunting establishment was called a ranch," and that such places offered a variety of merchandise in addition to fresh water, whiskey, and women.[1] Fellow traveler Robert Peck explained that such places were almost always surrounded by walls or other barriers to protect against Native attacks. In these remote places, working girls were most likely allowed to operate within the confines of the ranch as a means of protection. After all, the ranchers no doubt profited from a percentage of the money their girls made.

One notable "outpost," located forty miles west of Ellinwood, was Camp Alert, which was originally established along the Santa Fe Trail in 1859 at the mouth of the Pawnee fork of the Arkansas River. A short time later, the fort was moved three miles west. Left behind was a small encampment referred to as Pawnee. Prostitution was of course strictly forbidden at the new Fort Larned, but that did not keep some prostitutes from setting up housekeeping at Pawnee. The 1875 state census reveals four prostitutes living there. They were identified as Mrs. Sanford and her ten-year-old daughter Lydia, Elizabeth Norton, Georgie O'Dell, and Jennie Butler. All four women shared the same house and employed a servant, Mary Morris. Next door was a house occupied by two other servants, Sophia Vance and Jasper Colfak. It is just a guess, but a likely one, that Sophia and Jasper worked for the women next door. The women's ages ranged from twenty-four to thirty-five years, the latter being Mrs. Sanford's age. Because she is listed first, Mrs. Sanford likely served as the madam of the bunch.

The Santa Fe and other trails went hand in hand with the birth of the cattle trade in Kansas. Annual drives and round-ups were prevalent by the late 1850s, and although the Civil War temporarily interrupted the cattle industry, more and more cowboys began bringing stock into the state from Texas and other places. The early towns and cattle camps of Kansas were primarily populated by cowboys in numbers two or three times more than single women. The men worked hard, sometimes toiling for upwards of eighteen hours in a single day and making around $30 a month. The idea of occasionally having a drink of hard liquor, eating a real meal, and cavorting with a shady lady must have appealed greatly to them. But prostitutes tended to move around often, generally arriving in cattle shipping towns during April and May, conducting business all summer, and slowly vacating for greener pastures beginning in late September.

In 1867, Abilene (established in 1856) became the first of Kansas's cattle towns. In April that year, the Union Pacific began operations as ranchers and cowboys prepared to bring cattle in for shipping. Within a year, numerous shady ladies had made their way to town in anticipation of the hundreds of young cowboys that would soon be coming through. In July, Topeka's fledgling newspaper, the *Commonwealth*, noted that "Hell is now in session in Abilene." The paper was referring to the saloons and brothels that provided entertainment around the clock.[2] In 1869, a newspaper from another town claimed Abilene had three brothels and twenty-one prostitutes.

The city of Abilene, in anticipation of the influx of wanton women, began working on its first ordinances against prostitution in 1870. The laws were put into place shortly after the first dance house opened in 1871. Among the new madams was young Mattie Silks, who opened her first high-class brothel. Mattie called her fine, two-story yellow place the Gulf House and served only champagne, as well as ten beautiful young ladies. Notably, the well-known marshal, James B. "Wild Bill" Hickok, once fought with Phil Coe of the Bull's Head Saloon over Jessie Hazel, who worked for Mattie. The men settled their differences by gunfight, with Hickok the victor. That, along with a fatal shoot-out between prostitutes Louisville Lou and Jenny Lyons, drew the line for respectable citizens who successfully petitioned authorities to forcibly move the red-light district. As for Mattie, she eventually moved on to Denver, Colorado, where she reigned over the red-light realm for several decades.

During the spring of 1871, more soiled doves than ever flocked into Abilene in time for the cattlemen pouring into town from Texas to buy, sell, and trade their stock. While the city certainly appreciated the extra business the prostitution industry brought, the respectable women in town were subject to seeing "the garbed whores who paraded Texas Street, often in tipsy condition" who crossed their paths and sometimes hurled insults at them.[3] In short order, the *Abilene Chronicle* reported that one hundred proper women had signed a petition against the red-light district. Officials were initially apathetic. It was over a month before the city council finally voted to begin taxing prostitutes and gamblers, forming a segregated red-light district at the edge of town, and hiring two police officers to keep a handle on things. In addition, the city passed additional new ordinances prohibiting prostitutes from entering saloons. They also began requiring $100 license fees of the said saloons, which eventually increased to $500.

Not all of the city council could agree on the ordinances. Councilman S. A. Burroughs, for instance, was less than happy with the proceedings and marched off in a huff during the ordinance meeting. But his resignation meant the council had no quorum. He was physically brought back to the city chambers by Marshal Hickok. Burroughs ran off again and was once more wrangled by Hickok, who "carried Burroughs in on his shoulder and stood guard while the council transacted further business." But Mayor Joseph McCoy really took things too far when he commissioned a drawing of the incident and distributed it as far as he could. Some anonymous person lashed back by revealing in the *Topeka Commonwealth* newspaper that McCoy had recently been spied "with two harlots at once on his lap, one on each knee."[4] McCoy clearly wanted to make things as easy as he could for the harlots of his city, including arranging for them to be able to pay their fines annually at the courthouse. Doing so also saved the city money in the way of officers no longer being required to search for the women and extract their fines from them. In spite of the proceedings, the ladies of the town already had their routine set in place as the first cattle were being herded through Abilene. One settler noted that "each spring, coming most commonly from the cities of the Middle Border, gamblers, frequently accompanied by harlots, commenced their annual pilgrimage to bring tarnished glamor [*sic*] and manipulated excitement to the nondescript centers of the Plains."[5] Another, Theophilus Little, remembered that of the soiled doves flocking into Abilene, "I do believe there were hundreds of them."[6]

The influx of prostitutes went unnoticed by few, given how many folks commented on them in Abilene. When the first cowboys brought their cattle to town, they found "scores of poor fallen women—if not hundreds. The streets were lined and crowded with saloons, gambling houses and dives and vile holes of hell."[7] The city's first red-light district flourished north of town until Mayor McCoy, in an effort to keep the peace, made everybody move east of town but just inside the city limits. "McCoy's Addition," as it was first called, was soon known as Devil's Half Acre.[8] Eventually the city council leased forty acres on the south side railroad tracks running through town, specifically for the red-light district. The vast majority of the girls were urged to move there, while the respectable townsfolk kept to the north side.

At some point, a wall was built around the red-light district, which was home to about 111 women. The local madams were responsible for keeping their employees within its confines except when they went shopping in town. Abilene's tenderloin district was a raucous, lively place. Theophilus Little remembered seeing "beer gardens, dance halls, and dancing platforms and saloons galore there."[9] Of course, everybody north of the tracks knew about the red-light district, with hack drivers willingly taking passengers there day and night. At its height, Abilene's brothels numbered around thirty, each featuring between ten and twenty rooms where an amazing 200 to 300 girls worked in shifts so as to be able to serve clients twenty-four hours a day, seven days a week. Competition was fierce, with saloons offering their own "bar girls" and fancily dressed women who openly solicited from doors and windows.[10] Higher class saloons like The Alamo offered upward of 4,800 square feet in which to drink and gamble, with a connecting boardwalk out back leading to the closest bordello.

Abilene's days of rowdy cowboys and strumpets were relatively short. Mayor McCoy moved on to Wichita in 1872. In the wake of his departure, the city council immediately voted in more stringent liquor license fees and stiff fines against prostitution. The ladies began a mass exodus. The Farmer's Protective Association in nearby Dickinson County made their opinion on the matter clear by openly stating that cattlemen should stop coming to Abilene to sell their stock, because "inhabitants of Dickinson will no longer submit to the evils of the trade."[11] But the cattle trade was dying down anyway, and Abilene's city coffers floundered terribly with some 80 percent of the businesses in town shutting down due to a marked loss of income. The city tried, unsuccessfully, to lure the saloons and shady ladies back. But Abilene eventually lost its cattle trade to the railroad altogether when the shipping terminus was moved far south of the town and many businesses moved on to Ellsworth.

Ellsworth happily took over where Abilene left off. Although that town also would lose out on the cattle trade due to being bypassed by the rails, it did enjoy a short-lived time as a red-light center of Kansas. By 1869, there was at least one dance house/brothel. More wicked women came as the Kansas Pacific Railroad continued building west toward Ellsworth. Within a year, things were as crazy in Ellsworth as they had been in Abilene. One paper reported that "Thursday night last a terrible shooting affair occurred at a dance house in Ellsworth. Two men named Reed and Gardner and a female named Fanny Collins were killed, and another female named Nettie Baldwin, was shot through the stomach and breast, and the latest account was that she could not live."[12]

Ellsworth's town hall also would come up with laws against prostitution in 1871, but the citizens were far from prepared when the soiled doves from Abilene began flying in by the dozens the following year. The women's antics were amusing at first; one article in the *Ellsworth Reporter* told of a drunken prostitute being taken to jail by the marshal and his assistant. The officer "insisted on her walking and she insisted on being carried," the paper said. "As is always the way the woman came out victorious."[13] In another instance, a local soiled dove made good on a bet that she wouldn't walk down Ellsworth's main drag wearing nothing but a smile. She did, however, carry a pistol in each hand, and her "reputation for marksmanship was such that none of the men present dared to look her way."[14]

One memorable madam of Ellsworth was Lizzie Palmer, whose marriage was less than ideal. After her husband set fire to her brothel, Lizzie wrote him a most eloquent poem:

Take Me Back Home Again

Take me back home again, take me back home,
Hopeless and helpless, in sorrow I roam;
Gone are the roses that gladdened my life,
I must toil on in the wearisome strife.
Once I was happy and friends were my lot,
Now I'm a wand'rer, despised and forgot!
Lonely and weary, in sorrow I roam,
Take me back home again, take me back home.
George, dear George, so gentle and mild,
Look once again on thy pitiful child!
Since we were parted I never have known
Love and affection so pure as thine own!
Days of my childhood, I dream of you now,
While in my sorrow and anguish I bow!
No one to love me 'neath yon starry dome,
Take me back home again, take me back home.
Oh, could I live but the days that are flown,
Dearest and sweetest that ever were known,

Fondly I weep in my desolate pain,
Longing to be with my George again!
Weary, so weary, my heart yearns for rest,
Poor wounded bird that is robbed of its nest!
Child of affliction! dear George, I come,
Take me back home again, take me back home
Take me back home again, take me back home.

Lizzie's heart-felt poem was for naught. The day she presented it to her husband, he burned up her new house, too. Later, he was found murdered.[15]

By the autumn of 1873, the prostitutes of Ellsworth were receiving word that the cattle industry as they knew it would soon end. Little by little the ladies moved on. One of them, Kittie Snow, was on her way back to her home state of New York but fell ill and died at Iowa Point, just over 200 miles into her trip. The *Ellsworth Reporter* remembered her kindly, noting that Kittie "belonged to the demimonde, but was once an intelligent, accomplished lady."[16] Once the cattle trade officially ended in Ellsworth in 1874, the harlots of the town drifted off and, one by one, were forgotten.

Another town to spring up in 1867 was Hays. Elizabeth Custer, when she visited Hays in its infancy, recalled that "there was hardly a building worthy of the name, except the station house." The nicer structures were built of wood frame and canvas, but the "shanties" were constructed out of whatever the builder could find. Some of the roofs were made from flattened fruit and vegetable cans.[17] Hays, however crude, was soon attracting saloon and dance hall owners. When Josephine Middlekauf moved there as a child with her family, she recalled seeing no less than seven saloons, some with gambling parlors and dance halls, situated along the old main drag east of Chestnut Street. Catherine Cavender would also remember the wild side of Hays when she arrived ten years later. Catherine said that the saloons and dance halls were mixed among more respectable businesses along the north side of the "one wide street about a block in length," with the Union Pacific Railroad tracks running down the middle. Catherine's party had literally just arrived in town and were standing on the platform of the depot when a shot rang out on the north side of the street. "A woman in a low-neck, short-skirted dress rushed screaming through the swinging door of a saloon," she said, and "a man rushed out after her firing his pistol at her feet." The woman ran down the crooked boardwalk and into Mrs. Bay's dressmaking parlors, after which her assailant hopped on his horse and rode out of town, firing his six-guns and "whooping in glee." A railroad employee explained to Catherine's group that a drunk cowboy was just having fun, "shooting at the sidewalk to see her run."[18]

The town of Ellinwood was unique among Kansas's cattle towns in that its illicit nightlife was kept underground, quite literally. Founded in 1870, Ellinwood's first citizens were of German descent whose architectural styles emulated those in far-off Bavaria—including tunnels and basements under the streets. The tunnels originally ran on both sides of Main Street for two blocks, connecting legitimate businesses with each other. They were accessed by outside corner staircases. The passageways were well thought out, with windows for ventilation but also the town's wells. The ambient temperature underground kept the water from freezing during winter.

By the late 1880s, upward of eleven underground saloons, brothels, boot- and hat-makers, and other businesses were accessible to the cowboys who came through Ellinwood. The town appreciated the extra money, and respectable citizens liked the decreased risk of running into prostitutes or their patrons—although respectable women and their families were sometimes forced underground when tornados threatened the town. Customers in the tunnels could pop into Jung's Barber Shop where they could get their laundry done, or take a warm bath for just $0.15. Jung also was said to offer additional services in the way of prostitutes right up to when he retired in 1929. Other businesses of the Ellinwood tunnels included pool halls, barber shops, and even a bowling alley. But it was the bathhouse and brothels that brought the most men underground. A few saloons flourished among the respectable businesses along above-ground Ellinwood's streets too, some with brothels behind or underneath them. A fellow could enter the Wolitz Shoe Shop, John Wever's Sample Room, Petz Meat Storage, and Drummer's Sample

Room with seemingly respectful intent, only to access the tunnels from these places. During the 1930s, some of Ellinwood's underground businesses closed when coal, which was kept in the basements, ceased being used. The tunnels faded into history for several decades, but most of the surviving passageways are now open for tours

Although the state of Kansas outlawed all saloons beginning in 1880, a few remote outposts remained where a man could have a drink and female companionship. One of these was Coolidge, which was first called Sargent in 1877 before the name was changed in 1881. By 1884, Coolidge was known as being located in "No Man's Land," a large strip of land along the old Santa Fe Trail and the newer Atchison, Topeka, and Santa Fe Railroad. "No Man's Land" was the result of establishing territorial boundaries in 1854, which left a section of public land that would not be claimed until 1890.[19] Coolidge also happened to be located along the National Cattle Trail, which was widely used beginning in 1884 and 1885 when Kansas forbade tick-infested cattle from being herded across the state from Texas. Enter Trail City, which was located in Colorado, just across the border from Kansas and only a few miles from Coolidge. Trail City quickly became popular among outlaws and prostitutes, since one could enter the front door of a business in Colorado and exit from the back door literally within a few feet of the Kansas state line. On its wildest nights, horse races conducted from Trail City to Coolidge and back consisted of drunken cowboys with nude prostitutes riding on the backs of their horses.

The antics at Coolidge aside, some Kansas towns were notorious for violence in their red-light districts. At the mining town of Galena in 1897, a string of grisly murders were discovered which were so ghastly that they made the news for quite some time. Galena was established in the 1870s after travelers passing through spotted some sizeable chunks of lead lying around, which were mighty useful for making shot for pistols and rifles. Upward of 300 mines were established for extracting galena, the mineral lead is made from, and a town of the same name was in place by the early 1880s. Some thirty thousand miners called Galena home, and they were naturally treated to entertainment in the way of gambling halls, saloons, and brothels. An article in the *Galena Sentinel* later recalled how the main street through town was nicknamed "Red Hot Street" for all of the vice and violent mayhem that took place there.

In Galena, Nancy "Ma" Staffleback's brothel was the most notorious. The place was known far and wide as a drunken den of debauchery where only the very brave dared visit. In 1897, one of Nancy's girls, Lela Ann MacCombs, came to the police with a most riveting story. According to her, the body of Frank Galbraith, which had only recently been discovered floating in an abandoned mine shaft, was a victim of murder at the Staffleback house. It was ultimately revealed that Nancy and her husband, Charles Wilson, as well as Nancy's sons, George, Mike, and Ed Staffleback, schemed to rob and kill customers at her palace of pleasure. Galbraith was not their only victim, apparently, as other killings also were reported. In one story, Mike returned to the house and "found his girl sitting on another man's lap," according to the *Kansas Farmer and Mail and Breeze*.[20] The brute beat the girl to death with a six-shooter and killed another girl to keep her from telling anyone. Both bodies were hidden under a bed for the night before being dumped in a mine shaft. The *Wichita Beacon* also claimed that Mike Staffleback killed the man as well.

The authorities might not have known anything about the murders at the Staffleback house if not for Lela, who was told she would be killed if she said anything. But when George's wife, Cora, argued with Nancy and was thrown out of the house, Lela left, too. Cora corroborated Lela's story, as well as another prostitute named Rosa Hayne. All three ladies also verified that the Stafflebacks had killed "an old soldier" prior to their arrival in Galena, also that they killed and robbed a peddler before dumping his body into a mine shaft as well.[21] More of Nancy's girls were found to have been involved in Galbraith's murder (mostly luring him to the house), but they were never charged. Nancy and her sons were sent to prison, and it was guessed that together, the family had committed many more murders than anyone knew.

In 1911, the Kansas Council of Women was founded to assist the welfare of the public. Their work included "improvement of women in education and work," which included rehabilitating prostitutes.[22] The KCW, as the group was known, quickly evolved into a temperance union of sorts. But their main goal was that of eradicating not just promiscuity, but also venereal diseases that had wracked the state for decades.

Reasons for Prostitution in Kansas, 1911

(Based on answers given by 525 prostitutes interviewed)
Death of or desertion by husband: 87
Deceived or seduced: 72
Driven by drinking and drugging: 91
Economic need: 70
Forced into white slavery: 59
Influenced by "bad friends": 42
Seeking "easy money": 90
Supporting husband: 10[23]

In the end, it was the military which finally put a stop to prostitution during the first stages of World War I in 1916. Social diseases had long run rampant among soldiers, and military officers, so it was decided that the best way to battle these types of illnesses was to "temporarily 'confine' women considered lewd and lascivious" in order to prevent them from spreading sexually transmitted illnesses.[24]

Next, Kansas authorities tried forcing "reproductive sterilizations on those they felt could not be cured of their immoral behavior," a move that is now of course viewed as antiquated thinking and terribly wrong besides. Only "Lillian," an inmate of the Kansas State Industrial Farm for Women, was able to point out how social evils and social disease went hand in hand. In 1925, Lillian was accused of violating Chapter 205—Kansas's law against "lewd and lascivious behavior." She had been sentenced to hard labor at the Farm for the violation. But Lillian's letter explained very clearly what happened to her: "My husband gave me this disease and when I found it out I 'beat upon him' and I was then arrested for disturbing the peace," she explained.[25] Lillian's husband had likely contracted his illness from a prostitute, who likely got it from a male customer. Lillian's statement was a perfect illustration of an ugly cycle. By then, however, frontier prostitution as it was once known in Kansas was over anyway.

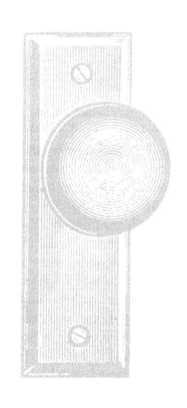

CHAPTER TWO

Wicked Wichita

As KANSAS GREW, SO DID THE NUMBER OF CITIES AND TOWNS THAT soon included city governments and proper society. One of the earliest communities, Wichita, was founded in 1868. The city grew quickly, with a population of 689 people within a year. By 1871, prostitution was rampant when a new marshal, Mike Meagher, was hired. Meagher was likeable enough, and immediately set up personal meetings with each madam in town. The marshal informed the ladies that there would now be a monthly fine system which must be adhered to by law. Those women who opposed the measure were told they must follow the new law or leave town. The marshal also assured the city council that the fining system would greatly reduce the number of newcomers. The proper ladies of the town watched the attempts to control the skin trade of Wichita for about a year, but were dissatisfied and ultimately petitioned the city council to close the local brothels altogether. But it was too late; a Topeka newspaper noted that one of the best-known dance halls in Wichita "is patronized mainly by cattle herders, though all classes visit it; the respectable mostly from curiosity." The place also drew cowboys and strangers from out of town. Each of them, said the paper, had "painted and jeweled courtezans [sic] for partners."[1]

To appease the discontented masses, Meagher successfully moved Wichita's red-light district to Delano, a budding neighborhood across the Arkansas River, in 1872. The editor of the *Wichita Eagle* expressed his satisfaction with the move, noting that "Delano is improving very rapidly and business is said to be very lively over there."[2] For all of the concern about

Wichita's shady ladies, however, there were only between five and seven prostitutes working in town when the first train rolled into Wichita in May of 1872. The cattle shipping season was just beginning, and by August, three brothels and thirteen prostitutes were counted in the city proper. The number would increase to four bordellos and fourteen girls, but would eventually decrease as the shipping season drew to a close at summer's end.

Even as the season rolled to its end, things remained rough in Delano. That August, two prostitutes who had indulged in several glasses of wine began arguing loudly. The spectacle attracted numerous men—several hundred in fact—who soon surrounded the ladies and watched eagerly as they went to blows. Not one stepped forward to stop the fight; instead, the women were allowed to carry on until all they were wearing were "shreds of their finery on soiled and wanton forms." In reporting the incident, the *Wichita City Eagle* did not blame the women, but shamed the men for being so uncivilized as to let such a fight happen, let alone watch it.[3] Surely the citizens of Wichita felt a bit of relief in November; when the season was over for the year, only two brothels and six women were left in town. But more than a dozen prostitutes were back by January 1873, when that many women perished in a hotel fire on 5th Avenue. At least one newspaper expressed much sympathy for the ladies, but not for the owners of the hotel who escaped the flames while the women died. Various charities paid for their funerals as the paper suggested spending more money for regular building inspections and fire alarms.

For his part, Marshal Meagher continued making sure that Wichita's wayward women duly paid their monthly fines. The standard fine was $8 per month per prostitute, and each woman was fined $2 in court costs each time she was arrested. Brothels paid an additional $18 each month. It cost another $25 if they wanted to legally sell whiskey. In August alone, the city made a combined $1,025 off of the prostitution and liquor industry. The amount was large enough that the treasurer's report showed that general business taxes were unnecessary. Whether the legitimate businesses in town were appreciative is unrecorded.

Even as Wichita's infrastructure benefitted from its shady ladies, the respectable women of the town not only took umbrage at the brothels in Delano, but also believed that not all of the prostitutes were paying their

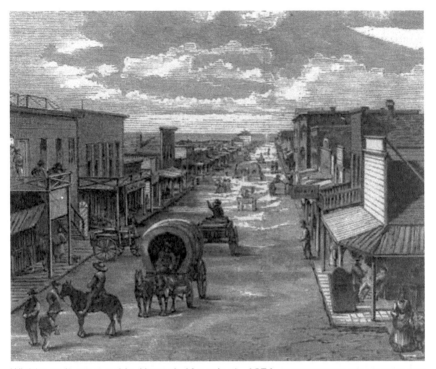

Wichita as it appeared in *Harper's Magazine* in 1874. COURTESY LIBRARY OF CONGRESS

dues. A petition filed with the city was signed by seventy-four women who urged the council to "take such steps as may be necessary or expedient for the enforcement of the Ordinances of the city related to Bawdy houses and houses of ill fame, And that such houses now in existence in our city may be suppressed, and the inmates of the same dealt with according to the law."[4] The good women did not seem to have a problem with Marshal Meagher, however, who was reelected that same year and continued doing his job as well as he could. He was not always successful. In October 1873, the *Wichita Eagle* reported on two dance hall owners, identified as "Rowdy Joe" and "Red," who shot each other. During the fray, a dance hall girl, Annie Franklin, was shot in the stomach and was not expected to live.

By 1874, Wichita's red-light district was well established. Beginning at the corner of Douglas Avenue and Water Street, also known as "Horse

Thief Corner," the district ran north on Water Street for some blocks.[5] In January, the *Wichita Weekly Eagle* announced that the city "is fast getting rid of that element which has proved such a curse to her prosperity, thanks to the county attorney and the improved sentiment of the place which is backing him up." Among those to leave town was a "Rowdy Kate" who, along with her husband, "Rowdy Joe" Lowe, had formerly run brothels in Newton and Ellsworth. The Lowes's departure transpired after Joe Lowe was taken to court for permitting "the corruption of good morals and the common nuisance of all citizens" because of "drinking, tippling, dancing, whoring, and misbehaving." What became of Lowe remains unknown, but Rowdy Kate soon left Wichita and may have moved on to Colorado.[6]

To the chagrin of city officials, for every "Rowdy Kate" who was chased out of Wichita, there was always another one to take her place. In April, the *Wichita Weekly Eagle* reported, "Again the music of their heels is heard upon our jingling sidewalks, and the libidinous cooings of jippoed [*sic*] doves increase with the shadows of each succeeding nightfall."[7] Two months later, Wichita's wicked women paid fines amounting to $514, nearly 65 percent of the total fines taken in. And a month after that, the ladies and the male gamblers of the town were paying roughly 80 percent of the city's budget income. Come September, of course, the raucous element of the town skedaddled out of town for the winter.

For three years, Marshal Meagher had done his best to maintain some sort of order over the red-light district. In 1874, however, he resigned to go into the livery business. Bill Smith was hired to replace him and hired various men to continue collecting fines. And that is when the trouble began. In 1875, Wichita's city treasurer found a glaring error in the books: Madam Georgia Williams had been dutifully paying her fines between June of 1874 and July of 1875. But the man who sometimes collected the money, John Behrens, had been turning in only a fraction of the total amount Georgia had given him. Behrens was investigated, a process that lasted into 1876 as councilman James Fraker introduced a new ordinance "To abolish the office of assistant marshal and regulate the fees of certain officers therein named." When Madam Mattie Wilson's brothel, the Gold Rooms, was shut down later that summer, it was noted that Behrens was her landlord. Mattie was apparently open again in August, when Behrens appealed to the court to make sure Mattie paid him his rent.[8]

Wichita would pass more ordinances against the prostitution industry. There wasn't really much sense in it seeing as the last cattle drive came through in 1876 and cattle were taken to Caldwell for shipping instead. But officials were determined to clean up Wichita, outlawing guns in 1877 and letting it be known that rowdy cowboys and wicked women were no longer welcome. Crime in the city declined as the soiled doves of Wichita flew elsewhere and seldom returned, at least for a few years. City fathers perhaps did not realize that with Wichita's growing population—nearly 29,000 in 1880—a whole new generation of harlots would soon make their way to town.

By about 1887, Wichita's wild women were back in great numbers—nearly 300. A grand jury investigation into their lives revealed particulars that remain fascinating today. The ladies testified that of the money they made, so much of it wound up in the hands of pimps, brothel owners, or hotels that there was little left to live on. At the time, many of Wichita's good time girls lived elsewhere, paying $3 to $5 a week for their rooms in respectable boarding houses. For work purposes, they rented a room from a hotel or a madam for $14 per week. Prostitute Millie Wright testified that upon renting her working room in a hotel, she not only paid rent but also gave the owner a third of her earnings there. Prostitute Myrtle Rapp recalled being brought to a room by a hack driver, in which an old man waited. She never learned the customer's name, but he paid the hack driver $5 for bringing Myrtle to him. What she was paid for her services is unknown, but a guestimate is that it also was around $5.

Sporadic efforts to close or suppress Wichita's bordellos continued throughout the 1890s. But the 1900 census, taken on June 8, shows that a total of seven brothels were still in business. Five madams: Kittie Miller, Lou Hall, Ollie Clayton, Nellie Orliff, and Carrie Glenwood, ran brothels ranging from plain to palatial. On North Water Street, Wessley and Julia Morris rented to seven women who lived in the main house but also four small outbuildings on the property; Wessley's occupation was that of a "rental agent" and the Morrises employed a cook named Julia Graham. Ruby Earnest was the only woman to live and work alone. All of the women were American born, the exception being Carrie Glenwood's cook, Russian-born Catherine Schuber. Most of the women were single, but a dozen of them were married. Four were divorced. At least one woman in each of the brothels (except for Ruby Earnest) was the mother of one or more children, some of whom had died by the time the census was taken. Notable is that laundress Emiline Wisher and musician Sterline Brown shared a house on North Water Street between Carrie Glenwood and the Morrises.

Local news articles about some of the ladies revealed more about them. Lou Hall was in Wichita as early as 1886, when she was fined $8 for working as a prostitute. By 1887, Lou was running her own place, the Iron Clad, when an unhappy customer had her arrested for running a brothel. The Iron Clad made the news again in 1899 when a client, Hughey Kistler, gave Lou's housekeeper a shot of morphine and she died. Interestingly the girl, Sylvia Rogers, actually used the alias of Blanche Porter while working in the red-light district even though she performed honest work. Sylvia was not the only woman to meet her end at Lou's. In 1901, the *Wichita Beacon* reported that one of Lou's girls, Grace Burk, was found dead in her bed. Her client woke up to find her sick, called for help, and left the house so fast he forgot his collar. Grace had recently visited her estranged husband in Oklahoma Territory, had returned in a despondent mood, and had been drinking, smoking opium, and shooting cocaine ever since. The newspaper noted how Grace's face looked very calm in death, and there appeared to be even a small smile on her lips. Three years later, Lou was dead, too. In 1904 she succumbed to dropsy at her home on Tremont Avenue, at which time her real name was revealed to be Florence Burton.

When twenty-three-year-old Carrie Glenwood first appeared in the 1895 census for Wichita, she was residing at the home of a Black man, seventy-year-old Clark Moore, with another young woman named Phillis Harmon. The ladies' occupations are not listed. Carrie had been married at the age of fifteen years, but her husband was nowhere to be seen when she took up her odd lodging situation in Wichita. In the 1900 census, it was noted that Carrie's sixteen-year-old son, Chauncey Glenwood (nee Chauncey Corey), lived with her at her brothel at 201 North Water Street and was her only child. But the boy apparently did a lot more than just occupy his own bedroom. In September, the *Wichita Daily Eagle* reported that Chauncey fired a .38 revolver at Dr. C. E. Hale. The incident happened at 2:30 a.m. The boy explained to police that the man had "been bothering his mother at their home and to protect her, he was forced to shoot Hale."[9] The *Wichita Beacon* gave further details. Hale, said the paper, had actually assaulted Carrie Glenwood. Young Chauncey had hit his mark, with Hale receiving a painful bullet wound that struck a rib. He was taken to the doctor and treated before both he and Chauncey were arrested. On the way to jail, however, Hale "broke away from Officer Aspy," drew his own gun, and fired at the lawman before escaping. Chauncey, meanwhile, was taken to jail and bonded out.[10] Whether Hale was ever apprehended remains unknown, but he was unaccountably shot again at Carrie's brothel in 1915. Whether the shooter was Chauncey also is unknown.

By 1903 Carrie had relocated to 239 Tremont Avenue in Wichita's expansive red-light district, and presumably Chauncey moved with her. The lady's bordello property was by far the largest in the Wichita demimonde. Sanborn Fire Insurance maps for 1903 show that address as the location of a large, two-story house with a porch and a bay window. When Carrie moved to a new house at 330 Tremont Avenue in 1904, the building was large enough to accommodate several women. The Kansas State Census of 1905 identifies Carrie and another woman, Mamie King, as sharing a house. Chauncey was there too.

Between 1906 and 1908, Carrie moved to another location in the red-light district. She was a good businesswoman, paying her fines and staying out of the papers for the most part. She was mentioned in the *Wichita Beacon* once in 1906, when she recovered a diamond that had been stolen from her and pawned. The following year, the city refunded $100 to her that she had paid during "the last administration."[11] That was in May; in June, Carrie was fined $25 for running her brothel. Two others at her address, Dollie Brown and Sam Edwards, also were fined. But in September, Carrie was tried and found not guilty of selling liquor when it was revealed that one Officer Nafziger had actually purchased liquor elsewhere and brought it to her brothel. And in October, cases were brought against her and Sam Edwards within a day of each other.

Wichita Resorts with Liquor Licenses in 1902

Orma Clayton, 238 North Main Street, 4 inmates
Madame Shirley, 324 North Main Street, 4 inmates
Maggie Manny, 118 North Market Street, 2 inmates
Mrs. Klouse, 140 North Water Street
Carrie Glenwood, 201 North Water Street, 5 inmates
Inez Miller, 219 North Water Street, 2 inmates
Madame Morris, 229 North Water Street, 3 inmates
Ollie Clayton, 139 North Wichita, 2 inmates
Mildred Miller, 229 Tremont Avenue, 3 inmates
Madame Hazel, 237 Tremont Avenue, 4 inmates
Ella Porter, 300 Tremont Avenue, 2 inmates
Ella Tossie, 301 Tremont Avenue, 4 inmates
Madame Verne, 305 Tremont Avenue, 4 inmates
Kittie Miller, 309 Tremont Avenue, 3 inmates
Bessie Armstrong, 311 Tremont Avenue, 4 inmates
Flossie Campbell, 316 Tremont Avenue, 2 inmates
Gertrude Barr, 317 Tremont Avenue, 2 inmates
Lou Hall, 324 Tremont Avenue, 3 inmates
Mrs. Trevor, 116 West Douglas Avenue, 3 inmates
One unidentified madam, 228 East Douglas, 2 inmates[12]

Sam Edwards, it turned out, was Carrie's boyfriend. By 1915 she was calling herself Carrie Edwards when she purchased more property in Wichita's red-light district. She was likely retired by 1917, however, when Chauncey registered for the draft and gave his mother's address as 1652 Market Street. The Edwardses would remain at the house on Market Street for the rest of their lives, and Chauncey continued living with them. But life on Market Street was not always serene; in 1923 the Edwardses made the paper after they apparently got into a brawl with their neighbors, W.S. and Nellie Fields. The Fieldses sued for $5,000 in damages, claiming they "received many blows over the head, shoulders and body," also that they were disgraced in front of their neighbors.[13] After Sam Edwards died in 1938, Carrie and Chauncey continued sharing the Market Street house. Chauncey was now gainfully employed as a carpenter, and duly enlisted for the draft again in 1942. He does not appear to have served in either World War I or World War II, but he did remain living with his mother until her death in 1952. Chauncey inherited everything, and continued living in the Market Street house until his own death in 1959. Mother and son are buried in Wichita Park Cemetery and Mausoleum.

By 1902, the public in general was fed up with the "appalling conditions" in Wichita's red-light district. An election was coming up and the *Wichita Beacon* was determined to make the public aware of how the "McLean administration" had mishandled the law, let the floosies and gamblers run amuck, and misallocated their fines and fees to the tune of $1,500 in discrepancies each month.

Wichita's Sanborn Fire Insurance map for 1903 shows the red-light district neatly spanning two full blocks along Tremont Avenue between East Williams and East Waterman. A total of forty-two bordellos, from small houses to grand, two-story affairs, flourished in the district. Nestled in between was a livery, a restaurant, and one laundry whose customers presumably consisted solely of prostitutes. Things had changed markedly by the time of the 1910 census, when only nine women were documented as prostitutes. They all lived in various rooming houses along North Main. Gone was the old red-light district, which by 1914 had pretty much disappeared as railroad operations expanded in the neighborhood. Wichita's early days of wickedness, as they were known in the wild west, were over.

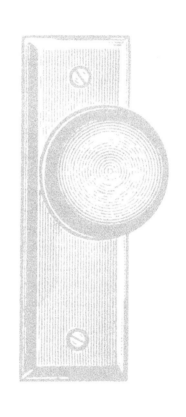

CHAPTER THREE

Jezebels of Junction City

SHORTLY AFTER FORT RILEY WAS ESTABLISHED IN 1852 ALONG THE Santa Fe Trail, pioneers began settling in areas around the fort. The closest locale was today's Junction City, which was still occupied by the Kanza tribe of Natives when the United States government built a bridge across the Republican River in 1853. Settlers began arriving the following year. Junction City was first known as Manhattan, then Millard, then Humboldt, and, finally, the name it is known by today. The townsite was officially laid out in 1857, and incorporated two years later. In time, a number of harlots would come to Junction City, and an official red-light district would be established along 9th Street. As of July of 1869, Mayor R. S. Miller put forth fines for prostitution in the city.

Fines for Prostitution in Junction City, 1869

Keeping a house of ill-fame or prostitution: $25 to $200
Working in a house of ill-fame: $10 to $100
Visiting a house of ill-fame: $10 to $100 for each infraction
Renting a house for the purpose of prostitution: $10 to $100
for each day[1]

The effort was a limited success; in December, Sarah Elizabeth Scott, also known as "Sarah Elizabeth Stone," "Sal Scott," "Black Sal," "Snowflake," and "Swamp Angel," was the first prostitute to make the papers after she killed soldier James Apgar.[2] The story went that a group of soldiers got terribly drunk at James King's "infamous dance house" just outside the city limits. On their way back to town, they stopped at Sarah's. When she refused them entry, the men broke down her front door. Inside, the group entered a bedroom and found Sarah with "a yellow woman" identified as Annie Grave. The women fled to Sarah's room and locked themselves in. Then the men locked the front door to the house and began making threats. Apgar and another man identified as "Bunkey" used heavy flat-irons to break through Sarah's bedroom door and began waving knives around and threatening to cut out the women's hearts. At that point Sarah, whom the paper described as an "old woman," drew her pistol and fired several shots into the group, hitting Apgar. Another shot hit a man named James Kraig and yet another soldier wound up with a broken jaw. The ladies then fled the house. By the time the authorities were summoned, Apgar was dead as Bunkey lay beside him totally incoherent from his drunkenness. Judge Gordon found Sarah not guilty due to self-defense.[3]

Sarah was still in Junction City during 1872 when there was a scuffle in city hall involving her. A man identified as the "Hon[orable] Mr. Tucker" was known to have a soft heart for the city's prostitutes. When Tucker approached Marshal Thomas Allen Cullinan, also known as "Tom Allen" about the treatment of Sarah, referred to as "poor black Sal," the marshal answered by "applying his boot to old Tucker's rear," and sent the man flying across the street.[4] A few days later, Sarah herself got into a scuffle with Allen, and "lost that exquisite chunk of stuffed rubbish used to ornament the back of the female head." In reporting the incident, the *Weekly Union* revealed that Sarah's mother, Henrietta, also had been jailed and that five children in her care had been taken to the poor house.[5] Sarah might have given up her career after this last incident; by 1873 she was in Solomon, where it was reported she broke into a Main Street building and resumed her business.

Stories are many of Marshal Allen's sometimes gentle, sometimes rough, approach to keeping the law. With regard to the red-light ladies, Allen began making sure Junction City's lewd women kept their businesses behind closed doors and ceased parading along the streets. One time, the marshal was summoned by some ladies who said a "six-foot tramp" was proposing "a beastly offense" to a small girl. Allen informed the tramp that he was not about to spend court time and money on arresting him, fining him, and incarcerating him—instead, he just beat the man senseless.[6] Tom Allen was a godsend in proper people's eyes, although many a citizen continued to openly voice complaints about the goings-on in Junction City's demimonde. In 1870, complaints were rampant about James King's dance hall. King employed nine women, according to the January 1870 census, all of whom ranged in age from seventeen to twenty-six years old. Two of them also had their young children living with them. The complaints about the dance hall focused on the pimps who forced the women to double as prostitutes and to steal from their customers. Also, it was charged, there was a "filthy outfit" conducting business down along the Smoky Hill River.[7] In addition, Junction City was fraught with violence and killings, including the shooting deaths of two policemen by a drunken soldier.

Allen did his best to stay on top of such outlawry. For its part, the *Weekly Union* continued beating its readers over the head with the ordinances against prostitution and editorials against the industry, which were published again and again. As for city officials, they were not above making examples out of the occasional citizen for various infractions concerning the ordinances. In March of 1872, for instance, George Eades was fined $50 for renting a house to prostitutes. For some reason, however, the fine was reversed. At a city council meeting a few weeks later, it was noted that the "case against Mr. Eades is the first prosecution that has ever been instituted and the first conviction that has ever been had under the ordinance." To ignore this and other abominations concerning vice in Junction City, said concerned council members, was as if to say, "Open your doors to vice and prostitution freely and without fear; our city ordinances are a farce, and we will remit all fines and penalties that may be adjudged against you." More arguments for and against Eades continued, until the council agreed that the final amount the man owed the court was $10 and costs.[8] A few months later, the city did update its prostitution ordinances to reflect the right to close brothels down and jail time for repeat offenders. Over the next year, city records reflected the arrests of four prostitutes, one person who was "keeping house of ill fame," and one other person for "harboring prostitutes."[9]

In addition to paying out fines, prostitutes also were the occasional victims of swindlers. In July of 1876, a "young man whose parents live near Council Grove" sauntered into Junction City and stayed overnight at a brothel. Come morning, the boy "made off with the girl's watch and chain, $50 in money, and a revolver." Officers tracked him to Americus and brought him back for trial with a $500 bond. The man claimed he was only sixteen years old, but the *Weekly Union* noted that he "appears much older."[10] The robbery of a prostitute does not seem to have disturbed the red-light community much. Even as Kansas Territory was officially designated "dry" during the 1880s, Junction City's demimonde and saloons carried on just as they always had. Even the city willingly issued annual liquor licenses, mostly as a means to keep soldiers from Fort Riley coming to town and spending their money.

Ida Blue is one of Junction City's best-remembered madams. The twenty-four-year-old Swedish lady was married but alone when she first appeared in Junction City during the 1880 census. At the time, Ida said she was a milliner. She was, perhaps, waiting for her husband, Charles Blue, to join her. When he didn't, Ida filed for divorce in December. Making ladies hats for a living was perhaps not as lucrative as Ida hoped. The next time she appeared in the Junction City *Weekly Union* was in September, when she was charged with "keeping a bawdy house."[11]

Unfortunately, there is no documentation of how many women worked for Madam Blue. Newspapers during 1882 do reflect that she sold liquor at her brothel, for which she paid the occasional fine of $14.90. In April, she was once again charged with running a bawdy house. This time, however, her fine was a whopping $175 including court costs, quite an exorbitant fee for the 1880s. But the city also exhibited some lenience on Ida; in 1883, another case against her was dismissed. Perhaps the city went easy on Ida since she was known for being quite intelligent, was willing and able to talk politics, and kept her brothel across from the Bartell House "as quiet and orderly as a house could be."[12]

Madam Blue did suffer the occasional indignity. One evening, in about 1884, Marshal Tom Allen was passing by Ida's brothel and noticed one of the madam's newest employees idly swinging on the front gate. The forthright officer told the girl she was not supposed to be out in front of the house, "and if she wanted to play she must go in the backyard." The young woman did as she was told, only to appear the next night doing the same thing. Again, Allen told her that loitering in front of the house was not allowed. But when he caught her doing it again on the third night, the marshal had enough. Marching into Madam Blue's, the lawman went upstairs, found the girl's room, and hurled her trunk through the window. Much of the window sash and glass went with it as it landed in the street. Allen ordered the young lady to take the next train out of town.[13]

Nothing more happened at Ida's, aside from her paying the occasional fine for prostitution and selling liquor illegally, until neighbor George Miller filed suit against the madam in March 1887. Although he occasionally used his building as a "wholesale liquor store," Miller claimed he could not find proper renters because of Ida's brothel. He was seeking to recover $1,200 in damages. Testimony showed, however, that Miller had received offers to rent his building, and Ida herself said she hadn't been in business for over a year. But the madam also had offered to pay Miller "his price for the building if he would let it remain idle and keep quiet." The jury sided with Ida as the Junction City *Daily Union* uttered its dismay.[14] A month after the trial, the *Weekly Union* announced that Ida had sold her property and was auctioning off everything in her house. She presumably promised Miller his money but left town soon after, leaving her business with both her house and the man unfinished. In 1890, Miller sued Ida again, but she never appears to have answered the charges. In December, Ida's property was sold at a public sheriff's auction. By then, however, the Swedish madam was long gone.

In the wake of Ida Blue's disappearance from Junction City, officers at Fort Riley apparently decided that the best way to keep their soldiers safe from the clutches of Junction City vice was to permit liquor on the post. That changed in 1901, when liquor was again banned from the fort and the Kansas Attorney General filed suit against Junction City and other towns for "open violation of the prohibition laws." Officials at city hall at long last gave in and closed their saloons.[15] One would think that was the end of prostitution in Junction City, but not quite. Beer baron

Adolphus Busch would soon appear on the scene and take one last stab at making sure Junction City residents and visitors to town were shown a good time.

Busch's interests lay in Bartell House, originally the site of a hotel known as Hale House at Washington and 6th streets. The building burned in 1875, and Bartell House was built on the site in 1879. It was, without a doubt, one of the fanciest hotels in Junction City with "55 rooms, a kitchen, parlors, offices, and a dining room with murals painted by Junction City artist Bertrand Hartman." Although Ida Blue's brothel was once located across from the hotel, Bartell House maintained a fine reputation for over twenty years. When Busch blew into town in 1902, he saw lots of opportunity for Bartell House. Purchasing the building, Busch remodeled the place inside and out, added a third story to part of it, and allegedly installed a "discreet bar" in the basement. Before long, it became known that services at Bartell House included ladies of the evening. Long after Busch sold the building and moved on, Bartell House remained tied to the prostitution industry. In later years, unfortunately, the hotel gained quite a seedy reputation and gradually fell into disrepair.[16]

Prostitution at Bartell House, as well as nearby 9th Street, remained a problem well into the 1970s. At the time, the owners of the hotel were trying to prohibit prostitution within the hotel but were technically prevented from doing so by anti-discrimination laws. After the upper floors were condemned, Bartell House closed and was eventually put on the block at a tax auction. It looked to be the end of the historic building until 2008, when Homestead, a senior housing company, purchased it. The former hotel was remodeled to reflect its former glory, and survives today as a senior retirement home called Bartell Place.

CHAPTER FOUR

Caldwell's Maggie Wood

IN ITS DAY, CALDWELL WAS NICKNAMED "THE BORDER QUEEN" AS THE last town along the famed Chisholm Trail.[1] The city was specifically founded in 1871 for the cattle trade, and actually managed to last roughly ten years longer—1885—than other Kansas cattle towns. Because it was the first town located north across the border from "Indian Territory," Caldwell became known as a wild place early on with shootings, mayhem, and other violence. Much of it was perpetrated by the cowboys galloping into town bent on a binge but also the shady ladies whom the men sought out for a good time. When the Atchison, Topeka, and Santa Fe Railroad reached Caldwell in about 1880, things just got wilder. Among the new ladies to town that year was Maggie Wood who, with her husband George, left an indelible mark on Caldwell.

Maggie and George Wood may have been new to Caldwell, but they were not new to Kansas or the flesh trade. Maggie was born Margaret Ann Gillion, circa 1857, in Arkansas to a large family. By the time of the 1870 census, the Gillions had moved to Butler County, Kansas, where Margaret's father, Isaac, toiled as a common farmer. Margaret, who preferred to be called Maggie, did not stay at home much longer, and perhaps left shortly after her father died in September 1872. By 1875, both she and George were in Wichita, where they appeared in the census as sharing a house with Laura Smith and Bessie Earp, the wife of James Earp whose more famous brother was Wyatt Earp. The women's occupations were listed as "sporting," the common euphemism for females who worked as prostitutes but also men who ran in such circles. Interesting is that there were two people named George Wood in the census: Maggie's husband, but also Maggie herself. It is interesting, too, that she appears as the first in the house to be listed, which census records usually use to denote the head of household. It is the first time Maggie appears in any documentation as Maggie Wood, although she had not yet married George.

Maggie's brothel was located on Water Street. In his book, *Notorious Ladies of the Frontier*, Henry Drago noted, "The toughest dive on Water Street was conducted by Mag Woods. She was arrested innumerable times and fined for conducting a disorderly house. Her husband, George Woods, an unsavory saloon character and two-bit gambler, ran her errands and did her bidding."[2] George was a Texas native and three years older than Maggie. His occupation in the 1875 census was listed as a laborer, but the man had a knack for making money. In September, he was able to buy a lot on Wichita Street as Wichita's demimonde expanded.

Right out of the gate, George and Maggie began expanding to other places, too. In 1876, Charles Francis Colcord and his father were driving cattle through Fort Worth, Texas, when the young man visited a dance hall run by Mag Woods. The building was still being constructed, with just a floor, roof and siding made from large sheets. The place must of have been huge, as the bar at one end could accommodate five bartenders, "all busy as could be." Mag had brought over some thirty girls with her from Wichita. Colcord recalled that the cost of a dance was "fifty cents a set" and that "it was a sight to see those old buffalo hunters, cowpunchers, and railroad men swing those girls." At midnight, a gunfight broke out. "The lights were shot out, one or two men were killed and several were badly hurt," Colcord said. Even Colcord had a dispute with a bartender over "something which I have forgotten." But the young man did remember that as he tried to yank the bartender over the bar by his shirt in order to "whip him," the man wrestled away from him and went for his gun. Colcord shot the bartender through the hand before he could fire, and even paid for his medical expenses to show he was a good sport.[3]

After her Fort Worth excursion, Maggie returned to Wichita. During her absence, George had procured another house at 12 Douglas

Avenue, which he had rented to James and Bessie Earp, as well as Wyatt and Mattie Earp. The Woods stayed there for a while, and when the Earps left town, George and Maggie simply took up business in yet another brothel. Maggie paid fines regularly, sometimes as a prostitute and other times as a madam. But her business does not seem to have been raided, perhaps because of George's diligence. Allegedly, during a scuffle with police in October 1876, George singlehandedly fended off the law by standing on the Douglas Avenue bridge with a six-shooter. But even he was not exempt from paying a fine in 1878 for running a bawdy house.

In May of 1879, George and Maggie's place on the corner of First and Wichita burned after a kerosene lamp exploded in the downstairs kitchen. The *Wichita Herald* noted that "a number of the demimonde" occupied the building, but they seem to have escaped. A crowd of fifteen hundred people gathered to watch the fire, which destroyed the whole building in just half an hour.[4] The couple wisely decided not to rebuild, as they heard that the city of Caldwell was preparing for the coming of the Atchison, Topeka, and Santa Fe Railroad. Maggie and George decided to explore their options there. Maggie had been to Caldwell before, so she and George explored other options on the way to Caldwell. In Wellington, some thirty miles from Caldwell, the couple purchased two lots but apparently never used them. Caldwell had much greater appeal for the couple, and besides, Maggie was tiring of her run-ins with the law in Wichita for operating a brothel, but also for being drunk and disorderly.

With the railroad coming, the town fathers knew well what to expect in the way of drinking, gambling, and prostitution. The city immediately penned ordinances against prostitution in particular. Fines between $50 and $100 would be levied against keepers of houses of ill fame, and the inmates would have to pay between $5 and $25 each. Caldwell newspapers, meanwhile, were soon abuzz about Maggie and George. The *Caldwell Post* already knew of Mag when she arrived in town "with several pieces of feminine frailty" and opened a temporary brothel just outside the city limits. She also was still very much with George, whom she finally married on December 8. Three months later, in March 1880, George purchased a piece of property on Chisolm Street in preparation for his next endeavor: the Red Light Saloon. The following month the

Post reported that "George Wood's two story building has been removed from Wichita to Caldwell. It is being erected, we presume for convenience sake, near the calaboose. If this building is built for the purpose of a dance house, we hope the mayor will keep the building on the move." Transporting an entire building was no easy trick, and it is not surprising that the structure needed work by the time it arrived at its destination. A week later, the paper reported that "three men working on the two-story building located near the calaboose fell off the roof last Monday afternoon. Two of them were quite severely injured."[5]

If Maggie and George were aware that Wichita's celebrated marshal, Mike Meagher, was planning to move to Caldwell, there is no record of it. But move he did, in April of 1880. Although Meagher opened his own saloon, the Arcade, he also was elected mayor in short order and served as city marshal for a short time. Just one month later, on May 1, Maggie was arrested in Caldwell for the first time, for being drunk and running a brothel. Maggie persevered, and about two weeks later, the all-new Red Light Saloon opened for business. Almost immediately, an unidentified visitor penned a letter to the *Caldwell Advance* about his visit to the Red Light Saloon. He stated that the "scenes there presented reminded me of the early times in Cheyenne, when murder ran riot and the pistol was the only argument." Even so, in the next sentence, the writer admitted that "the assemblage was sober, orderly and [it was a] quiet Saturday night." But the prospect that mayhem might break out any minute, said the writer, should be enough for the city to "at once take measures to close all such places."[6] The writer was not alone; in the same issue of the newspaper, a complaint commanded the place to "stop that 'dance house' racket."[7]

How many wanton women were actually operating in Caldwell during 1880? One undated police report listed thirty-seven prostitutes living in the town of seven hundred people. Another source says Caldwell's court dockets listed twenty-five prostitutes between April and August of 1880. Yet another source stated that the city collected fines from seventy-six women during the year. Only George and Maggie's place listed any ladies on the premises during the census in June. There were only four in all, and the occupation for each of them was documented as "dancing." Still, the size of the rest of the staff insinuates that the Red Light Saloon operated on a large-scale budget. Aside from the dancing girls—Mary Babize, Lucy Moody, Belle Piper, and Lizzie Roberts—there was also a cook, a house servant, and two bartenders besides George Wood. Two men, Henry Cabden and George Reed, were also listed and might have been customers. Most curious was the presence of a six-year-old boy identified as George Brower, who does not appear to have been related to any of the other residents.

At least some of the residents at the Red Light Saloon bear more looking into. George Reed, for instance, was employed by the city as a full-time policeman whose job it was to perform various odd jobs and, perhaps, serve as a bouncer at the Red Light. Over time, Lizzie, Mary, Belle, and Lucy were each arrested as "inmates of houses of ill fame," while Maggie and even her Black cook, Becky Banks, were arrested for *keeping* a house of ill fame. In twenty-four-year-old Becky's case, her arrest may have transpired because, sometime in the recent past, she had worked as a madam and was once fined $10 more than her Anglo counterparts. There is little doubt that Maggie's dancing employees doubled as prostitutes, as the upper floor of the Red Light contained seven beds, each with a wash stand and mirror, that were separate from the furniture owned by George and Maggie.[8]

The Red Light Saloon eventually was known as the largest dance house in the state of Kansas. But it was also commonly referred to as the "worst whorehouse in Kansas," a place of "obscene and violent action."[9] Maggie and George were arrested on numerous occasions. Maggie's offenses were "unrestrained carousing and fighting," and George was arrested on three occasions for riding his horse on the sidewalk, carrying a concealed weapon, and assault and battery.[10] Even George and Maggie occasionally butted heads. Once, in July of 1880, George took out an ad reading, "Notice is hereby given that all persons are cautioned against trusting my wife, Maggie Wood, on my account, as I will not pay any debts of her contracting."[11]

Meanwhile, the occasional bad guy made an appearance at the Red Light. In September, W. F. Smith got drunk and was riding through town waving his gun around. "Of course he struck the 'Red Light,'" sniped the *Caldwell Post*. "They all do it." Policeman Frank Hunt ended up shooting

Smith in the knee and shot his horse, too. "A great deal of sympathy was expressed for the horse," the paper said. A month later, Hunt was sitting in the Red Light near an open window when someone shot him from outside. Hunt died, and one David Spear was arrested for his murder. The *Post* also talked of another recent killing at the Red Light, concluding that "if the Council had listened to our protestations against the running of the 'dance house,' this murder would not have happened in our place."[12]

Perhaps in need of a break, George and Maggie traveled to Eureka Springs, Arkansas, later that month. Since Maggie had been born in Arkansas, one must wonder if the couple happened to visit any of her relatives while there. Left behind, albeit briefly, was the debauchery that reigned almost constantly at the Red Light Saloon. In October, the city, tired of the constant troubles, issued three new ordinances prohibiting houses of prostitution, their prostitutes, and any other woman working "in a hotel or tavern" who attempted to seduce men for money. The fines ranged from $10 to $100.[13] The ordinances were of little use; in January of 1881, a petition was brought before Caldwell's city council asking for suppression of the brothels in town. Officials were not controlling such places, it was charged, and they were a blight to the local residents. When a gunfight broke out later that year, killing a saloonkeeper and a former mayor, citizens demanded that all saloons, gambling, and prostitution be outlawed.

This time, the city took more effort to propose stronger ordinances. The first order of business was to officially outlaw saloons, as well as gambling and houses of prostitution. Next, a police judge ordered all wanton women to leave town while citizens themselves forced the one dance house in town to close. But raids on the saloons were wanting for actual convictions by December, when saloonkeepers and others petitioned to let Caldwell's more notorious businesses resume operating. Casino owner George W. Reilly maintained that the ordinances had caused losses for legitimate businesses. George and Maggie felt the pressure and, in February, purchased property in Hunnewell some ten miles from Caldwell to build an all-new combination saloon, dance hall, and brothel on what was known as "Smoky Row" at the corner of Oak Street and Sixth Street. It, too, was named the Red Light Saloon, and the Woods offered stage service between their place in Caldwell and the new place in Hunnewell for $0.50 one way, or $1 for a round trip.

Hunnewell turned out to be a good investment for the Woods, at first. In 1881, George partnered with Fred Kuhlman, a former cowboy who owned the Kentucky Saloon in Caldwell. Kuhlman purchased a half interest in the Hunnewell Red Light, but only a month into his ownership he was shot dead right in front of the place. At issue was a Miss Mattie Smith, one of the girls from the Caldwell Red Light who had been arrested at least four times for prostitution and was apparently seeing Kuhlman. But a local herder, Ed Stokley, also liked Mattie—enough to walk right up to Kuhlman and shoot him in the chest. Hunnewell's only marshal was out of town, enabling Stokely to calmly purchase more ammo and a gun before riding off into the sunset. George Wood obligingly paid for Kuhlman's funeral, right down to his casket and burial clothes. As a precaution, George next hired James "Big Jim" Cavner to assist Maggie in Caldwell while George took over management of the Red Light in Hunnewell.

The arrangement appears to have been temporary. Maggie also served as administratrix of Kuhlman's estate and tried to officially end his partnership with the Woods' Red Light in Hunnewell. She told the court that the building was actually "unoccupied and has been for a number of months last past and that the same is deteriorating very much in value, that the same is becoming rickety; the windows and sash are being stolen and taken out, and that the same is liable to fall down during any hard storm . . . that to repair the same would be a greater expense that it could be sold for after the same should be repaired."[14] Maggie was apparently hoping to sell the Red Light Saloon in Hunnewell, but it appears she did not get her wish. Whether her statements about the building were even true is questionable, for George was soon running the place again—or had never vacated it to begin with.

On the first day in August 1881, Maggie, Big Jim Cavner, and Lizzie Roberts decided to go visit George in Hunnewell. Lizzie was more than an employee to Maggie: the two were also good friends. Hunnewell's marshal, Joseph Dolan, had started his law career in Caldwell even as he himself was occasionally arrested for disturbing the peace. Dolan knew

Lizzie well, having arrested her at least six times either for prostitution or being drunk. Upon her arrival in Hunnewell with Maggie and Big Jim Cavner, the party began. Soon, Dolan apparently arrested a man, believed to be Cavner, who was fined $21 and released. Cavner invariably resumed his drunken tear, this time resisting arrest when Dolan attempted to take him in a second time. This time Maggie, Lizzie, Cavner, and even George, who had just recently lent Dolan money, jumped in. The threesome "did strike, pummel and severely beat Joseph Dolan," and were arrested upon their return to Caldwell.

Perhaps due to a request for a change of venue, the case against the Red Light bunch was moved to nearby Wellington. Their attorney, Samuel Berry, was no better than his clients. After a night of drinking with the Red Light foursome, a hungover Berry penned an amusing poem to Judge Ike King:

Apostrophe to the Court

Oh, Ike King
I hope you'll decide to my liking
For I'm sleepy and tired
And I want to be fired
Out of court (for a spell)
Over prairie and dell
Over morass and fell
Till I light in Caldwell
In the Leland Hotel
And sleep forty winks without waking
Oh, Ike King, Oh, hell.

An amused King scribbled his own note on the back of the poem regarding Attorney Berry: "He danced all night till broad daylight / And defended the whores in the morning."[15]

Berry lost his case. Cavner was fined $100 and jailed for ten days. George was fined $25 and appealed but was made to remain in jail. Maggie paid a $2,500 bond for his release as the appeal was considered by the court. Wellington's newspaper willingly published a comment Berry had made about Maggie, wherein he opined "that her only fault was—that she is intolerable and curst [sic], and shrewd and forward: So beyond all reason, that were my state far worser than it is, I would not wed her for a mine [of] gold."[16]

Maggie and George returned to Caldwell. Later that month, a young Texas cowboy named Charlie Davis talked Lizzie Roberts into coming to live with him. Davis had been enamored with Lizzie for nearly a year, giving her money and gifts. She initially accepted his offer but ultimately decided to go back to Red Light Saloon. Davis soon appeared at the Red Light too, demanding that Lizzie go home with him. George Wood overheard the conversation and intervened to say that Lizzie didn't have to go anywhere at all if she didn't want to. The argument escalated and George ordered Davis to leave. And that's when Davis whipped out a revolver and shot George Wood in the stomach. The bullet passed through Wood's body, but he continued wrestling with Davis. The two wound up outside; Davis managed to get away but immediately turned himself in to a policeman. George, meanwhile, managed to stumble back into the Red Light before he fell. He died a short time later after telling Maggie to make sure Charlie Davis was prosecuted and to "keep all the property, do the best she could, and be a good girl." As a coroner's jury concluded that death came by murder, Davis managed to escape.[17]

The *Wichita City Eagle* respectfully reported that George had "died with his boots on" in recounting the shooting affray. The paper did not name Davis, but called him a "cow-boy crazed with whiskey" whom George had only asked to quiet down before being shot. The article also claimed that Davis had escaped by making the officers "throw down their arms and throw up their hands." The *Eagle* viewed this as cowardice, stating that "had Mike Meagher been City Marshal no such humiliating episode would have occurred." Meagher, unfortunately, had resigned some months before.[18] Kansas governor John St. John, meanwhile, offered a $1,000 reward for the capture of Davis, and Maggie put up another $500.[19]

As much as he got into trouble when he was alive, George Wood was remembered kindly in death. In December the *Wichita City Eagle* noted that Maggie had gathered $550 to purchase a "monumental arch of Kimberle & Adams, the magnificent piece work which took the premium at fairs last fall" in George's memory. "It does not make so much difference what field one dies upon," lamented the paper, "it's the kind of friends he leaves behind."[20] Maggie also ordered a fine marble headstone for both George Wood and Fred Kuhlman to share, and eventually had one or both men's bodies moved to Caldwell's newest cemetery in March of 1882. They were reburied side by side.[21]

Maggie tried her best to carry on without George. Her clientele continued to include such roughnecks as Jim Talbot and his friends, who enjoyed taking Maggie's harlots out on the town and hated Mike Meagher, who was back in town and had recently served as interim marshal of Caldwell for Mayor W. N. Hubbell. Maggie had hired George Spears to manage the Red Light's bar, which was probably a mistake; in December 1881 both Spears and Talbot began firing their revolvers outside while yelling, "Hide out, little ones!" This time, marshals and citizens alike took up arms to quell the shenanigans. Shots were exchanged for some time before Talbot and Meagher dueled it out. Meagher was killed. Talbot escaped. Understandably, and perhaps rightfully, the *Caldwell Post* blamed "that sink-hole of iniquity, the Red Light dance house." Talbot was later tried for the murder of Meagher, but was acquitted in 1895. He was later killed during a saloon fight in Texas.[22]

Maggie seemed understandably unnerved by the Talbot shootings, and contemplated moving her business to Wellington even as Caldwell's new mayor, Cass Burrus, received a mysterious letter. The note advised Burrus to either resign or repeal Caldwell's three ordinances outlawing prostitution, or "we will find some mode to remove you that won't be very satisfactory to your hide."[23] What happened next is unknown but Maggie warily watched as Caldwell's city council, newspapers, and citizens fussed over the legalities of prostitution within the city limits. In April of 1882, a new, morally correct mayor, Albert Colson, and council were elected and set about making more stringent laws and penalties pertaining to vice. But another more personal matter would soon catch Maggie's attention, and it wasn't pretty.

In May, the *Caldwell Commercial* revealed that shortly after Meagher's death two men, Dave Sharp and George Spears, were accused of digging up George Wood's body and stealing a diamond stickpin from the corpse. The paper went into great detail on what happened, explaining that Maggie discovered that Spears's girl, Blanche Stevens, knew all about the theft and gave specific details: the men had broken the lid off the coffin, afterward chucking it in the remains of their small campfire at the grave and throwing dirt on top of the coffin. Maggie duly requested officials to look into the matter. Upon examining the grave and Wood's body, they corroborated Blanche's account. The trials for the theft began as Maggie, who had fallen out of favor with Caldwell's new marshal, George Brown, was arrested for running a brothel in early June. Two weeks after that, some customers were creating a disturbance upstairs at the Red Light Saloon. Brown boldly strode into the place, marched upstairs, and attempted to subdue three men. Their reaction was brief and bloody, and by the end of it, Brown lay on the floor, dead from a gunshot wound to the head. The men escaped.[24]

This time the good citizens of Caldwell were completely fed up with outlaws, the Red Light, the tenderloin ladies, and especially Maggie. The madam finally threw in the towel and advertised the Red Light for sale on June 22. Citizens quickly rallied to gather $400 to buy the building and turned it over to William Corzine for sale to any respectable party. Whatever Corzine got would be divided among those who donated the $400. But even the most meticulous buyer could not help but see the *Caldwell Post*'s caveat that "that old building has been the cause of more murders than any other house of the kind in the Southwest."[25] The building finally sold in July, and Maggie left town. One story goes that as Maggie headed to the train station, she was followed by a crowd of angry citizens. But as the group looked back, they discovered Mag had set fire to the Red Light, and she "was said to have a smirk on her face as the train pulled out."[26] It sounds exactly like something she would do, but little else was heard about her until George's killer, Charlie Davis, was finally caught in Albuquerque. Or was he? The *Caldwell Commercial* revealed that, figuring that any witnesses against him were long gone, Davis had actually conspired with a fellow named Stewart to pretend he had arrested the murderer in order to collect the reward money from both the governor and Maggie. The men would then split the money and go their separate ways. Fortunately, the sheriff had caught on to the game and refused to play along. Davis and Stewart did leave town, but with no money in hand.

In 1883, Maggie married Big Jim Cavner in Wellington. They were back in Wichita in 1885 when Maggie was involved in a wild and violent scuffle with a prostitute named Lizzie Dale. For reasons known only to Lizzie and herself, Maggie and one of her servants appeared at Lizzie's house late one night. Pistols were fired between the two before Maggie and her employee gave Lizzie a severe beating. A reporter from the *Wichita Eagle*, who saw Lizzie afterward, said she suffered from a broken leg, injured spine, dislocated shoulder, and a head "covered with lumps." Police were called and Maggie was arrested. She paid a $500 bond, plus another $100 for her servant. In court, Lizzie pleaded guilty and, between herself and Cavner, whittled the fine down to just $5 and costs.[27] Lizzie sued Maggie in 1885, but the outcome of her case is unknown.

Maggie continued making the papers. In August of 1885 she was fined for prostitution, filed for divorce from Jim Cavner in Wichita, and put her property on Wichita Street up for sale. The divorce from Cavner, however, was apparently never finalized, and Maggie also remained in business. Newspapers show she paid various fines between November of 1885 and April of 1886. During 1889, two of Maggie's customers turned her in for some infraction. And then, a turn of fortune occurred that was so amazing that Maggie must have been absolutely bowled over.

In 1888, Maggie discovered she could be a party to a lawsuit against Jerome B. Wheeler, a one-time partner of Macy's Department Store in far-away New York who had invested much of his money in the gold mines of Colorado. He was among the state's wealthiest citizens, erecting buildings in Aspen and Manitou Springs. Now, one Charles E. Wood of Denver, along with other family members, was suing Wheeler to the tune of $3.3 million for his share of the Aspen Mine. Charles was an heir of William J. Wood, who had invested in the Aspen Mine of which Wheeler was a one-third owner. William was George Wood's father. And when William passed away, nobody in his family knew he was a part owner of a rich gold mine in Colorado.

Wheeler had since sought out William Wood's heirs, which included Maggie who received $2,500 to sign away her rights to the mine. But the family soon caught on that the Aspen Mine was worth much more than Wheeler's attorneys had told the heirs. Wheeler was ordered to pay everyone their rightful share of the profits, hence, the lawsuit amount of $3.3 million. Maggie and Big Jim Cavner soon hastened to Colorado City, the wild town west of Colorado Springs where brothels, saloons, and gambling houses flourished with much vigor. The couple lived in a house on Colorado Avenue, where Cavner quickly became "well known in sporting circles as one of the late proprietors of the Crystal Palace variety theater." The Cavners also had been running a bordello "near the old plaster mill" in Colorado City.[28] But Maggie was also described as living "in the most straightened circumstances" as she awaited her part of the settlement.[29] Their abandoned Wichita property, meanwhile, was sold at a sheriff's sale. Maggie was believed to be headed for Denver in anticipation of receiving her money and, perhaps, taking up residence there.

It would be nice if this story had a happy ending, but most unfortunately it does not. It is unclear why, but Maggie never received the proposed $200,000 in the Aspen Mine settlement, equivalent to just over $6 million today. She did not move to Denver, but remained in Colorado City with Cavner. The couple did their best to make a life for themselves, and Maggie gave birth to three children between 1891 and 1895. None of them lived, and the burial records about them are quite puzzling. The oldest, a daughter who was also named Margaret, died on May 16, 1894 at the age of two-and-a-half years. On that same day, too, a son, also named James, died at birth. Both children were buried in the same lot and block at Evergreen Cemetery in Colorado Springs. The third child, whose name was spelled John "Kavanaugh" in the death records, succumbed to a premature birth and died at 26 W. Rio Grande Street in Colorado Springs on November 6, 1895. This child, however, was buried in a different area from the other two in Evergreen Cemetery. Then, just a few weeks later, Maggie herself died, too.

On November 30, 1895 the *Colorado City Iris* reported that "Miss Maggie Cavner died in this city Wednesday morning, after a protracted illness."[30] Sadly, she was only thirty-eight years old. So, what was the protracted illness? The answer perhaps lies in the burial records for Evergreen Cemetery in Colorado Springs, but even Maggie's burial records bring forth more questions than answers. Maggie's name was misspelled. Her occupation was that of a housewife, and the date of her funeral, December 7, is also listed as her date of death (which cannot be true, seeing as her death was initially reported in November). She was buried in the same lot and block number as her first two children. St. Mary's Church appears to have seen to the funeral arrangements and may have been responsible for the misspelling of Maggie's last name, which appears in records as "May Margaret Cavanaugh."[31] Nor is there an explanation as to who Ed M. Cavner, who died in 1896 in Missouri and was buried next to Maggie and her children, was. Today, no headstones appear to mark any of the family graves. As for James Cavner, he eventually moved to Pueblo, remarried, and ran a restaurant for many years. He does not appear in city directories with his wife, Florence, after 1917, and what became of him is unknown. The second Mrs. Cavner was alone when she died in La Junta in 1944.

CHAPTER FIVE

Dodge City's Demimonde

ONE HUNDRED AND SEVENTY-FIVE MILES WEST OF CALDWELL IS Dodge City, long known to history buffs as one of the roughest, toughest towns in the wild west. It is true that the likes of Bat Masterson, Wyatt Earp, and their cronies have helped spur Dodge City's rowdy reputation. Without these men, who later became the stuff of numerous dime novels, books, movies, and television shows due to Earp's friendships in Hollywood, Dodge City might appear as just another wild west town in Kansas. But Dodge City indeed earned its ornery reputation in its own right, with thousands of naughty ladies trailing after cowboys and other men in an effort to part them from their hard-earned money. And as with the other towns of Kansas, Dodge owed much of its red-light success to the annual cattle shipping that took place there.

When H. L. Sitler built a simple sod house just west of Fort Dodge in 1871, he was in exactly the right place at the right time. Situated along the Santa Fe Trail, Sitler's place soon blossomed into a small community complete with a general store—as well as three dance halls and six saloons. By 1872, the fledgling town was known as Buffalo City, the place where the drinks and dancing that were forbidden at Fort Dodge could be found. But there was already a post office called Buffalo elsewhere in Kansas, so the name was changed to Dodge City. Dodge's progression was quick; soon Texas cowboys were herding their cattle along a shortcut off the Chisholm Trail. Known as the Texas Trail, the path wound its way through Dodge City beginning in 1872, just as the Santa Fe Railroad rolled into town and built a large stockyard. Gambling and carousing with women were soon the major pastime.

Dodge City was in Ford County, which did not have its own sheriff. Likewise, Dodge City had no law enforcement during its formative years. The saloons, gambling houses, and shady ladies ran wild, and within a year's time, there were nineteen murders in the town. Not until June 3, 1873, was Sheriff Charlie Bassett elected to oversee Dodge City, and by 1876, the city was a major player in the cattle trade. The weekly influx of cowboys was a boon to the prostitution industry, seeing as the men were often paid upon their arrival in town. Naturally, this displeased certain elements of the town, who resented a bunch of dirty cowpokes who spent most of their money on good time girls. But a lot of the men's hard-earned cash went to local businesses as well, and complaints against them fell on deaf ears. Over the next three years, an average of between 48 and 108 prostitutes worked in Dodge City each summer. In time, the townsfolk would come to trust a group of lawmen who were hired in quick succession to oversee Dodge City and Ford County. They were Wyatt Earp and the Masterson brothers: Ed, Bat, and Jim. Of these, Earp and Bat would ingrain themselves within Dodge City's prostitution industry.

Wyatt Earp's stint as assistant marshal in Dodge City began sometime in 1876, after serving for about a year on the Wichita police force. Bartholomew "Bat" Masterson was just a young army scout when, in 1876, he was involved in a Texas shoot-out over dance hall girl Molly Brennan. Masterson managed to shoot his two opponents and wound up severely wounded himself. Thereafter, he decided to follow the law to the letter and work as a policeman. He soon made his way to Dodge City, and when Charlie Bassett became county sheriff in 1877, Bat Masterson was elected as his undersheriff. Dodge City liked Masterson, until he interfered with the arrest of a man by Marshal Larry Deger in June. Bat was arrested as Dodge City's newest assistant marshal, Bat's brother Ed, wrangled in Deger's suspect. Wyatt Earp, meanwhile, drew unwanted attention in July when, as a temporary "ex-officer," he slapped prostitute Frankie Bell after she "heaped epithets" at him. He was fined a dollar, while Frankie spent the night in jail and paid a fine of $20.[1]

Frankie Bell was not the only wayward woman to cause trouble in Dodge City. In October, the *Dodge City Times* reported on a man identified only as "Fritzie," who "has a black eye, caused by a heroic attempt to separate a half dozen pugilistic courtezans [*sic*] who were indulging in a free fight." A "Miss Fannie" jumped forward and gave the man "two or three center shots about the head, closing one of his blinkers, and otherwise marring his beautiful countenance."[2] It is unknown whether the Miss Fannie mentioned in the article was the same one who was identified as a "woman of color who worked at Beatty & Kelley's, a local restaurant attached to the Alhambra Saloon."[3] That Miss Fannie once appeared at the city attorney's office with a black eye. According to the *Times*, Fannie was performing some ironing at the home of a Mrs. Curly when a man named James Cowan busted through the door. Cowan was terribly drunk and threw the woman to the floor. Next, the man "elevated her paraphanalia, [*sic*] spanked her, and finally busted her a left hander in the right eye, accompanying the same with a kick in the stomach."[4]

Attacks on women of questionable character in Dodge City were reported with alarming frequency, but sometimes the ladies themselves were clearly guilty of crimes too. At other times, newspapers merely commented on the women's life choices. One article in the *Dodge City Times* reported on Susy Haden, a "beautiful Creole maiden of this city." Commentary was made that Susy was "casting fond and loving glances upon our modest but susceptible young friend, Bobby Gill," and that someone saw them "occupying positions relative to each other of such a delicate nature as to entirely prohibit us from describing in these chaste and virtuous columns."[5] Susy's tryst with Gill was a matter of fact as far as newspapers were concerned, and it was public knowledge that certain men in official capacities—including the mayor, two police officers, and the vice president of a local bank who was a partner in the Long Branch Saloon—even lived with prostitutes. One visitor to town commented that "Even the Mayor of the city indulges in the giddy dance with the girls and with his cigar in one corner of his mouth and his hat tilted to one side, he makes a charming looking officer."[6] Inexplicably, the Long Branch Saloon—one of Dodge City's most famous watering holes—was

The infamous Long Branch Saloon as it appeared in Dodge City during 1874.
COURTESY WIKIMEDIA COMMONS

said to have barred prostitutes and dance hall girls from doing business inside.

Besides certain saloons barring painted ladies and women in general, plenty of Dodge City's respectable ilk also objected to the prostitution industry openly flourishing throughout town. By 1878, certain Dodge City residents were openly resenting the annual cattle drives through town due to the unhealthy element of wicked women who increased in number each summer. The trouble was that several men identified as "the Gang," including Mayor James Kelley, Wyatt Earp, and Bat Masterson, were ruling over Dodge City's official affairs. It was well known that certain Gang members were known to make their money by rigging their games of chance, acting as outright con artists, duping victims in land deals, and even staging holdups. Eventually, however, reformers were at least able to talk Kelley into taxing Dodge City's gamblers and good time girls.[7] Of course this did little to quell the quarrelsome women who continued engaging in public fighting and other nuisances, nor did it prevent newspapers from reporting on them, tongue-in-cheek. In January, two soiled doves got into a heated fight at the boarding house of a "Mrs. W.," identified as being in Dodge City's "Tin Pot Alley." The *Ford County Globe* would bear witness to the incident, explaining in great detail that "When we heard the noise and looked out the front window, it was a magnificent sight to see. Tufts of hair, calico, snuff and gravel flew like fur in a cat fight, and before we could distinguish how the battle waned [*sic*] a chunk of dislocated leg grased [*sic*] our ear and a cheer from the small boys announced that a battle was lost and won. The crowd separated as the vanquished virgin was carried to her parlors by two 'soups.' A disjointed nose, two or three internal bruises, a chawed ear and a missing eye were the only scars we could see." Despite the paper's grisly description, Dodge City newspapers blatantly regarded prostitution as a "minor concern" when measured against more serious crimes.[8]

Some of the troubles with Dodge City's wayward women extended to those trying to infiltrate Fort Dodge. In March, the *Dodge City Times* reminded its readers that "No heavy wagons or wagons containing prostitutes are allowed to be driven through the Fort Dodge garrison."[9] The so-called cat wagons simply moved on to Dodge City.[10] But when the *Hays City Sentinel* claimed that there were some 120 wicked women living in Dodge City, the *Dodge City Times* retorted, "Divide that number by three and you get at the right number."[11] The true prostitution population, said another editor, was closer to forty.

In spite of the apparent low numbers of prostitutes, they were indeed a problem. The *Dodge City Times* duly published the ordinances against bawdy houses in August. But was Dodge City passing new ordinances because the city was overrun with harlots, or for another reason? The *Dodge City Times* answered that question, noting that "the city was running heavily in debt necessary to keep up a large police force. The ordinary revenues of the city were not adequate to the demand of so great a force to a small town . . . the fines are extended to the houses of ill-fame and those who inhabit them. The frail humanity will respond to the demand of the depleted city exchequer, remembering that the wages of sin is death." By the day of the *Times* retort to the *Sentinel*, authorities had already collected over $200 in fines.[12]

The bickering between Dodge City's newspapers was temporarily set aside in 1878 with the tragic death of Dora Hand. Dora has been one of a handful of shady ladies to eventually capture the hearts of historians and writers alike. Nevada has Julia Bulette, the famed courtesan who was mysteriously murdered in Virginia City. In Bodie, California, Rosa May has been courted by both magazine writers and authors. Like them, Dora's story has been told so often through time that the facts of her life have been mixed with enough fiction to make the lady appear a saint in the mesh of sinners around her. Only by examining the few facts about her life does her actual story emerge, beginning with her birth in New York, circa 1844, as Dora Crews. By 1870, she was in Omaha, Nebraska, where she worked as an "actress" at a theater known as the Academy of Fun. No matter how refined she might have been, however, Dora did turn to prostitution as needed; the 1870 census found Dora in Sedalia, Missouri, where she occupied a small brothel with fellow prostitute Stella Allen and a Black servant, Ida Watson.

A year later, Dora was in St. Louis when she married Theodore Hand. But Hand does not appear to have been with his bride when she appeared in Dodge City in July of 1878. The *Dodge City Globe* gave her a nod under her stage name, Fannie Keenan, in describing the Lady Gay Theatre Comique with some of "the best show entertainment ever given in Dodge."[13] Notable is that Dora's friend, Fannie Garretson, was included in the Comique's lineup of entertainers. It is she who was said to have encouraged Dora to come to Dodge City. Did Dora know that Fannie Garretson was most certainly the same woman who had recently been caught up in a fight with another prostitute in Deadwood, South Dakota, and that she had actually bit off a chunk of her opponent's ear? Perhaps not, but Fannie was as good a pal as any in Dodge City's red-light realm. Dora, however, was quite more genteel than her rowdy friend.

Almost all accounts of Dora Hand describe her with words like gracious, beautiful, charitable, and kind with a stellar singing voice, and her manner of dress was far more refined than the average Dodge City prostitute. The *Topeka State Journal* described her as "a brunette, very fine looking and about twenty-six to twenty-seven years of age" and called her "a vocalist and actress, well known in St. Louis and Cincinnati."[14] The description seems to be what Dora aspired to be, versus the hardened harlots who worked in Dodge City's demimonde. Among her suitors was

Mayor James Kelley, who enjoyed watching her sing at the Comique and was soon "squiring Dora around town." Dora also was known to spend lots of time at Kelley's cabin behind the Great Western Hotel. But there was, unfortunately, another man in her life: Spike Kenedy, a common cowboy who became infatuated with the woman. But the smitten fan was a troublemaker, to the effect that, one night in July, he was arrested by Wyatt Earp for waving a pistol around. The following month he was arrested again for being drunk "and so attentive to Dora Hand, that Jim Kelley threw him out." Afterward, Kenedy confronted Kelley in the Alhambra Saloon, during which the mayor warned him that local law enforcement had a job to do and that he'd better behave, or else. This time Kenedy tried to fight Kelley, only to be beaten up and tossed in the street. A defeated but furious Kenedy rode out of town.[15]

Unbeknownst to anyone, Kenedy had vowed to kill Mayor Kelley. As for Dora, she must have felt closer to Kelley than ever before, as she filed for divorce from Theodore Hand on October 1 and published her intention in the *Dodge City Globe*. Kelley, meanwhile, was suffering some sort of intestinal trouble which required a trip to see an army surgeon back at Fort Dodge. In his absence, he offered his cabin to Dora and Fannie Garretson. The *Dodge City Times* told what happened next: in the early morning hours of October 5, an unknown assailant rode up to Kelley's cabin, fired shots through the front door from his horse, and quickly rode away. Unbeknownst to the shooter, Fannie occupied the bed in the front room of the house while Dora slept in the back room. Quite by chance, one of the bullets passed through Fannie's bedclothes but missed her, penetrating the thin plaster wall between the rooms instead and hitting Dora "on the right side under the arm" as she slept. She died instantly.[16] Upon hearing the gunfire, Fannie got up to check on her friend and found her dead.

Although nobody saw Kenedy, Wyatt Earp and Jim Masterson soon surmised that Dora's unstable stalker had done the deed with the intent to kill Kelley. By that afternoon, a posse consisting of lawmen Bat Masterson, Charlie Bassett, Earp, Deputy Duff, and William Tilghman were in pursuit of the killer. Within hours, Kenedy was caught after rifle fire from the posse hit him in the shoulder and his horse was shot out from under him. He was brought back to Dodge City and deposited in jail, a good thing since public sentiment was running very much against him. Dodge City, meanwhile, remained kind to Dora Hand even in death. Rather than bury her in Boot Hill with the ruffians and scallywags of Dodge City, Dora's body was taken to Prairie Grove Cemetery instead. Her funeral was said to have been one of the largest in Dodge City's history, with upwards of four hundred men on horseback following behind the spring wagon carrying her body to the cemetery.

Although Kenedy was eventually acquitted due to insufficient evidence, the gunshot wound from the posse was so bad that a portion of his arm was amputated the following December. Dora Hand remained as a folk hero of sorts. In 1887, her body was moved to the all-new Maple Grove Cemetery, although she has no headstone today. Two movies, *The Woman of the Town* and *Wyatt Earp's Revenge*, as well as an episode on the 1950s television show *The Life and Legend of Wyatt Earp*, have paid tribute to Dora Hand—the harlot who went straight, and lost.

During 1879, it was guessed that forty-seven prostitutes lived in Dodge, while the city's population hovered around seven hundred. Some of them worked out of dance houses, one of which was described by the *Dodge City Globe* as "a long frame building, with a hall and bar in front and sleeping rooms in the rear. The hall was nightly used for dancing, and was frequented by prostitutes, who belonged to the house and for the benefit of it solicited the male visitors to dance. The rooms in the rear were occupied, both during the dancing hours and after, and both day and night by women for the purpose of prostitution." The lucky owners of such places made money off the dance fees, the drinks their girls sold, and the sex they were paid for.[17]

During the 1880 census, there were three to six times more men between the ages of twenty and forty-nine years in Dodge City than there were women in the same age bracket. Notable, too, were six prostitutes listed in the census as "sporting" who lived in various parts of town. Other prostitutes, however, were documented as concubines when they were found living with certain citizens. Among these were Bat Masterson who lived with Annie Ladue, his brother James who lived with Minnie Roberts, barkeeper Charles Ronan who resided with Laura Campbell, and another saloonkeeper, W. H. Harris, whose "concubine" was identified as C. C. Henderson. Any other women in the sex trade went undetected in the census, perhaps demurely giving their occupations as those of respectable women. Curious too is that the *Dodge City Times* published stories about local prostitutes only twice during 1880, and that one of them merely jabbed at the editor of the *Ford County Globe*: "The *Globe* editor makes frequent visits to Tin Pot Alley, we should judge, from his frequent allusions."[18]

After James Kelley was voted out of office in 1881, his successor, Alonzo Webster, immediately announced that "thieves, thugs, confidence men, and persons without visible means of support" were no longer welcome in Dodge City. A ticked-off James Masterson wired brother Bat, who was now in Tombstone, Arizona, tattling about the new mayor's plan to clean up Dodge City. Bat came in on the next train, but although a few shots were fired upon his arrival, Webster was able to organize a special posse to escort the Masterson brothers and two of their buddies out of town. Afterward, Webster beefed up his police force. Still, prostitution and wild cowboys remained a problem as some 500,000 cattle were brought through town during 1882.

By 1883, Webster was owner of a saloon himself when he found new enemies in the way of two men who owned an adjoining drinking hole: William Harris and his friend, the noted gunfighter Luke Short. Webster finally had enough and chose not to run for mayor again. His efforts to squelch prostitution had been for naught, for his successor, Larry Deger, came into office only to find that prostitutes were still running rampant around town. Deger passed all new ordinances prohibiting prostitutes from entering dance halls, saloons, and other places that may offend respectable people. Furthermore, all but one dance house was closed, and it was agreed that the surviving place would close on November 1, after the cattle season had ended.

Dodge City's immoral population was not going down without a fight. Almost immediately, William Harris was raided for violating the ordinance and three working girls were arrested and fined for being inside his saloon. But other saloon owners, like Webster for instance, were getting away with the same thing. Harris and Short felt picked on.

During what was known as the Dodge City War, Short was actually in a gunfight with a policeman. Nobody was hurt, but Short was arrested along with several sympathizers and thrown out of town. Short declared he would be back with several others as citizens cowered in their homes for a time and requested militia protection. Unwilling to have the situation escalate, authorities allowed Short to return peacefully and resume his business. Unfortunately, however, word of the Dodge City War reached newspapers as far away as Chicago and New York, much to the chagrin of Santa Fe Railroad officials. Dodge City was their major shipping point for cattle. The railroad demanded action from the city and threatened to change shipping points. Officials complied by closing businesses on Sundays, forbidding music in saloons and dance halls, and relegating gambling to back rooms out of public view.

Business owners only complied with the new rules for a short time before resuming their usual activities. News of wicked women continued appearing in newspapers throughout 1884. One article told of Sadie Hudson and Bertha Lockwood, whose jealousies over the same man led to a fight. When Sadie slapped Bertha, the woman went after her adversary with a knife and stabbed her three times. Sadie was expected to live. There might have been more scuffles, but cattle drives through Dodge City would cease in 1885, following the quarantine law that banned Texas cattle from entering Kansas. That may explain why the 1885 Kansas census failed to list any shady ladies. Kansas Governor Jeremiah Strang himself noted the absence of cowboys in Dodge City, writing that they, as well as "the gamblers and prostitutes will find their occupations gone, and, from necessity, must follow." Mayor Robert Wright answered that "We have always been a frontier Town, where the wild & reckless sons of the plains have congregated, their influences are still felt here, but we are rapidly overcoming them, let us alone & we will work out our own salvation."[19]

Wright appears to have been true to his word. Prostitutes, at least, bore very little mention during the next several years, except for a few incidents. Those who remained in town obviously had a hard time of it. In one incident during 1886, a Black prostitute was actually shot while trying to wrangle a customer. This and other incidents continued to plague Dodge City for a time, but frontier prostitution as it was known was drawing to a close. Most historians agree that after 1887, Dodge City melded into a quieter, safer place. But where did the ladies of Dodge City's demimonde disappear to? One answer may lie in a 1912 article in a Dodge City newspaper. The editor was new and decided to regale his readers with stories about the city's brothels and dance halls of the 1880s, including raids and arrests on such places. How could he know that some of the shady ladies from Dodge's early days had managed to marry well and still lived in town? Alas he did not, and not until someone pointed out the public slight did he cease writing the stories.

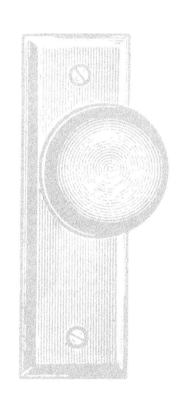

CHAPTER SIX

Mattie Blaylock, Little Girl Lost

IT IS IMPOSSIBLE TO CONSIDER THE HISTORY OF DODGE CITY WITHOUT Wyatt Earp, his brothers, and the men's various wives. Two of them— Nellie "Bessie" Bartlett Ketchum, wife of James, and Celia Ann "Mattie" Blaylock, wife of Wyatt— are well known for their careers in Kansas's prostitution industry. The women were vastly different, even though they most certainly worked together. Bessie was a madam and lived out her life with her husband. Mattie was eventually abandoned by Earp and died under tragic circumstances in a raw Arizona desert town.

Mattie's life began as Celia Blalock [*sic*] in Iowa in January of 1850, where she was born to farmers Henry and Elizabeth Blaylock. Growing up, Mattie was called Celie by her friends and family. The Blaylock farm was busy, what with a main wagon road and other farms nearby. Most researchers

This is believed to be the earliest known image of Mattie Blaylock.
COURTESY WIKIMEDIA COMMONS

believe that Mattie and her fifteen-year-old sister, Sarah, left home sometime during the summer of 1868. Another of Mattie's sisters, Tony May, would later say that the girls "left very suddenly."[1] It is possible that neither girl could stand their strict Lutheran lifestyle. Life on the road for two teens with limited experience was no doubt difficult, and it has been widely believed the girls dabbled in the prostitution industry during their time away from home.

Two years after the girls' departure, Sarah Blaylock decided to return home. She was there by the time the census enumerator visited the Blaylock farm near Iowa City on July 28, 1870. Where Mattie went after Sarah left her is a puzzle. Most researchers believe she was in Fort Scott, Kansas, during 1871, when she had a full-length photograph taken of herself at J. T. Parker Ltd. It is also believed that while in Fort Scott, she began going by Mattie. And, it is believed by many sources that Mattie first met Wyatt Earp at Fort Scott as early as 1870.

By the time Earp allegedly met Mattie, he was a widower, had been fired from his job as a constable in Missouri for embezzling city money, had escaped from jail in Arkansas where he was arrested for stealing horses, and is believed to have been living with his brother, Newton, not far from Fort Scott. Although it is undocumented whether, where, or when the couple married, Earp did introduce Mattie to Newton and his family during the summer of 1871, and they are said to have "accepted her as his wife." Newton's family liked Mattie and she was known to have stayed with them on two separate occasions.[2] By today's standards, Mattie and her man should have married proper. In frontier times, however, it was indeed acceptable for couples living in remote areas to simply marry by common law, without the sanctity of a church or certificate. Two of Earp's brothers lived with common-law wives: James with Alvira "Allie" Sullivan, and Morgan with Louisa Houston. It would not have been unusual that Mattie and Wyatt Earp were never officially wed in a ceremony.

For Mattie, the union meant that she now had a man to take care of her. It must have meant a lot to her that Newton Earp and his family liked her, as did Morgan when Mattie met him in Peoria, Illinois, during the autumn of 1871. Within a few months, Wyatt and Mattie would themselves relocate to Peoria. It is unknown how Mattie felt when she and Earp, instead of finding a house together, moved into Jane Haspel's brothel, Haspel House, on Washington Street. Morgan, it turned out, was well known in Peoria's demimonde and soon formed an investment partnership with Wyatt and one George Randall. Jane's house was the investment. Formerly the abused wife of Frederick Haspel, Jane had been in Peoria since 1865 and filed for divorce in 1871. Fred Haspel had deserted her after nine years of marriage back in 1864, she said, also that on New Year's Day in 1865 he "struck, kicked, choked & beat" her, knocking her to the floor. Three children came of this tumultuous reunion: Sarah, Edward, and Mary.[3] What were the men's roles as the investors in a house of prostitution? Plenty of men owned bordello properties in the west, although the majority of them seldom lived on the property. Although Morgan Earp seems to have lived elsewhere, Wyatt and George Randall were clearly an exception. Since their paramours worked at Jane's brothel, the men lived there too. Their jobs were to keep the peace within the house when customers were present, negotiate with city officials on behalf of the women, pay for fines and licenses as needed, drum up business outside of the brothel, and perform other duties to assure the occupants of the house stayed out of trouble while generating income.

Only Wyatt Earp and Jane Haspel appeared at Jane's house in Peoria's 1872–1873 city directory, but that isn't so unusual. Mattie was not in the directory, but at the time, wives typically were not listed alongside their husbands unless they were legitimately employed. Jane, however, would have appeared as head of the household. Mattie's presence at Jane's is verified by her arrest in February of 1872, along with Randall's wife, Minnie, Carrie Crow, and another woman named Sarah. The Earp brothers and George Randall were arrested too, and the whole bunch was taken to court. The Earps and Randall were charged as keepers of Jane's brothel, and the prosecuting attorney explained to Jane that it was the men he wanted. If Minnie would testify against them, the ladies of the house would go free. Surprisingly Jane agreed to the deal, but the men successfully petitioned for a change of venue, and by way of the judge's error, were only fined $20 each.

Probably due to Jane's agreement with the prosecuting attorney, Wyatt and Mattie were on the outs with her when they, along with Morgan and the Randalls, moved to another brothel soon after their court case was over. The madam of the new place, called the McClellan Institute, was Jennie Green. All was well until April, when Minnie Randall spent the day partying at Jennie's and accidentally overdosed on opium. Morgan, Mattie, and Wyatt were all called to testify at an inquest over Minnie's death. A month later, Wyatt and Morgan were arrested once again, at Jennie's. The *Peoria Daily Transcript* reported on the raid, stating, "That hotbed of iniquity, the McClellan Institute on Main Street, near Water, was pulled on Thursday night, and quite a number of inmates transient and otherwise were found therein. [Wyatt] Earp and his brother Morgan Earp, were each fined $44.55 and as they had not the money and would not work, they languished in the cold and silent caboose."[4]

When the Earp brothers were released in June, they, along with Mattie and George Randall, moved to Beardstown some seventy-seven miles southwest, to a floating bordello on the Illinois River known as the Beardstown Gunboat. John Walton owned the boat, and his wife ran the brothel onboard. Wyatt was already familiar with Beardstown, having been involved in an 1869 shooting scuffle there with one Tom Piner after the man called him "the California boy."[5] The Beardstown Gunboat was nicely outfitted, with a saloon and dance floor on the lower deck and a series of small rooms on the upper deck. Walton could maneuver the boat to different locales, thereby evading the law. All was well until August, when George Randall, Mattie, and Wyatt went ashore and were spotted talking with two sixteen-year-old girls by the sheriff. The group was hauled in for questioning and released. But when a big party broke out aboard the Beardstown Gunboat in early September, Walton and the Earps were arrested.

This time, the group appeared in court and were duly reported on by the *Daily National Democrat* on September 10. Interestingly is that one of the women, when asked her name, responded, "My name is Sarah Earp. I am Mrs. Wyatt Earp." But the paper also reported that "Sarah Earp, alias Sally Heckell, calls herself the wife of Wyatt."[6] Several theories guess at whether the woman in court was Mattie: the Peoria 1870 census reveals

Sally Haskell, a sixteen-year-old prostitute, working at the separate brothel of Madam Thankful Sears. Did the census taker perhaps mis-hear or misspell Sally's name? A few lines up in the census, ten-year-old Mary Haspel, Jane Haspel's daughter, is documented as a domestic in the house (and most interestingly, the census taker wrote "God pity you" next to her occupation). Because Jane's other daughter, Sarah, called herself Sally during an 1871 court appearance, some researchers believe she was the one in court that day. Alternatively, there is also the chance that Mattie said her name was Celie in court, and it was misspelled.

All that is known for sure is that Mattie, along with Mrs. Walton, was fined $24. Notable too is that Sarah Haspel was not recorded as being aboard the Beardstown Gunboat when it was raided. John Walton and Wyatt Earp paid $43.15 and $44, respectively. Earp paid his fine and that of Mattie's, and the couple returned to Kansas to live with Newton for a time. A short time later, Wyatt rented a small farm where the couple remained until 1873. The Earps likely had no intention of farming for long and, as the autumn months set in, Earp's brother James summoned him to Wichita. Earp left in November as Mattie stayed behind to settle their affairs and joined him in December. By the time she got to Wichita, Earp was dealing faro at a local saloon. And, it turned out that James's new wife, Bessie, was herself a madam.

Bessie was Nellie Bartlett when she first began working in the prostitution industry as a teenager. She was a widow with the last name of Ketcham when she met James, perhaps as early as 1864, but had only recently moved in with him. By January of 1874, James, Bessie, Wyatt, and Mattie had rented a brothel at 12 Douglas Avenue from George and Maggie Wood. The house was big enough to accommodate several people, including the four Earps, James and Bessie's two children, the Woods, and three prostitutes, including Georgie Wood and Laura Smith. The third woman was "Big Nose Kate" Haroney, who also had long been a prostitute on her own before coming to Wichita. A number of historians have long speculated that in his first months in Wichita, without Mattie, Wyatt Earp carried on an affair with Kate. The romance was cut short with Mattie's arrival, which Kate did not like. Whether Mattie was aware of the affair is unrecorded, but Kate remained an inmate of what soon became known as "Bessie's Whore House."[7] Also unrecorded is how Kate felt about working under Wyatt's girl, since it was soon clear that Bessie and Mattie ran the brothel as partners.

Per a city ordinance, Mattie dutifully registered with the other women from Bessie's at the Wichita police station in January 1874—under the name Sally (her nickname, Celie, might have again been misspelled) Earp—and paid her fine. Wyatt, meanwhile, aspired to work in law enforcement in Wichita. In March, it was announced that Wichita city marshal Mike Meagher was leaving to become a US deputy marshal. Earp ran to take his place. But his application was rejected, probably due to his association with Bessie's Whore House, and Bill Smith took Meagher's place instead. Earp might have been hoping to better control the fines imposed on Bessie and her girls, for in May, Bessie and "Sallie" Earp were both fined for prostitution. The ladies paid, but on June 3, they were arrested again on the charge that they "unlawfully and feloniously set up [a] bawdy house or brothel and did appear and act as mistress and have the care and management of a certain one story frame building situated and located North of Douglas Avenue."[8] In court, Bessie and "Sallie" pleaded guilty, but were ordered to stand trial anyway as their bail was set at $500. Wyatt and James were able to come up with the money as the trial was set for September. Judge Mitchell warned the women that a condition of their release prohibited either of them from "acting as madams."[9]

Mattie and Bessie soon found a way around the judge's order by "hiring" one Madam Mattie Bradford to run the brothel. Madam Bradford would run the house, pay the fines, and keep the girls in line, thus enabling Mattie and Bessie to work as "common bawds" within the confines of Wichita law. What the law did not know, however, was that Mattie Bradford did not exist. Her name never surfaced in newspapers, official documents, or city directories. Although fines were paid on her behalf, the madam herself never appeared in court. Mattie Bradford, some historians challenge, was almost certainly a made-up persona, designed by the Earps to appear as though it were she who was running the house. The ploy worked.

At their trial on September 15, Bessie and Mattie appeared before Judge William Campbell, who demanded to know where the witnessing officers were. A bailiff was sent to find them but returned empty-handed. The women's attorney, William Baldwin, immediately stepped forward and asked Campbell to dismiss the case. Campbell was in no mood for this waste of his time; not only did he dismiss the case but he also decreed that the prosecuting witnesses who failed to show would have to pay the court costs. Just why the witnesses never appeared remains unsolved, and it is just a guess that Wyatt and James Earp had something to do with it. Bessie and Mattie happily returned as reigning madams of their own court, and the fictional Mattie Bradford magically "disappeared" after her final court costs in the last week of September were paid by lawyer Baldwin.[10]

The law eventually caught up with Big Nose Kate, who somehow missed out on the arrest of Mattie and Bessie but paid a $10 fine in June. When she was arrested in August, Kate was identified as Kate "Earb," or Earp.[11] Did Kate say her name was Earp because she was still carrying on with Wyatt? Or because she was one of Bessie Earp's girls? Or, perhaps, because she was being defiant over Wyatt going back to Mattie? Whatever her reason, Kate paid her fine and soon left Wichita. Later in her life, Kate would claim that Wyatt was once her customer until he "went back to prostitute Mattie Blaylock," also that she didn't even meet Wyatt and Mattie until she had moved on to Fort Griffin, Texas, and met her new paramour, Henry "Doc" Holliday.[12]

Bessie's house remained mighty popular, although she and Mattie (still as Sally or Sallie Earp) paid fines for prostitution in February of 1875. But in March, the Kansas State Census found only Bessie Earp, George and Maggie Wood, Laura Smith, and M. Blackman, the latter a fifty-two-year-old Black servant. Interestingly, James and Wyatt were documented as living elsewhere in the census. Mattie's name does not appear in the census at all, and whether the census taker merely missed her somehow remains a mystery. In April, Wyatt finally achieved his dream of working in law enforcement again when he was appointed to serve as a policeman under Mike Meagher, who had returned to his duties as city marshal. As a result, neither Bessie nor Mattie paid another fine in Wichita. Wyatt remained marshal of Wichita for about a year before he was accused of punching Marshal Bill Smith in April of 1876.

Meagher, who was running for marshal against Earp, was forced to testify against his friend. Worse yet, the only reason Earp smacked Smith to begin with was because he uttered some insult against Meagher. Earp was found guilty, fined for the incident, and fired from his position.

Earp continued running his faro game, but his luck ran out within a few months. Those who had soured on the entire Earp family in Wichita were soon watching him closely. It was no secret that Wyatt was suspected of pocketing certain fines and fees he had collected in the red-light district, and the city treasurer soon verified it was true. Earp had no choice but to offer up the money, although he did ask that no charges be levied against him in return. Wyatt now was the shame of Wichita, and in May, the Earp brothers split up and left town—James and Bessie to New Mexico, and Wyatt to Dodge City, with Mattie in tow. Wyatt had a good reason to go to Dodge City: his brother Morgan was there. Here too, Earp would get another job as a deputy and run his faro bank. By November of 1876, city marshal Larry Deger and Wyatt, said the *Atchison Daily Champion*, were competently keeping the peace at three rowdy dance halls in Dodge City "discreetly, firmly, and [humanely]."[13]

Mattie and Wyatt remained in Dodge City for about three years. Mattie no longer worked as a prostitute, and her letters home to sister Sarah consistently bore the return address of Mrs. Wyatt Earp. The Earp home was located just two blocks from Front Street's saloons, so there is a chance that Mattie occasionally accompanied Earp on his excursions there. The money Wyatt made enabled one or both of them to take extended trips. During their first winter in Dodge City, for instance, Wyatt and Morgan traveled to Deadwood, South Dakota, to cut and sell wood. Also, the *Dodge City Times* confirmed in July 1877 that Wyatt had been away for a while. "Wyatt Earp, who was on our city police force last summer, is in town again," the paper said. "We hope he will accept a position on the force once more. He had a quiet way of taking the most desperate characters into custody."[14] Earp did rejoin the force, but just two weeks later the *Times* reported that he slapped prostitute Frankie Bell.

It is unknown whether Mattie accompanied Earp on his trips, but it is verified that he spent more time away from Dodge City. In January of 1878, he was known to have just returned from a visit to Fort Clark,

Texas. And in May, he had apparently been gone for some time when he returned to Dodge City from Fort Worth, Texas, and "was immediately appointed assistant marshal."[15] That he was very well thought of is evident by a note in Wichita's *Weekly Eagle*, which reported two days later that Earp had been offered a whopping $200 per month. But the story seems to have been no more than a rumor, for the *Dodge City Times* would verify in June that Wyatt was still employed as assistant city marshal at just $75 per month.

A short time later, Kate and Doc Holliday showed up in Dodge City, at Wyatt's invitation. The Earps seemingly enjoyed their time with Kate and Doc; Kate would later recall that Mattie and Wyatt often dined or attended the Comique Theater with Wyatt's friends in the sporting crowd. What Dodge City's denizens thought of Kate and Doc is unrecorded, although even the *Wichita Eagle* did note that Earp was doing a bang-up job as assistant marshal. Kate and Doc seemed quite content with Dodge City, if Doc's advertisement for dentistry in the June 8 issue of the *Dodge City Times* is any indication. Doc's office was at Dodge House, a primitive hotel with a billiard parlor with sample rooms on the northwest corner of notorious Front Street and Railroad Avenue.

Doc's advertisement appeared in the newspaper but twice. He apparently preferred playing cards, and Kate spent her time entertaining men. Both of them, especially Doc, were also involved in various skirmishes and petty crimes during their time in Dodge City. Whether Mattie joined the couple on their escapades is unknown, although a descendant of Mattie later implied that Mattie got into a lot of trouble in Dodge. Yet her name does not surface anywhere in Dodge City. There may be a reason for that, as Wyatt was purportedly carrying on with a prostitute known as Lily "Dutch Lil" Beck. If that story is true, Mattie likely would have preferred to stay at home rather than face the fact that her man was seeing another woman. There was, after all, nowhere else for her to go. And she was probably quite relieved when at last, in December, Kate and Doc left Dodge City and headed for New Mexico.

By April of 1879, Wyatt had truly redeemed himself as an upstanding lawman in Dodge City. A visiting reporter from the *Atchison Champion* later commented that "Before going to Dodge I was told to stay away;

that it was not safe to be on the streets after night; and that it was run by robbers, pick-pockets and rowdies. Just the reverse of this is true."[16] Yet Wyatt was restless, later telling others that "Dodge was beginning to lose much of the snap which had given it a charm to men of restless blood, and I decided to move to Tombstone, which was just building up a reputation."[17] In September, the *Dodge City Globe* announced, "Mr. Wyatt Earp, who has been on our police force for several months, resigned his position last week and took his departure for Las Vegas, New Mexico."[18]

The rest of Mattie's life is much more documented in western annals than her time in Kansas. In Las Vegas, she and Earp met up with Doc Holliday, Big Nose Kate, James and Bessie Earp, and their daughter Hattie. Everyone went on to Prescott, where Wyatt's brother Virgil and his wife, Allie, were waiting. The party planned to travel to Tombstone together. Allie later remembered how the three women—Mattie, Allie, and Bessie—teamed up to sort through and pare down the best of their wares—rolling pins, a commode, and a sewing machine—for the remaining trip to Tombstone. Although she had little to offer, Mattie is credited for convincing the men to take along the sewing machine. "Oh, we can get it in someplace," Wyatt finally said, and muttered quietly, "but I don't know where."[19] Kate also remembered Wyatt opening a trunk which revealed a stash of "false mustaches, beards and wigs and he asked me if I knew what they were. I said, 'Yes, I think I do.'"[20] Clearly, Wyatt was still on the hustle.

As the Earp party prepared to leave Prescott, Kate decided to go to Globe where she could make some good money, and Doc chose to remain in Prescott because he was on a winning streak. The rest of the party continued south, arriving in Tombstone on December 1. Virgil secured a job as US marshal for the Tombstone district and Wyatt eventually became a deputy sheriff for Pima County. That was the end of Bessie and Mattie's foray in the prostitution industry for the time being. Instead, the pair made a handsome profit taking in sewing for others, including a canvas tent for a new saloon.

Was Mattie bored in Tombstone? Not at first, since she had the other Earp wives to keep her company—especially Allie. "That was our life: workin' and sitting home," Allie later said. "Good women didn't go any place." Allie also had kind words for Mattie, calling her "as fine a woman as ever lived," who stuck with Wyatt "through thick and thin."[21] For a time, Mattie was content and resumed writing letters to her sister Sarah.

As of the 1880 census on June 2, Mattie and Wyatt were sharing quarters with James and Bessie. Notably, Mattie's birthplace was given as Wisconsin. Also, the birthplaces of both Mattie and Bessie's parents were left blank. This seems to indicate that the women were not present when the census was taken, and that one of the other occupants of the house gave the enumerator the information. The following day, the census taker was in another part of town when he documented James, Bessie, and Hattie at a different address.

Mattie and Wyatt eventually purchased an adobe house together, and many historians claim that Earp even named one of his mining claims the "Mattie Blaylock." Later that year, Morgan Earp and Louisa Houston arrived in town too. Now, the Earp family was all together in one place, and Mattie likely felt quite at home as one of them. When Wyatt resigned his position on the police force and took a job as a Wells Fargo detective, she must have been mighty proud. But that would soon change.

In addition to his new job, Earp also began running a game of chance at the Oriental Saloon. He began coming home later and later; eventually the Oriental was his primary occupation. Meanwhile, Mattie started suffering terrible headaches, which has been attributed to migraine headaches, painful gum disease, or even female troubles. By day, she was able to go shopping and to lunch with Allie. Once, the ladies decided to take a walk around town and wound up getting a bit tipsy on wine. When they finally toddled home, they went straight to bed in hopes their husbands wouldn't be the wiser. Wyatt and Virgil, however, came home earlier than expected and found them out. Allie later remembered Wyatt's attempts to sober Mattie up as she was "spillin' the coffee Wyatt was makin' her drink."[22] Allie would also remember how Wyatt treated Mattie after the wine drinking incident. "I told you to keep out of town and not to show your face on the streets," Allie remembered him bellowing, "I told you!"[23] He also berated Mattie about her being so passive. But it was indeed rare for Wyatt to come home early, and Mattie's nights were indeed lonely without him. To combat her pain, and also her loneliness, Mattie began taking various drugs and drinking, which is perhaps why she appeared so passive to her husband.

By the spring of 1881, the relationship between Wyatt and Mattie was steadily going downhill. Enter Sarah Josephine Marcus, the girl-friend of sheriff John Behan who first appeared in Tombstone in April. By August, she and Wyatt Earp were an item, and Wyatt spent more and more late nights away from home. "We all knew about it and Mattie did too," Allie said of the affair. "That's why we never said anything to her. We didn't have to. We could see her with her eyes all red from cryin', thinkin' of Wyatt's carryin' on. I didn't have to peek out at night to see if the light was still burnin' in her window for Wyatt. I knew it would still be burnin' at daylight when I got up."[24] Allie also recalled horrible fights between Mattie and Wyatt, as well as being with Mattie when she once spotted Josie in a local shop.

Then came Tombstone's most notorious day in history, October 26, when the Earp brothers, Doc Holliday, and John Behan were involved in the famous shoot-out near the OK Corral. The Earp ladies were at home, and Allie would later explain that Mattie had her hair in curlers when the gunshots rang out just blocks away. Mattie ran outside, but quickly came back in and nervously waited along with Allie and Louisa until the injured Virgil and Morgan were brought home. The ladies tended to the men's wounds as news stories about the shoot-out were literally published around the world. The months following the shoot-out were quite intense, and Mattie's drinking continued—often in the company of Allie. When Wyatt heard there was a hit list with the Earps' names on it in December, most of the family moved into the Cosmo-politan Hotel. Wyatt commanded Mattie to stay in their room and not wander around town. Sure enough, Virgil was shot and severely injured on December 28.

In February of 1882, financial woes forced Earp to sell his share of the Oriental Saloon. He also took out a loan for $365 and put the adobe house up for collateral. But one source states he had sent Mattie to Iowa to see her family, and as half-owner of the house, her signature was required on the loan papers. Earp signed the papers on February 13. A second source states Mattie returned from Iowa on February 22. Was

Mattie's Time in Tombstone

December 1, 1879—Mattie arrives with Wyatt in Tombstone and, with Allie Earp, begins sewing to make money

June 1, 1880—Mattie and Wyatt purchase a home together; Wyatt is listed in the census as a "farmer"

October 28, 1880—Wyatt is appointed deputy sheriff

November, 1880—Wyatt quits his job and begins working late at the Oriental Saloon; Mattie takes up drinking

August 1881—Wyatt begins an affair with Sarah Josephine Marcus as Mattie's drinking and drug habits increase

October 26, 1881—The shootout at the OK Corral occurs

March 1882—Mattie goes to the Earp family home in California to await Wyatt.

she even aware of what Wyatt had done? That's a mystery that will never be solved.

After Morgan Earp was shot and killed in March, things moved very quickly. James accompanied his dead brother's body to his family's home in California, followed by Virgil, Allie, and Louisa, who left on March 19. Mattie and Bessie followed on March 27. Mattie likely had no idea that it was the last time she would see Wyatt Earp. For several months, Mattie stayed with the Earps and waited for Wyatt to come for her.

At first, Wyatt sent Mattie a little money to live on. But that gesture eventually ceased, and the loan on Mattie and Wyatt's little house in Tombstone was never paid and went into foreclosure. Earp, meanwhile, was dodging bullets and arrests as he ran all over the west. Mattie must have been frantic as newspapers were riddled with misinformation. In early May, for instance, it was reported that Earp had been killed. A week later, however, another newspaper reported he had been arrested. In July, he was reported as the new marshal of Gunnison, Colorado. None of these reports were correct. What is known for sure is that sometime around August, Wyatt finally headed to California—but to San

Francisco, not the family home, and moved into an apartment with Virgil and Warren. It was no coincidence that Josie Marcus had also moved back to San Francisco. Mattie eventually realized that Wyatt Earp was not coming for her. Brokenhearted and with no place else to go, Mattie contacted Big Nose Kate in Globe and caught a train to Arizona. There, she resumed the only real job she ever knew: working as a prostitute.

In Kate, Mattie found a better friend than she expected. The women had obviously remained in touch, and Kate respectfully referred to Mattie as "Wyatt Earp's wife" when talking later on about their time in Globe. Mattie had perhaps reached a very sad conclusion: she was no longer a part of Wyatt Earp or his family, although she did stay in touch with Allie Earp and Wyatt's sister, Adelia. There is nothing to indicate she remained in contact with Bessie, her long-ago partner in the prostitution industry. In the end, Mattie turned to the only other person she knew who could help her find a way to make a living. That person was Kate.

Mattie remained in Globe for about four years, and she had the only other known portrait of herself taken at The Photograph Gallery there in 1885. But she talked more and more about how she lost Wyatt Earp as her drinking and drugging increased. In 1887, her only other longtime friend, Bessie Earp, died. Then Big Nose Kate left for Colorado, where Doc Holliday was dying. Now truly alone, Mattie remained in Globe until October when she inexplicably moved to Pinal, a milling town in the hot desert between Globe and Phoenix that was quickly fading. Why Pinal? The guesses are many, including that Mattie intended to go on but decided to stay, or ran out of money and was forced to stay. Either way, she is believed to have initially checked into the Pinal Hotel until she found a two-room cabin she could afford with her wages as a prostitute.

Mattie did make a few friends in Pinal: county sheriff Pete Gabriel, Dr. Thomas Kinnaird who treated her illnesses, a Mexican couple, and a mine laborer named Frank Bueler. Wyatt Earp is rumored to have sent her money now and then, but her mantra, "Wyatt Earp wrecked my life," exhibited Mattie's deep depression and bitterness at how sad her life had become.[25] Finally, on July 3, Bueler fetched some laudanum for Mattie. Sometime later, a man named T. J. Flannery appeared, saw that something wasn't right with Mattie, and summoned a doctor. But there was nothing anyone could do. In the hours after Mattie died, two Mexican women who were friends with her dressed her body for burial before turning her over to the undertaker, who placed her in a pine coffin and took her for burial in Pinal's cemetery. The county paid the cost.

The most intriguing end to Mattie's story is that of her two trunks, which Coroner Benson sent to her sister Sarah. Upon receiving them, Sarah and her husband relegated them to the attic where they were subsequently forgotten about until 1952. Sarah had died in 1906, leaving her estate to her son, Osmond Hiram Marquis. He knew about the trunks, who they belonged to, and what happened to Mattie. One of the trunks had inexplicably been given away by the time Marquis decided to look inside the one that remained. There he found a packet of letters that included Coroner Benson's letter to Sarah, Mattie's clothing, and a small Bible inscribed to Wyatt Earp by "Sutton and Colburn." Seeking more answers, Marquis next wrote to Merritt Beeson at the Beeson Museum in Tombstone. It would be three years before Beeson's wife wrote back and successfully requested copies of everything Marquis had. Mattie's things (except for her letters, which were passed on to her family) were donated by Marquis's widow to the Arizona Historical Society, and her trunk was eventually sold at a wild west auction in Pennsylvania. Today, historians still debate whether Earp really married Mattie Blaylock, and few want to admit he deserted her in her time of need.

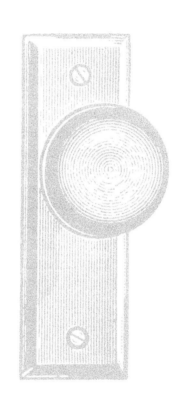

CHAPTER SEVEN

The Story of Squirrel Tooth Alice

THE LIFE OF LIBBY THOMPSON IS QUITE REMARKABLE. AS A CHILD, SHE was kidnapped by Natives in her home state of Texas. Back from captivity, she ran away from her parents' home and wound up working as a prostitute and madam for over six decades. The only real man in her life was a wild, often violent gunslinger who kept her on the run, and she amazingly found time to give birth to nine children during her time with him. In spite of her rough, rambling life, Libby died just two years short of her one hundredth birthday. Yet with all of her accomplishments, the lady might have easily slipped through the cracks of history if not for her charming, enigmatic nickname: Squirrel Tooth Alice.

Libby was named Mary Elizabeth Haley, after her mother, when she was born in Belton, Texas, in 1855. Her father, James, toiled as a farmer. In spite of their humble existence, the Haley family was a busy one. They were living in Johnson County during the 1860 census, receiving their mail at the Comanche Peak post office. Although James Haley's real and personal property was worth $1,423 at the time, the family would lose nearly everything after the Civil War broke out in 1861. Everything about the Haleys was seemingly routine for the era—until 1864, when a group of Comanches raided the family farm. Although there is no newspaper documenting exactly what happened, Libby would later say the Natives took her with them when they left. She was just ten years old. For the next three years, Libby's frantic parents toiled to come up with enough money to purchase their daughter back from the Comanches. They finally succeeded, but Libby would later recall that "Through no fault of my own I was seen as a marked woman after my release. Though only thirteen years-old most people assumed that I had been 'used' by the Indians during my captivity and I was shunned and ostracized from society."[1]

Libby's father especially seemed determined to keep Libby, an unwilling victim, in a life of shame. An oft-cited story goes that when an older man began courting the girl, James Haley suspected the worst of him and shot him to death. The incident is most likely what inspired Libby to leave her parents' home and strike out on her own in about 1869. Nearly five hundred miles later, the teenager was working as a dance hall girl and prostitute in Abilene, Kansas. Here too, she would meet the love of her life: William "Texas Billy" Thompson.

Born in England in 1845, Thompson immigrated to New Orleans in 1952 with his father and an older brother, Ben Thompson. He was in Austin, Texas by 1860, and both he and Ben volunteered for the Confederate Army during the Civil War. The brothers also enjoyed gambling and the sporting life. By 1868, Billy had already been in the first of many shooting scrapes, which occurred in Austin, Texas. Earlier in the day, he had tangled with a soldier named Burke over a prizefight, but the two were on friendly terms at a local bordello when Burke allegedly began threatening Thompson. Shots were fired, Burke died, and Thompson fled to Rockport, Texas. Two months later, he killed one Remus Smith for slapping his horse.

Thompson was still wanted when he met Libby, but she didn't seem to mind. Besides, Thompson appeared to go straight by taking a job cowboying along the Chisholm Trail between Abilene and San Antonio, Texas. Libby traveled the trail with him, plying her trade along the way. The two posed as husband and wife, and Libby was using Thompson's name when she was found in the July 1870 census. Enumerator S. Jackson found Lizzie and three other harlots residing with a farmer named George Palmer and his wife, Elizabeth, in Ellsworth, Kansas. Jackson obviously took his job seriously, recording the occupations of those he interviewed in more detail than the average census taker. But he also had a sense of humor; in the case of Lizzie and her friends, Jackson recorded the following:

Libby Thompson, age 18, born in Missouri, "Diddles"
Harriet Parmenter, age 23, born in New York, "Does horizontal
work"
Lizzie Harris, age 24, born in Ireland, "'Ogles' Fools"
Ettie Baldwin, age 23, born in Illinois, "Squirms in the dark"

Interesting, too, is that there was a four-year-old child, John Edward, living in the Palmer house as well. There is no clue as to whose child he was or why he was there. Libby was recorded by the census elsewhere, too. On October 2, she was found at the house of her parents in Mead County, Texas, where she appeared under her given name, Elizabeth, and was recorded as being age sixteen. This second census record is most interesting, an indication that Libby perhaps was not at odds with her family as much as historians believe. Both listings in the 1870 census also bring forth the question of Billy Thompson's whereabouts, since he is not included in the 1870 census at all. Certainly, he and Libby were together, for she was using his name.

Around the same time as the 1870 census, Libby earned her famous nickname: Squirrel Tooth Alice. Various historians have attributed the name to Libby's use of "Alice" as a pseudonym, a common practice among prostitutes. Others also surmise that Libby's pet prairie dog, who appears in the only known images of the lady, was mistaken by others for a squirrel. That and the small, protruding gap in Libby's front teeth have

Libby "Squirrel Tooth Alice" poses with her pet prairie dog. COURTESY KANSAS HISTORICAL SOCIETY

been attributed to the birth of her famous moniker.[2] Newspapers during Libby's life, however, do not seem to have used the nickname. Not until later was she identified in western annals as Squirrel Tooth Alice.

Libby and Billy Thompson remained in Ellsworth until 1873. Libby could prostitute herself as Thompson worked the gambling tables. When Ben Thompson joined the couple in June, the brothers earned their way as the "house gamblers" at Joe Brennan's saloon. They also formed a friendly alliance with Sheriff Chauncey Whitney. Unfortunately, during a fracas between Ben Thompson and a gambler who stiffed him, a drunken Billy accidentally shot and killed Whitney during a fray that included Ellsworth police officer John "Happy Jack" Morco. The officer was known as a blowhard who claimed he'd killed upwards of a dozen men. He also had previously arrested Billy for "carrying a weapon in town limits."[3]

At Ben Thompson's urging, Billy left town and stayed on the run. Libby must have gone with him, for she gave birth to her first baby, a son named Rance, later that year in Oklahoma. The baby lived only a year, dying while the couple was somewhere in Texas during 1874. It is known that in June of that year, Libby and her beau traveled through Austin, where Thompson was almost caught, also Mountain City where Thompson was caught but escaped, and San Antonio. At this latter place, Thompson drew the attention of two police officers after he hit a prostitute at the Long Horse brothel. Either way, Thompson escaped from the clutches of the law once again.

While on the road, Libby gave birth to another baby, Leander, in July. Exactly where this happened remains unknown, although various researchers have said that Libby and her man went on to Sweetwater, or perhaps Dodge City, Kansas. Only newspapers of the time tell the real story: Thompson, at least, was in Travis County, Texas, in October when the law caught up with him and another man. The pair had nearly one hundred head of stolen cattle. Thompson pleaded innocent and was released, only to be immediately arrested for the death of Chauncey Whitney and taken back to Ellsworth.[4]

Many historians suppose that despite Thompson's penchant for drunken violence, Libby did marry him in 1876. The union allegedly occurred in Grimes County, Texas, between William E. Thompson and

Mary E. Lacey on December 1. Unfortunately, that can't be Libby and Thompson, since the latter was still awaiting trial in Ellsworth. The trial was still going on as of March 1877, while Thompson was still incarcerated. Libby, meantime, had given birth in February to yet another child, Cariozonia "Carrie" Thompson, in Hood County, Texas. It must have been a great relief to her when Billy Thompson was at last acquitted, and the duo took to traveling once more.

How did Libby feel about Thompson, who had a violent temper and a penchant for shooting people? He had hit a prostitute in San Antonio; did he also hit Libby? Nobody knows, but certainly the lady must have continued in her profession while Thompson was on the run and during his time in jail. But news items about her exact whereabouts are scant, and newspaper stories about Thompson give only small clues. He was, for instance, in Dodge City in September of 1878 when he visited with a friend. One historian says Thompson says he was arrested by Marshal Martin Duggan in Leadville, Colorado, during December of 1879, for disturbing the peace. Was Libby with him? Most writers suppose she was, working as both a prostitute and dance hall girl to help the family finances. Yet lugging her children along as she traipsed after Thompson had to have been difficult at best.

The easiest way to track Libby is by looking at where and when the rest of her children were born. She was in Texas during 1879 when the next of her children, William R. Thompson Jr., came along. If she had enlisted the help of her mother in raising her children, that ended when Mary Thompson died in June 1880. At least Thompson was back with her when the couple and their children appeared in the 1880 census on June 26, in Callahan County, Texas. Something had temporarily turned in Thompson, who was documented as a farmer while Libby kept house and tended to toddlers Leonidas, now age six, Cariozonia, who was three, and baby William. Sadly, the latter child would die before the year was out and there is no way of knowing whether Libby was with Thompson in July, when he next got into yet another shooting scrape in Ogallala, Nebraska.

According to the *Weekly Democratic Statesman* in Austin, Texas, Thompson was in a saloon when a drunken barkeeper, Bill Tucker, cussed at him. One thing led to another and Thompson shot at the man, severely wounding his hand. Tucker then chased after Thompson and fired a load of buckshot into his back. The altercation, according to some historians, was over a prostitute known as "Big Alice." Ben Thompson, now a well-known gunslinger, decided to stay out of it and instead requested his buddy, Bat Masterson, to come from Dodge City to settle things. The two men arrived back in Dodge City later that month. "The latter [Billy] has recovered from his wounds," the *Dodge City Times* reported.[5]

For about a year, things were quiet for the Thompsons. Libby did give birth to her fifth child, Ofilea, in Texas during May of 1881. In March of 1882, the *Brenham Weekly Banner* in Texas announced that Billy Thompson was at last returning to Aransas County, Texas, to answer to the long-ago killing of Ramus Smith. "He claims self-defense," the paper explained and, just as Thompson hoped, he was acquitted of the murder.[6] And in February of 1884 Libby had yet another son, also named William. Barely a month later, however, Thompson was in trouble yet again. This time, he was in San Antonio when brother Ben was shot to death.

According to the *San Antonio Light*, Billy was at the White Elephant Saloon when he heard a commotion at a nearby theater. He knew Ben was in town, and must have instinctively gone to see what the fuss was about. The paper said Billy "was met on the steps by Billy Simms with a cocked six-shooter, and behind Simms several men had guns." Before Thompson could react, policemen at the scene took him back to the White Elephant. The marshal warned Thompson to stay there, and that if he appeared on the streets, he would be shot on sight. Although the newspaper stated their source was another newspaper and doubted its veracity, Thompson does not appear to have done anything to avenge his brother's death. The murder of Ben Thompson did, however, take the wind out of his brother's sails. The *Light* verified that, sick from the death of his brother, Billy Thompson retreated to a room at the Cloud Hotel where he "talks very calmly, shows no disposition to discuss his future movements and was perfectly clear of threats of any nature."[7]

Thompson eventually left San Antonio and, for a time, wandered aimlessly around the west. He allegedly spent time in Cripple Creek, Colorado, as well as different cities throughout Texas. Certainly, his time in Texas must have been spent with Libby, since she continued giving birth to his children.

Libby Thompson's Children Born Between 1887 and 1895

Birthdate	Name	Birthplace	Comments
1887	Robert Thompson	Texas	Died as an infant
1887	Charles Martin	Milford, TX	
1890	James Healey	Cleburn, TX	
1893	Fain Eugene	Granbury, TX	
1895	Thomas	Texas[8]	

In 1897, Billy Thompson suddenly died. Surprisingly, his death did not come at the end of a gun, but a serious stomach problem while he was in Houston. Without him, Libby, who was pregnant yet again, moved to Fort Hood where she was found in the 1900 census—living with her once overbearing father. Also in the house were Libby's surviving children. The census was taken in June; sometime after that, James Haley died. Libby was now completely alone in the world, and appears to have been largely dependent on her relatives for assistance. One of her descendants recalled that during the early 1900s, Libby lived for a time with the family of her granddaughter, Virginia Thompson Chulufas. By 1910, she was living in Oakdale, Oklahoma, where the census recorded more interesting facts about her. Libby, who now went by Mary E. Young, said she had been married for six years—although her husband was not living with her. She also verified that of her thirteen children, eight still lived, and three of them—Fain, Thomas, and David—resided with her. Also in the house were Libby's niece, Mary Johnson, and Mary's daughter Sadie. And although several sources believe Libby continued running a brothel, there is no hard evidence to prove she did so. There are also questionable claims that "most of her sons had turned to a life of crime and her daughters became prostitutes."[9]

What is known for sure is that Libby eventually moved to California. Years of living with Billy Thompson, traveling all over the west, and popping out babies left and right had taken their toll on the woman. She was living with family; granddaughter Virginia Chulufas recalled how the elderly Libby asked her to buy snuff for her, and that she sniffed it "threw [*sic*] the nose." She also, unfortunately, was in the habit of whacking Virginia with her cane any time she walked too close by to Libby. Virginia surmised that "Grandma Thompson lived a very hard life and . . . that's why she was so mean." When Libby died on April 13, 1953, she was living in the Sunbeam Rest Home in Los Angeles. Her obituary in the *Los Angeles Mirror* was short and to the point, revealing that Libby had suffered "a long illness" before she passed away, and had lived in Los Angeles County for the last thirty-one years.[10] Not until several decades later would historians unearth Libby's story and the days when she was known by Squirrel Tooth Alice.

CHAPTER EIGHT

Naughty Nebraska

BORDERED BY TODAY'S SOUTH DAKOTA, IOWA, MISSOURI, KANSAS, COLorado, and Wyoming, early Nebraska was long occupied by a number of native tribes. They survived quite nicely along the rolling hills and prairie that were watered by the Missouri and Platte rivers as well as several smaller natural tributaries. The budding state was known as Nebraska Territory by 1848 when thousands of Anglo settlers came through on their way to the California Gold Rush. Some of them stayed or later returned, and by the 1860s, a territorial capital had been established at Omaha. Discouraged male gold miners were aplenty, but there was another type of gold digger putting roots down in early Nebraska: prostitutes who saw the state's growth as a way to ply their wares in the small but growing demimondes throughout the territory.

One of the earliest accounts of prostitution took place in about 1860, when famed frontiersman "Wild Bill" Hickok arrived at Rock Creek Stage Station in today's Johnson County to regain his strength after being attacked by a bear. Soon after he arrived, a Pony Express rider named Doc Brink mentioned that Rock Creek's station boss, David McCanles, kept a "mistress" named Sarah Shull. Sarah had apparently "fled" with McCanles from North Carolina back when he was a sheriff. Unfortunately for Sarah, Mrs. McCanles eventually showed up at the station and was none too happy to see the strumpet with her husband. Even after she faithfully reunited with McCanles, Brink said, Mrs. McCanles "still yowls about 'that whore.'" But the woman apparently left at some point, for she no longer appears in the telling of what happened next.

It seems that Sarah Shull and another possible prostitute, Sarah Kelsey, stayed on at Rock Creek Station to comfort the common-law wife of Horace Wellman, who was there to assume duties as manager. Wellman had taken a quick trip to the company offices when, much to McCanles's chagrin, Sarah Shull, Sarah Kelsey, and Mrs. Wellman suddenly took over the station and locked McCanles out. Over the next several days, they say that McCanles "pounded the doors daily," screaming at the women to "Give me back my station!" The ladies refused to budge. But when McCanles next accused Mrs. Wellman's father of horse stealing and beat him senseless, a furious Horace Wellman made a swift return. In preparation of Wellman's wrath, McCanles rode off and returned with three armed men: James Gordon, James Woods, and his own son, William. "You little rat," he bellowed at Wellman. "If you don't clear my house of all your whores right now, I'll blow you apart with this scattergun!" But the women themselves were not to be fooled with; hearing McCanles's words, Mrs. Wellman stepped out and faced McCanles herself, declaring, "You filthy beast! If you raise that gun, I'll rip your eyes out!" At this, McCanles retorted, "My business is with men, not whores!" Then Hickok stepped up, urging Mrs. Wellman to "go home while you still can."

Next, McCanles requested a cup of water from the house, and Hickok stepped into the station house to fetch it. Then, McCanles suddenly remembered how Hickok had looked at Sarah Shull upon his arrival. His temper got the best of him and he "jerked his shotgun up." That was a fatal mistake, as Hickok immediately shot McCanles neatly through the heart. James Gordon now rushed in, and Hickok shot him, too. Mrs. Wellman, overcome with both fear and anger, next rushed out screaming, "Kill them! Kill them all!" In her fury, the woman took up a hoe and went after James Wood who was also wounded, and "chopped" the man to death. Hickok, Brink, and a stage driver named George Hulbert next went looking for James Gordon, who was hiding in the brush, and finished him off as well. Although Mrs. Wellman seems to have escaped arrest, Hickok was later tried for the killings. He pleaded self-defense, the case was dismissed, and the noted gunman moved on to Fort Leavenworth, Kansas.[1] At least that is one version of the story.

On March 1, 1867, Nebraska was officially admitted to the Union. Within a few years, red-light districts and houses of prostitution were popping up everywhere. At Grand Island, founded in 1857 along the Platte River, the new town benefitted greatly by the coming of the Union Pacific Railroad in 1868. The citizenry numbered around eleven hundred by 1870, and Grand Island incorporated in 1872. Within a couple of years, the first brothel was built by William and Anna Anderson at a spot just north of the railroad tracks on the outskirts of town. The Andersons called their brothel "Prairie House."[2] A short time later another couple, John and Sarah Gettle, built a brothel too. Together, these houses of ill-repute comprised Grand Island's early red-light district which would eventually grow around them into what would become known as the "Burnt District."[3]

Both the Andersons and the Gettles seemingly were accepted by Grand Island, seeing as their bordellos were located just on the city limits, and besides, the men of the houses were respectable saloon owners. Not until 1881 did the city pass its first ordinance against prostitution, with fines ranging from $5 to $25 that were used for school funding. The ordinance was basic, forbidding houses of prostitution within the city limits but also becoming "an inmate or frequenter of any house, room or rooms" used for selling sexual favors. The procedure for collecting fines was fairly standard, patterned after other American cities: the ladies were rounded up each month, taken to court, pleaded guilty, paid their respective fines, returned to their brothels, and resumed business. Likewise, men associated with the demimonde also were fined regularly. As long as they stayed out of trouble, the ladies could continue to conduct business in this fashion month after month. The exceptions were women who could not pay their monthly fine, in which case they were given a certain time by which to pay up or leave town.[4]

Grand Island's fining process appears to have worked quite well— that is, until a soiled dove named Nell Thompson flew into town. Little is known about Nell, except that she first began paying fines for prostitution in about 1892. But when the lady suddenly began moving from brothel to brothel in 1894, it bothered not only the public but also Nell's competitors. Other brothels began lodging complaints against her, and city officials agreed that Nell's erratic behavior was somehow unbecoming. On June 29, Grand Island's *Evening Times* reported that the police had raided Nell's place in the Burnt District because she was "causing a disturbance." Nell and her girls, Rosa Ford and Minnie St. Clair, were arrested and bonded out as a court date was set for the next day. The ladies' attorney managed to move their hearing to the following week. In the meantime, Nell's piano player, identified only as "a young lad," also was arrested "for being an inmate of house of ill-fame."[5]

As one might guess, the proceedings did not set well with Nell. On July 4, it was reported that the madam had retaliated against the other ladies in the Burnt District by swearing out her own complaint against them. Now the whole red-light district was in an uproar, a predicament that the Grand Island *Daily Independent* judged would "only prove detrimental to themselves."[6] Indeed, within a day, other brothel keepers were being arrested as well, and the *Evening Times* reported that "Nell's efforts at reforming this part of the community by closing them out of business is a great 'hit.'"[7] Nothing more was reported on the matter, nor did the papers have much else to say about Nell Thompson. Presumably she moved on to the bawdy district in Omaha, where, in 1900, it was reported by the *Omaha Daily Bee* that a woman by her name got into a fight with another woman named Elsie Smith. Elsie was at Odin's Hall when she dared Nell "to knock a chip from her shoulder." In the ensuing fight, Elsie's "new 'Ladysmith' hat was trampled in the mud."[8]

In the wake of Nell's departure from Grand Island, William Henry Thompson was elected mayor of the city. In 1895, spurred on by a petition from respectable residents around the Burnt District, Thompson went after the local red-light ladies in full force. The irate residents were not without reason, for teachers and students at a nearby school not only witnessed the goings-on in the district, but were sometimes accosted by prostitutes. Surprisingly, however, the city's biggest targets were the long-standing, respected brothels owned by the Gettles and the Andersons—the latter whom retired and simply continued living in their former brothel. The city council also voted for prohibiting any more bordellos from opening. By September, the Burnt District was no more, and prostitution was seemingly nonexistent in Grand Island. But a railroad worker named Millard Boquette, who had been in and out of Grand Island since 1879, was about to change all that.

Boquette had first appeared in Grand Island newspapers in 1893, when prostitute Goldie Gray's property was sold at a sheriff's sale to settle a debt she apparently owed to the man. Just a few months earlier, Goldie's brothel had been extensively damaged by fire, and the *Omaha Daily Bee* mentioned that this was the second time a fire had been set at the house. Boquette's suit against Goldie continued into 1894, when he was awarded her property in June—but only one cent for damages. Everyone knew that Boquette dabbled in the red-light district, but when he was arrested for being in the wrong place at the wrong time in September, the man openly complained to the *Grand Island Daily Independent* about it. And, after marrying Sophia Husmann in 1895, Boquette made Grand Island his permanent home.

As Boquette and his wife settled in, some of the ladies ousted from the former Burnt District quietly moved to an area south of the Union Pacific tracks. Boquette had already purchased two houses and had them moved to the new area. The cat-and-mouse game between the red-light ladies and the police began anew. Beginning in March of 1896, three brothel keepers were arrested. It is believed that some women escaped prosecution since publicly transporting them clear across town to the court offices was viewed as "distasteful." The arrests would gradually increase in the coming years, and law enforcement also began focusing on illegal games of chance and liquor that was being offered around town.[9] Boquette, meanwhile, kept a low profile for many more years by operating a blacksmith shop and playing family man with four children. Real estate transactions in the local newspapers, however, show he also continued selling properties, almost exclusively to women.

Grand Island, and the rest of America, were seeing serious changes in attitudes toward the prostitution industry by 1912. In July of that year, Boquette was the owner, and builder, of the Bell Hotel when it was raided by authorities and netted five men and six women. Boquette was out of town at the time, so it was Sophie Boquette who paid nearly $100 in fines for the ladies. Subsequent raids in the red-light district took place in August 1912, March 1913, and, finally July 1913. The rest of Grand

Island's wayward women would eventually move on when the Boquettes relocated to Iowa for a time before eventually returning to Grand Island. After Sophie died in 1938, Millard lived in the Bell Hotel until his death in 1940.

When Grand Island enacted its first laws against prostitution, the state of Nebraska must have been listening. In 1885, the secretary of state decided to "extend powers and duties to city/village officers to suppress Houses of Prostitution."[10] It wasn't just a matter of respectable citizens objecting to the skin trade in their midst; there were other problems, too, that would continue for several more years. In 1887, the Omaha and Winnebago Agency for Natives submitted several reports of venereal disease outbreaks on the reservation. The prostitution trade also remained a continuing problem in certain remote Anglo towns, including Red Cloud where one woman was told to leave town "in the absence of filthy lucre to liquidate her fine," and three others at nearby Dutch Flats who were brought into court.[11] In Columbus, the chief of police was ordered to submit a report to city council of just how many houses of ill fame there were in the city limits, and how many women were openly living with men "in a state of fornication or adultery."[12] And then there was Covington, referred to by one writer as "Nebraska's sinful city."[13]

Originally called Harney City and Newport, Covington was finally named for the Covington, Columbus, and Black Hills railroad in 1856. The community was located across the Missouri River from Sioux City, Iowa, with a ferry service eventually taking folks between the two towns. Quite some time would pass before Covington would become what former *Sioux City Journal* editor Willis Forbes called one of the "three wickedest places in the world," comparing the river town to San Francisco's notorious Barbary Coast and the waterfront clear over in Hong Kong, China.[14] The root of the problem with Covington was that it was once a blossoming metropolis with a narrow-gauge railroad passing through on the way to several other counties. When the railroad "fell into litigation," service stopped, leaving Covington "the only dead and dilapidated town in Nebraska."[15] Had it not been easy to access Sioux City right across the Missouri, Covington likely would have quickly become a ghost town.

Instead, revelers on both sides of the river found a place to party, away from the nosy eyes of the law.

If nothing else, the various characters of Covington identify with the town's wickedness. Colorful names like "Beefsteak Bod Thompson," "Black Diamond Nell," "Dutch Mary," and "Winnebago Jane" are peppered throughout the community's history, where bawdy houses, burlesque theaters, gambling houses, and saloons flourished.[16] Even storekeepers were subject to sinfulness; in 1880, the *Platte Valley Democrat* in Columbus revealed that a grocer named Drown was jailed after his wife appeared on the scene with the husband of the man's mistress. Some of the riff-raff came across the river from Sioux City as a means of escaping the law. In 1886, the *Custer County Republican* reported that five hundred residents of Sioux City had taken "several dozen kegs of beer and other lubricants" over to Covington in a "full-fledged protest against Sunday closing."[17] If folks in Sioux City couldn't drink to their hearts content on Sundays, they seem to have had no problem doing it in Covington.

By 1888, there were two grocery stores, two hotels, two saloons, and a blacksmith shop in Covington. As anti-saloon crusaders began converging upon Sioux City, more and more of the "tough element" found a home in Covington as one of the saloon owners, John Peyson, was elected mayor. The number of drinking holes quickly grew to six, including Peyson's new place, the Tontine. Peyson and the others continued to openly defy Nebraska's Sunday drinking laws for some time. In 1889, the *North Nebraska Eagle* published a scathing editorial about Covington: "Covington is the veritable hell. No man or woman of decency is safe upon the street day or night. The city is entirely given over to drunkenness, debauchery and prostitution." Life was so fast and fuzzy in Covington that visitors had trouble even identifying the actual numbers of saloons and brothels there.[18]

Covington's eventual downfall proved to be South Sioux City, which had incorporated nearby in 1887. South Sioux City offered everything Covington did not: churches, a newspaper, and an actual bridge across the Missouri to Sioux City proper. More and more respectable folks began settling in the area, to the extent that the wicked citizens in Covington began moving over to another nearby community, Stanton. By the time another railroad, the Pacific Short Line, was built through Covington it was too late. Respectable people were now in great numbers, and local law enforcement had a jolly time chasing the gamblers, illegal boozers, and prostitutes throughout Covington, South Sioux City, and Stanton. Inhabitants of the latter two towns soon grew weary of the goings-on with Covington's residents; on the evening of January 18, 1891, five buildings in Covington were set on fire. Nine other buildings were found with oil-filled auger holes in the walls, to which a match had not yet been lit. One of the buildings was the Little Allen, a bordello leased by Lillie Langworthy. But the arsonist who set the fires failed; all of the structures were saved by the formation of a bucket brigade to extinguish the flames.

One popular theater in Covington was the Fashion Theatre which opened in 1891 and provided bawdy entertainment and prize fights. It too was set on fire by arsonists in 1892, along with the Ferry House and a saloon. This time the buildings burned, but the Fashion rebuilt and was soon known for its racy comedians and scantily-clad burlesque dancers. Newspapers across Nebraska, meanwhile, continued reporting almost daily on the prize fights, illegal gambling, and other illicit happenings in Covington as whispers of annexing the town to South Sioux City began. Meanwhile, things just got worse in Covington. In 1892, Nell Johnson was madam of a brothel called the Oak when one of her girls, Ida Stewart, was murdered by a customer. Even city officials were corrupt; later that year, Covington's town marshal was charged with robbery. Something had to give, and it did. More fires contributed to the destruction of Covington, as well as the overflowing banks of the Missouri River which eventually washed away most of the downtown area in 1893. "The street where stood the Red Light and vaudeville theatre has long since drifted downward," reported the *Dakota County Democrat*. "The 'Glory' of Covington has departed." Soon afterward, Covington was officially annexed to South Sioux City, its bawdy history forgotten.[19]

Covington was not the only town to welcome prostitutes and their cohorts. At Crawford, in the northwestern section of Nebraska, working girls during the 1890s were allowed on the streets if they were "properly attired," although they were prohibited from entering most saloons or being a public nuisance. Dr. J. Walter Moyer remembered one time, however, when "a razor-wielding prostitute" was seen walking down a main street yelling profanities. "She was literally tripped up with a rope by Marshal Charles Spearman and his helper," Moyer said, "and taken into custody." Many of the ladies were addicted to various drugs, which they could be seen purchasing at the local pharmacy around noon each day. Those who used needles to get their fix, Moyer recalled, "had the most dreadful looking arms."[20]

At the town of Sydney during the late 1870s, robberies, fights, and a fair amount of shady ladies ran wild throughout the town. Robberies in particular got so bad that trains coming through town locked the doors on their cars and refused to even stop there. Outlaws enjoyed spending time at places like Joe Lane's Dance Hall, where "Soldier's Night" each Sunday permitted only servicemen to saunter upstairs for a good time with the ladies. One of them was James "Doc Middleton" Riley, an escaped convict from Texas who wandered into town around 1875. The women at Joe Lane's liked Riley, but he left town after coming in on Soldier's Night one evening and ending up in a fight with Private James Keith. Apparently, Keith didn't like it that some soiled doves were flocking around Riley. After a brief fisticuff, Riley shot the man and fled.

Another time, a ruffian named Jack Nolon was challenged by his lady of the evening to kill a Mexican, Jose Valdez. Apparently, the woman had an issue because Valdez was in a room with her friend, who was white. After much berating, Nolon knocked on the door of the room Valdez occupied, but the Mexican refused to open it. Nolon shot through the door and hit Valdez in the abdomen. He died shortly afterward. Nolon was arrested but escaped.

A similar incident happened in 1879 when the mistress of one Charley Reed, known as Mollie, invited a group of men into her parlor. Among them was a respectable man named Henry Loomis, who was about to be married. When Loomis found out the nature of Mollie's party, he told the harlot that he and his friends "didn't associate with other men's women," and moved on. A furious Mollie summoned Reed and told him Loomis had "insulted her." Reed, who did not realize how well-liked Loomis was, ran after the man, hit him on the back of the head, and shot him in the thigh. Reed was arrested as an angry mob formed. The sheriff was still try-ing to figure out how to get the prisoner out of town when Henry Loomis died. Over two dozen men converged upon the jail, secured Reed, and forced him to jump to his death at the end of a noose. Mollie was given a bit of money and ordered to leave town.[21]

There were more: in 1894, in the small town of Elm Creek, two barbers were run out of town after their barbershop was converted into a brothel. At Ogallala in 1895, the nine-year-old daughter of a prostitute, identified as Rosa Belle, was left in the care of a man named Shiffield. A musician by trade, Shiffield took the child with him as he played at various brothels and "carousals" until his sister-in-law, Mrs. Nellie Shif-fold [*sic*] apparently took Rosa Belle to the Nebraska Children's Home Society as she petitioned for custody.[22] And in Nebraska City, twenty-two-year-old John Ricker was shot by Madam Anna Smith (nee Mrs. Anna Sopher) after he and some friends were denied entry to her brothel in 1896. The group was drunk, and when they refused to leave Anna "opened fire on them with a 32-caliber revolver, firing five shots one of which struck Ricker in the back just below the neck near the spinal column." Anna tried to blame her piano player for firing the shots as the women of the house were arrested.[23]

As the new century dawned upon Nebraska, reformers began taking a harder look at the prostitution industry. In 1900, Sioux City's *Dakota County Record* called out the corrupt chief of police, and his officers were "recently raked over the coals" for attending a prize fight while a murder was committed just two blocks away. The officers had also been taking "presents" from the local soiled doves as a form of protection, while the men themselves were known to visit such places.[24] Angry wives came for-ward too: in 1902, Ida McGill filed for divorce from her husband Perry because he contracted venereal disease. Likewise, Crete King also filed for divorce in 1903 after she "contracted gonorrhea from her husband who frequented prostitutes."[25]

In 1907, a new state statute provided for a "Nebraska Industrial Home" at Milford for "shelter and protection" while providing employ-ment "for penitent women and girls, with a view to aid in the suppression of prostitution."[26] Two years later, national legislators were able to pass the first official "Red Light Abatement law," parts of which were eventually copied over to the law books of Iowa and, in turn, Nebraska in 1911.[27] It is true that in 1915, Nebraska's Red Light Abatement was challenged when the Supreme Court found that a $300 tax provision within the law violated Nebraska's constitution. But reformers in the state had a strong foothold and converged on the prostitution industry with a vengeance in 1917. When certain madams tried to evade the law by moving to other places in their cities, the reformers went after their landlords. Some of the madams gave up and left the state; one of them traveled from Lincoln to far away Portland, Oregon, where she resumed business.

Finally, military officials during World War I tired of their men going AWOL and contracting social diseases, and began working in earnest to shut down prostitution across America. The effort was a success in many ways, although some women of the night continued finding ways to continue business on the down-low. "We must face this problem resolutely, frankly, and fearlessly," commented a Nebraska police superintendent in 1921, "molding public opinion as we go, but never turning back on the program started by the Government during the war."[28] The military's efforts also strengthened groups like the Women's Christian Temperance Union, and similar groups. Concentrated efforts were now being made to assist prostitutes through reform and medical help.

Occasionally, such efforts were protested by citizens who just wanted the women to go away. In Omaha during 1919, for example, Police Commissioner Ringer was attacked when he supported "the continued existence of the women's detention hospital," because patients sometimes included those with social diseases. Mayor Edward Smith flatly told Ringer, "I don't want Omaha advertised as a place where diseased prostitutes can come to be cured. I want the burglar, the bootlegger, the pickpocket, and the prostitute to understand that we will not tolerate their presence in Omaha if we can help it." Ringer pleaded for compassion and told Smith his attitude was "unchristian." The hospital, unfortunately, was closed anyway.[29]

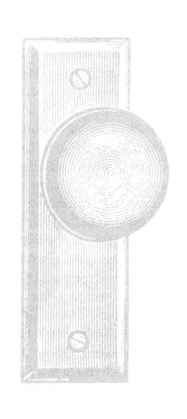

CHAPTER NINE

The Adventures of Octavia Reeves

NEBRASKA MADAM OCTAVIA REEVES IS A MOST INTERESTING STUDY. She was mysterious yet forthright, demure yet violent, a cheater of death who left a trail of blood behind her. She also was one of the most successful Black madams in the west for a time. But was it her fault that men were killed at her various hog ranches and bordellos? Who can say? What happened to her son and husband(s)? Nobody knows. Even where and when she died remains a mystery. One thing is for sure, however: throughout her travels as she traipsed through Colorado, Wyoming, South Dakota, and Nebraska, Octavia left a lot of intriguing clues about her existence, but also lots of questions.

Because the 1880 census documents Octavia as being a widow, Reeves was most likely not her maiden name when she was born in Missouri around 1851. Also, there are only subtle hints about her when she first surfaced in Denver, Colorado. Was she the "Mrs. O. Reeves" who departed for Central City via John Hughes & Co.'s Stage Line in 1869?[1] Or the lady of the same name who received letters in Denver in January and June 1873? Did her career in the prostitution industry begin with a job working for Denver madam Lizzie Preston, where "Octave Ruse," a Black woman the same age as Octavia, appears as the chambermaid of the house in the 1870 census? These teasers, as well as some known facts about Octavia, certainly bear looking into.

It is known without a doubt, for instance, that Octavia was living in Denver in November 1873, when a lawyer identified as L. K. Smith apparently stole a "dust brush" from her. The item would have proven useful to a chambermaid, but how Smith laid his hands on it is unknown. The *Rocky Mountain News* did have great fun in reporting the theft, however. The article called Octavia Reeves "a lady of dusky color" when she "missed her dust brush, and being a tidy person about her house, complained of its loss to a policeman." Smith was fingered as the culprit by witnesses, arrested for petit larceny, and fined a "nominal sum" by the court before being discharged. The dust brush, after all, was only worth a mere fifty cents.[2]

The cost of Octavia's dust brush actually says a lot about her in her chambermaid days. A fifty-cent brush of 1873 would cost around $12 today, enough to mean something to someone who makes minimal wages. That Octavia sought the assistance of the police to recover the item implies that she was definitely not well off and likely wanted something better for herself in the way of income. She would not get it for some time; the *Denver City Directory* for 1874 gives her address as 472 Holladay Street, the locale of the city's notorious red-light district. Even after she moved to Cheyenne, Wyoming, in 1875, Octavia was still retained as a servant. Notable is that she was identified as being white in the Wyoming state and city censuses, a sign that the woman was likely of mixed heritage. A year later, the said "Mrs. O. Reeves" had a letter waiting for her at the Cheyenne post office.[3] The next time Octavia received any communication, it was a telegraph sent to her at Deadwood, South Dakota, in September 1877. And, she would soon no longer toil as a chambermaid in a bawdy house.

In January 1878, a most interesting article appeared in the *Black Hills Weekly Times* that verified Octavia was now a madam. The article described Octavia as the hostess of a "colored ball," who was trying to break up a fight when a barber by the name of Sims fired his .38 Smith & Wesson at somebody. The bullet missed its mark, accidentally striking Octavia instead. Imagine the gasp of the crowd as the bullet struck Octavia right in the chest—only to be stopped by her corset, the slug "barely reaching the flesh."[4] Indeed, Octavia survived most swimmingly, and later that year she began buying and selling lots in Deadwood. After selling property to Julius Burns for $300, Octavia turned around and purchased another lot from G. E. Breckenridge for just $150. The lady certainly knew how to invest her money. According to Deadwood's city directory, she also ran a restaurant and saloon.

Octavia was clearly climbing the ladder within the red-light realm. In June of 1879, the *Daily Deadwood Pioneer-Times* reported she had arrived back in town but did not say where she had been. Deadwood citizens soon knew why she had taken the trip, however, when an advertisement appeared in the Black Hills *Daily Times* three days later, on Friday the thirteenth: "Saturday night dance at the New England Hall, China Town, Octavia Reeves, proprietor, everybody invited. A new arrival of ladies of color in attendance. Come one, come all. Good music."[5] Chinatown happened to be located right on Main Street, so it would have been difficult to miss the party Octavia hosted.

Octavia's party, and others like it, were most certainly a success. By September, she owned five houses in all. Unfortunately, four of these, along with the furniture inside them, burned on September 26, when a fire began in a bakery on Sherman Street. Over three hundred buildings were reduced to ruins. The value of Octavia's losses was set at $3,000. The one surviving house, she apparently felt, was not enough to make the money she wanted. So, Octavia did what any other madam in her position would do. She began anew, in another town. By 1880, she was in Cheyenne, Wyoming, where the census identifies her as a "mulatto" widow who employed five "mulatto" girls. Also present was Octavia's one-month-old son.

Since nothing is known of Octavia in the nine months between the 1879 fire in Deadwood and June of 1880 when the census was taken in Cheyenne, it is difficult to say just who baby William's father might have been. No marriage records have surfaced linking her to anyone in Colorado, South Dakota, or Wyoming. Also, there is no record of what became of William. Whatever the truth of the matter was, Octavia was in Cheyenne during a time when the city was in the midst of a "colored campaign" to rid itself of Blacks. Octavia must have been targeted, as well as Pauline Alexander, a second "mulatto" madam who employed four prostitutes. Both Octavia and Pauline also employed servants, attesting to their wealth at the time the census was taken. The failure of the "colored campaign" was blaringly apparent: of the

Occupants of Octavia Reeves's Brothel on June 11, 1880

Octavia Reeves, age 29, born Missouri, mulatto, widow, keeping house

William C. Reeves, age one month, born Wyoming, mulatto, son

Fannie Reeves, age 20, born Missouri, mulatto, married, prostitute

Mary Brooks, age 34, born Ohio, mulatto, married, prostitute

Maggie Cartwell, age 22, born Missouri, mulatto, married, prostitute, cannot read or write

Laura Copeland, age 25, born Ohio, mulatto, married, prostitute

Willie Young, age 21, born Arkansas, mulatto, married, prostitute

Sallie Barney, age 23, born Missouri, Black, single, servant, cannot read or write[6]

only three brothels in Cheyenne in the census, two were occupied by "mulatto" women while only one was occupied by Anglo women. Also, the numbers of white versus Black women were nearly equal at fifteen to twelve, respectively.

Indeed, Octavia was doing so well that she cared little when her house back in Deadwood was put up for auction during a sheriff's sale in October. But she also cared little for Cheyenne; by 1881, Octavia had moved again—this time to her own "ranch" near Fort Laramie. The men who visited Octavia's ranch were a rough bunch. One November day, a man identified as A. H. Smith rode in and "put up" his team and horses at Octavia's. Smith was quite quarrelsome, squabbling with others and running up a stable bill to the effect that he signed his team over to Octavia to settle what he owed.

After another squabble, Smith was ordered to leave. Before he could do so, another man named Matt Hall showed up. Hall claimed that Smith's team was not even owned by the man, and had been hired for use at Fort Fetterman. Furthermore, Hall said, he had already walked six miles and wasn't leaving without the team. Octavia, however, refused to let the team go without settling the stable bill, and Hall too was ordered to leave. Outside, Hall drew his pistol on a soldier, which was taken away from him by others before he left. Nothing more came of the incidents until Christmas day, when a drunk man named Crawford next appeared and said he was there for Hall's pistol. Octavia told him to relay a message to Hall that he should come get his gun himself. Crawford rode away, muttering something to the effect that he "would have the pistol or kill a nigger."[7]

That evening, Matt Hall showed up at the ranch and asked for Octavia. He was directed into the barroom, where he demanded his gun. When Octavia said it wasn't there, Hall drew another pistol and shot at her. The bullet missed, hitting prostitute Georgie Cox instead. Hall was detained only until a doctor was summoned and verified that Georgie would live. On January 6, however, Georgie died from her injuries. After a month of chasing Georgie's killer around the region, Deputy John Field finally apprehended Hall but he was inexplicably acquitted of killing Georgie.

The day after Hall's acquittal, officers descended upon Octavia's little hog ranch. "Yesterday Octavia Reeves was placed under arrest for keeping a place of bad savor near Fort Laramie," announced the *Cheyenne Daily Leader*. "It was at this place that the row occurred in which one of the inmates was killed, and for which Matt Hall was acquitted by the jury yesterday." If officials could not put Hall behind bars, arresting Octavia for running a rowdy operation would have to do. "The prisoner was placed under $200 bonds," the *Leader* went on, "in default of which she was taken in charge by Sheriff Sharpless. An examination will be held to-day."[8]

In the end, Octavia paid fines amounting to a total of $114.90. But her publicized arrest apparently cost her more than just her hard-earned money, and by 1883, she had moved to Laramie proper. With her was Hattie Turner, a prostitute who, like Octavia, had formerly worked in Cheyenne. Laramie was not as friendly as Cheyenne had been; between January and April of 1883, Octavia and at least seven other prostitutes were arrested on three different occasions. Paying three separate fines in four months was making a serious dent in Octavia's profits. The madam decided to move once again, this time to Nebraska.

By 1886, Octavia was once again running a hog ranch outside of Crawford, in the northeastern corner of the state. The town was relatively new, initially established as a tent city along the Fremont, Elkhorn, and Missouri Valley Railroad. Crawford was quite rowdy right out of the gate, with fifty buildings that mostly housed saloons and a few brothels. Nearby was Fort Robinson, whose soldiers regularly visited Crawford, as well as Octavia Reeves's hog ranch along the aptly named Soldier Creek. The hog ranch was even wilder than any of Octavia's other demimonde dives, with "thieves, pimps, tramps, vagabonds, and white and colored prostitutes." One visitor proclaimed that "In this vile den of iniquity social equality exists in the broadest terms, in one corner of the dance hall can be seen a wench of the blackest type sitting on the lap of a white man, while near by can be seen a white woman adorning the knee of a colored patriot."[9] Octavia apparently didn't care what color a person's skin was, as long as they had sex to sell and money to burn.

Scenes of violence were soon the norm at Octavia's place. In January, according to the *Gothenburg Independent*, "Edward Anderson, a stage driver, turned up his toes at the notorious hog ranch of Octavia Reeves, in Sioux City, [*sic*] recently. The dive is the headquarters of the worst gang of toughs alive. There was a general fusilade [*sic*] of guns when Anderson dropped and the murderer cannot be apprehended."[10] News of another shooting at Octavia's on June 23 reached as far as the *St. Paul Daily Globe* in Minnesota. This time the victim was C. L. Bradley, a "colored gambler" who ran Octavia's poker table. He also was formerly a sergeant in the Ninth Cavalry. The unfortunate man had a knack for being in the wrong place at the wrong time; he had previously been in eight other "shooting scrapes," wherein he was wounded by a bullet each time. In the last gunfight, some six months before, Bradley was wounded four times and found a bullet lodged under the coating of his own tongue after feeling something "curious."

On the day of the June shooting, Bradley was snoozing on his cot when one Thomas Shotwell unaccountably, and literally, filled the man with bullets. The first shot went into the back of Bradley's head, "tearing off the outer plate of the skull." As Bradley raised up, Shotwell fired four more times, hitting the man once in the back, again in one eye, yet again

The United States of America.

CERTIFICATE No. *[handwritten]* | **To all to whom these presents shall come, Greeting:**

Whereas, *Octavia Reeves of Dawes County Nebraska*

ha*s* deposited in the GENERAL LAND OFFICE of the United States a Certificate of the Register of the Land Office at *Valentine Nebraska*, whereby it appears that full payment has been made by the said *Octavia Reeves*

according to the provisions of the Act of Congress of the 24th of April, 1820, entitled "An Act making further provision for the sale of the Public Lands," and the acts supplemental thereto, for *the West half of the South West quarter; the South East quarter of the South West quarter and the South West quarter of the North West quarter of Section twenty three in Township thirty one North of Range fifty three West of the Sixth Principal Meridian in Nebraska containing one hundred and sixty acres*

according to the official plat of the survey of the said lands returned to the General Land Office by the Surveyor General, which said tract ha*s* been purchased by the said *Octavia Reeves*

Now know ye, That the United States of America, in consideration of the premises, and in conformity with the several acts of Congress in such case made and provided, HAVE GIVEN AND GRANTED, and by these presents DO GIVE AND GRANT, unto the said *Octavia Reeves*

and to *her* heirs, the said tract above described: To HAVE AND TO HOLD the same, together with all the rights, privileges, immunities, and appurtenances, of whatsoever nature, thereunto belonging, unto the said

Octavia Reeves

and to *her* heirs and assigns forever.

In testimony whereof, I *Benjamin Harrison*

PRESIDENT OF THE UNITED STATES OF AMERICA, have caused these letters to be made patent, and the seal of the General Land Office to be hereunto affixed.

Given under my hand, at the City of Washington, the *Sixteenth* day of *January*, in the year of our Lord one thousand eight hundred and *ninety*, and of the Independence of the United States the one hundred and *fourteenth*.

[L. S.]

BY THE PRESIDENT: *Benjamin Harrison*

By *J. M. McKean* Secretary.

J. M. Townsend

Recorder of the General Land Office.

In 1890, Octavia Reeves filed for a homestead plat surrounding her remote bordello. COURTESY BUREAU OF LAND MANAGEMENT in his forehead, and last into his right arm—a total of five shots. Quite by some miracle, Bradley did not lose consciousness as Shotwell hopped on his horse and escaped. The *Falls City Daily News* and other Nebraska newspapers clarified that the man already had some twenty-five bullet wounds from the other shootings. This time, Bradley died of his injuries, and there was no news of whether his killer was ever caught.[11]

Following Bradley's death, newspapers declined to comment on Octavia's whereabouts, period. She did file for a homestead for her land, just about five miles from Crawford, and was granted ownership in 1890. She also reappeared in South Dakota during the state's 1905 census. The record found Octavia living in Central City, an early gold boom town just a couple of miles from Deadwood that had burned in 1888. Much of it had not been rebuilt. Puzzling is that Octavia's occupation in Central City was that of a nurse. Had the fifty-something madam given up her notorious life in favor of helping others? Nobody seems to know, and Octavia disappeared from record after that. Octavia, much like the ashes from Central City's fire, seems to have just floated off in the wind.

CHAPTER TEN

Ornery Omaha

JUST LIKE NEBRASKA'S BAWDY COVINGTON AND THE LATER TOWN OF South Sioux City, Omaha also is located directly across the Missouri River from a major city: Council Bluffs, Iowa. Omaha was founded in 1854, just a month after Nebraska Territory was formed and President Franklin Pierce ratified a treaty with the Omaha Native tribe to open the land for settlement. The land rush was on, with businessmen who had long wanted the land finally staking their claim on what would become Omaha. Almost immediately, the city was declared the territorial capital, and lots were given out free to anyone willing to improve a piece of property. By 1859, prospectors were streaming through town on their way to the Colorado goldfields as Omaha dominated the steamboat trade along the Missouri. The infant city must have looked quite enticing to the harlots venturing west, for Omaha's fallen flowers soon blossomed like no other in Nebraska.

By 1865, Omaha's demimonde had grown to the effect that several cases of venereal disease caused marked concern. The city passed an ordinance prohibiting "houses of prostitution," but the new law proved ineffective due to inconsistency in enforcing the law. The lack of law enforcement led to such stories as one newspaper account in 1869, which reported on a "disgraceful fracas between a party of women connected with rival establishments," wherein they "indulged in several rounds of pulling hair and scratching faces. Ball dresses were torn to tatters."[1] More laws were passed in 1871 and again in 1876.

As Omaha's respectable element waged their battle against the city for the suppression of prostitution, other concerns about the cleanliness of the demimonde and the city in general also surfaced. The unpaved streets often "overflowed with mud and sewage, so thick lace-up boots would be suctioned right off of the feet of the women who wore them." As for the red-light district, one writer in an 1869 issue of *Harper's* magazine wrote that it was a place "where everything is overdone and everyone is underpaid. If not take heed to what I'm saying, you will find it just as I have found it, and if it lies upon your way, for God's sake readers, go around it."[2]

Added to Omaha's troubles, too, was losing its capital status to Lincoln in 1867 as Nebraska was admitted to the union. Yet the city continued to prosper, and the sordid ones continued to make Omaha their home. Sometime around this time, Omaha's demimonde was finally relegated to what was called the "Burnt District," a popular euphemism for the demimondes of the Great Plains. The district would eventually span an amazing six blocks, encompassing an area north from Douglas Street to Cass and from 16th Street west to the railroad tracks along the Missouri River.[3]

Laws against prostitution during the 1870s brought some fairly stiff punishments for offenders. Fines could range between a dollar and $100, plus ten days in jail. Madams were charged another $100 for each day they remained open after being ordered to close. Dance halls, however, were another matter. In these places, girls could dance with a man and entice him to engage in sex elsewhere. Sometime around 1872, one young man later remembered, a pretty dance hall girl asked him the time and thereby struck up a conversation with him. The two chatted for a little bit before the girl invited the man to go home with her. His response was that he had a train to catch, but the girl tried to entice him further. She "wanted me to go a piece with her," he explained. She also tried to get him to let the train "go to hell." It took a bit for the naïve young gentleman to figure out just what the dance hall strumpet was after, at which time he declined her offer. Before parting, the young lady asked for "a quarter for luck." This was given to her, which appeased her. "Good-bye, baby," she said.[4]

The 1880 census might reveal a lot about the Burnt District had the census taker not had such a hard time gleaning the necessary information from its residents. On June 8, the *Omaha Daily Bee* interviewed a census taker who was tasked with recording residents in the district. He told the newspaper that "he was much impeded by the deplorable obtuseness of many people he had occasion to question." The bottom line was, residents of the district were suspicious of the man's motives and feared their information would be reported to the authorities. The 1880 census itself confirms that almost all of the women working in Burnt District brothels told the census taker they were employed as shirt makers, dressmakers, or milliners. Although many ladies indeed did their own sewing on their wardrobes, these occupations were most certainly made up.

The census taker also caught grief from the many denizens who hotly objected to being woken up in the morning hours, since most of them had been up all night. "I meet with many abusive people, and am frequently insulted and loaded with epithets of no flattering nature," the

---

A Woman's Outfit from the Ground Up in the Victorian Era

1 pair of pantaloons (underwear which did not feature a sewn-in crotch until the late 1880s)

1 pair stockings (knitted and held up by garters)

1 chemise (a long, flowy blouse with a wide neck and short-sleeves)

1 corset (made with hard "stays" of metal or whale bone to keep it in shape and make the waist look small)

1 loose shirt (worn over the corset)

1 bell-shaped "cage crinoline" (a stiff, skeletal-looking skirt to hold up the outer skirts)

1 or more petticoats (frilly slips that go over the cage crinoline, usually several)

1 dress (slipped on over the head with several buttons to fasten it)

1 pair high-button shoes[5]

---

man complained. Furthermore, many residents of the red-light district seemed not to know where they were born, or exactly how old they were. The enumerator's task was tough too, because the Burnt District was so large. During the first three days alone, he said, "I took between 400 and 500 names." And despite the often-squalid conditions he encountered, not one resident reported so much as an illness or death in the district.[6]

Given what the census taker described, it is no wonder that fines and jail times increased during the 1880s and 1890s. The authorities also began evicting "habitual offenders" from the city. But law enforcement still lacked in many areas, the main issue being consistency in the way of raids, arrests, and imprisonment. It could not have been easy to keep track of each brothel, saloon, and gambling house, nor the drug abuse, crimes, suicides, and other characteristics that were the norm in what was now alternately called "Hell's Half-Acre." It is entirely possible that the police force was simply overwhelmed by the goings-on in the district, combined with issues of starvation and poverty that also were rampant throughout Omaha at the time. When Methodist minister Charles Savidge arrived in 1882, he found a substandard welfare system that was in dire need of assistance by local churches and "private philanthropic organizations." Although some of Omaha's wealthy citizens lent a hand, one Omaha historian noted that "most unfortunates were left to fend for themselves."[7]

Although Savidge repeatedly used his observances in his sermons, another culprit in the mix was soon discovered: law enforcement. It was 1885 before a city councilman outright charged a local marshal with letting brothels and other bawdy businesses run rampant, and demanded an explanation. The councilman was likely referring to Omaha's standard policy of collecting $5 from every madam and a dollar from every prostitute each day. Apparently, the ladies willingly paid. They were also subject to monthly raids, for which they were given advance notice. This practice seemed acceptable to both the law and the women of the demimonde, although the Burnt District continued to be plagued with social issues. And then, Elia Peattie came to town.

Elia and her family arrived in Omaha from Chicago in 1888. She had already worked for the *Chicago Tribune* and was immediately hired by the *Omaha Daily Herald* as the city's first female reporter. Elia had a special spot in her heart for the underdogs of her new hometown, especially for prostitutes and unwed mothers. She openly supported the "Open Door," a charity which provided medical assistance to unwed mothers and she also publicly campaigned for affordable housing for single women. Most importantly, Elia recognized that prostitutes in general were victims of their own mistakes but also suffered from "society's double standard."[8] A prime example was M. F. Martin, a man who built the "Castle," which functioned as a hotel. As of 1894, however, half of the structure was rented out as a brothel for $200 a month. Martin and his wife eventually owned nearly all of the Burnt District, which now spanned several blocks in the vicinity of Ninth Street, Douglas, Capitol Avenue, and beyond. Their seventeen bordellos ranged from a rickety three-story building, to a dilapidated two-story brick affair, to six one-story "flats" containing three rooms each and sparse furnishings. The flats rented for $3 a day, but other of the Martins' holdings rented for as little as $2.50 per day.

In an 1894 editorial, "No Need of Prostitution: Mrs. Peattie Refuses to Accept the Claim That the Wanton Is a Necessary," Elia expressed her shock at the decision of Lincoln's mayor, Austin Weir, to close every brothel in his city as of March 1. The proclamation would affect two hundred women working in Lincoln's demimonde. Elia rightfully pointed out that Lincoln's businesses would suffer, that Lincoln's illicit ladies would simply work on the sly or drift into other cities such as Omaha, and—most blatantly—that "real politics appear to have difficulty in proceeding without the aid of prostitution." After all, who else had the most knowledge of the inner workings of government? The ladies who were largely aware of the laws in place and who entertained men during legislative sessions, that's who. And, to the chagrin of the general public, legislators felt most comfortable making important decisions within the brothels of their city, for the madam and her girls knew how to keep their secrets.[9]

Everyone knew, Elia wrote, that prostitution was a "necessity" as a means to prevent sex crimes. That included respectable wives whom, Elia realized, had their own "black leaf of shame" in the way of husbands who sometimes cavorted with prostitutes. "When a pure woman thus condones sin," she wrote, "it is because her husband or son is a sinner, and she had to do one of two things—disapprove of the sinner or approve of the sin." Doing so made for some mighty unhappy home lives for married women due to their men's indiscretions. But for a woman of the nineteenth century, it was better to live with skeletons in her closet (as well as any social diseases) than to bear the loss of her social position and steady income for her household.[10]

The truths Elia wrote about certainly shocked the public, but there does not seem to have been any retaliation against her. Too many women, both those in the respectable element and those in the demimonde, knew that she was exposing the true facts about the prostitution industry. There was no arguing with a woman who could cite the fate of three girls, all age sixteen or younger, who were "ruined" by much older men but found safety at the Open Door and another state-run home in Milford. The girls were cared for and taught skills in hopes of finding respectable employment in the outside world. Elia was ultimately selected as president of the Omaha Women's Club in 1896. Shortly afterward, however, she and her family returned to Chicago—perhaps to the relief of officials and others who were outright shamed by her words.

Elia Peattie was not the only one to focus on Omaha's wicked women. A year after her arrival, Methodist pastor Frank Crane also moved to town. Like Elia, Crane was also soon made aware of Omaha's vice, but the two would soon become adversaries due to their points of view. Crane had little to say about the city's prostitution issue until 1893, when mayor George Bemis lambasted reformers wanting to close the Burnt District, telling them that "instead of building fine churches on the hills, build a home, a mission in the burnt district, and let the society women go there and take the social outcasts by the hand." Crane openly objected to Bemis's plan, arguing that prostitutes had no place in society or the church. They were, according to him, "unpardonable," and the city was only encouraging those sinning soiled doves by regulating them. Others, however, favored Bemis's opinions and for a time the city was divided as the two men sparred in the local newspapers. Crane finally left town in 1896, just after Bemis served his final term.[11]

The women in the Burnt District must have watched intently as the likes of Elia Peattie, Frank Crane, and George Bemis battled it out. But the ladies also had their own business to tend to, including staying within the confines of the law to continue working and making money. Some, such as Ada and Minna Everleigh, worked in Omaha just long enough to learn the trade before moving on, or so they would have everyone believe. In the real world, the girls were born to George and Virginia Simms in Greene County, Virginia. Their great-grandfather was Greene County's first sheriff. The girls later claimed they visited former Virginia governor James Kemper's fancy mansion in Madison County. Here, some historians surmise, the ladies got their first taste of the finer things in life. While performing in a singing troupe with two other sisters, Ada and Minna traveled around. In New Orleans one of the sisters, Lulu, died but a few months later the surviving girls, Ada, Minna, and Flora, were noted in the *Weekly Town Talk* as having performed in the nude.

The Simms Sisters, as they called themselves, remained in New Orleans until at least 1889. Flora was no longer with them, however, when Minnie and Ada inexplicably wound up in Omaha, circa 1890. "Minnie" and "Rae" Everly, as they were now called, resided at 822 Dodge in the Burnt District (the girls eventually took their grandmother's valediction at the end of her letters, "Yours everly," and began using it as their last name). During their stay in Omaha, the girls also acquired "a run-down parlor house" at the corner of 12th Street and Jackson. And in 1895, the ladies paid for "two rather risqué painted portraits" of themselves. But the Everleigh Sisters, as they became known, really shined in 1898 when they were said to have inherited $35,000. The pair next acquired a house at 14th Street and Dodge, remodeled it, and opened the fanciest parlor house they could muster in preparation for the world-famous Trans-Mississippi and International Exposition.[12]

Between June and November, some 2.6 million people visited the fair, and many of them saw advertisements for the "Everleigh Sisters" exhibit. The "exhibit" was actually the girls' parlor house with only the most talented, beautiful, and refined women they could find. Admission was $10, and within three months the girls managed to make an amazing $70,000. As the fair closed, the Everleigh Sisters wisely reckoned they would never make that sort of money in Omaha again. On the advice of another madam, Ada and Minna relocated to Chicago where they built the lavish parlor house of their dreams and remained highly successful for several more years. Between the two of them they literally made millions, were able to retire and travel, and both lived until the mid-twentieth century.

Of course, no other soiled dove in Omaha ever came close to making what the Everleigh Sisters made. They are, however, remembered today by way of snippets of history, handed down stories, and photographs. In the latter category is Goldie Williams, a Black prostitute from Chicago, who might have been forgotten if not for her most unusual mugshot in Omaha. According to her arrest record, for vagrancy, Goldie also went by "Mag Murphy." The petite lady stood only five feet tall and weighed in at just 110 pounds. Her admission to working as a prostitute, a broken index finger, and a cut on her wrist all attested to her rough life. She also said her home was in Chicago.

Goldie Williams's mugshot shows an angry young prostitute. COURTESY NEBRASKA HISTORICAL SOCIETY

So, who was Goldie really? Although there are vague clues as to her existence, none of them really pan out. In 1894, for example, the *Herald-Sentinel* in Cordell, Oklahoma, noted that a Goldie Williams had "opened up in the Brennon stand a first class saloon."[13] But the woman in the article was not identified as being "colored," the slang term newspapers nearly always used to identify Blacks. More telling is an article in the *Chicago Chronicle* from April of 1896, which detailed how upwards of one hundred men were chasing down a Black man for robbery in the area of State and Taylor streets. While doing so, the group happened across two other "colored" women identified as Celia Smith and Maggie Murphy at 480 State Street. The two were fighting; Celia fired a gun at Maggie twice but missed. Maggie retaliated by bashing Celia in the head with a beer mug, cutting her forehead.[14] In September of 1897, one Maggie Murphy was arrested after J. C. Curry of New York reported he was robbed of $175 at No. 120 Custom Place, one of Chicago's many "resorts" run by Mamie Boyd. Curry expressed his surprise that the thief did not make off with the numerous diamonds he wore.

Was the Maggie Murphy of Chicago the same person who, as Goldie Williams, was arrested in January of 1898 in Omaha? It is hard to say, but Goldie's mugshot says a lot about her. She was, for instance, wearing a fancy hat with satin ribbons and a feather plume. In her ears, were thick hoop earrings. Even her dress appears expensive, and this only known image of her might prove most appealing if not for her pose: Goldie had not only defiantly crossed her arms but also puffed her small lips out in an angry grimace for the camera. Prisoner #228, as the image identified her, did not take lightly to being arrested.

How did Goldie get to Omaha, and why was she there? The answer remains unknown although one writer supposes that Omaha's Black population grew during the 1880s, largely due to expanded stockyards and railroad systems which provided more labor opportunities. Goldie may have seen her chance to make money from the laborers flocking into Omaha. Or, she may have continued traveling. In July of 1898, Chicago's *Inter Ocean* newspaper reported that a Maggie Murphy and Barney Talbert of 203 Plymouth Place in Chicago were charged with "implication in the theft of" money from a man named Samuel Dunno. Maggie received $395 for her part, but claimed she was robbed of $100 by Matt Driggs, "a colored habitue of the place."[15] Maggie, notably, was not identified as "colored," but another woman by her name was identified as such in October when she and another "negro" woman were arrested in Georgia for disorderly conduct. In that case, Maggie paid a $2 fine.[16] And finally, an article in the *Omaha Daily Bee* in April of 1902 noted that "Miss Maggie Murphy, aged 25," of 812 South 11th Street had died.[17] If that was indeed the same woman, the young girl took her secrets with her to the grave.

It is no wonder that there were hundreds of women just like Goldie Williams in Omaha, whose stories were scant or never told at all. Author Ryan Roenfeld rightfully submits that for decades, the city's demimonde ran rampant, what with saloons and brothels brazenly operating all day and all night, and where "strangers were victimized by every scheme going."[18] It was the perfect recipe for the likes of Tom Dennison, a professional gambler who arrived in Omaha shortly before Goldie was arrested. By 1900, Dennison was in the thick of the city's politics and prostitution industry, and would rule over the underworld for the next thirty years. Dennison and his associates, known simply as "the Gang," became well known around Omaha. The man not only ran a series of gambling joints, brothels, and speakeasies, but he also was extremely friendly with everyone important, including those in the police department and judges in the courts. The law couldn't touch him, and he became commonly known as "the power behind the throne." No law or court, it seemed, could make a move without his approval.[19]

Dennison's wealth easily procured anything he wanted. By making large campaign contributions and contributing to the welfare of the demimonde, he was able to control the votes of any given election. It didn't hurt either that he bought the support and friendship of the *Omaha Bee*'s publisher, Edward Rosewater. Add the purchased support of Mayor Frank Moores, and here was a perfect storm raining pleasantly down on the bawdy element of Omaha. Subsequent Omaha mayors would follow suit as Dennison garnered support for his illegal actions by giving immigrants and other poor residents jobs to sway their votes, paying off police, and doing whatever he needed to do to stay in control of Omaha vice. And amazingly, he did it without ever holding a public office. When Rosewater died in 1906, Dennison simply continued his antics with Victor Rosewater, the publisher's son and heir of the *Omaha Bee*.

Not everyone supported Dennison, of course. Madam Josie Washburn of Lincoln would later recall how a "Man-Landlady" controlled Omaha, and she most likely was talking about Tom Dennison. Josie called the Man-Landlady, and men like him, "the most despicable member of the underworld." Indeed, by about 1907, Dennison had been joined by a number of other men who also owned and operated cribs in the red-light district. The cribs, according to Josie, were comprised of "two small rooms, about six feet height; a door and window forms the whole front. Each crib has a projecting corner, and a casual glance down the line gives it a scalloped appearance, which is meant to be artistic." The cribs were located along paved alleys with "heavy iron gates at each end." One of them even had a "fancy roof," red in color and lit by electric lights.[20]

The women working in Omaha's cribs, according to Josie, were anything but gay. Some of the veteran prostitutes in these alleys were addicted to drugs and alcohol. Many more crib girls were younger and swept away by the excitement of the alleys at night, dancing to the "cracked electric piano in each crib" as epithets and obscenities reverberated through the alley. Many had a male lover or pimp who took their money, and few of the girls practiced safe sex. Anything could be had inside the cribs, each of which featured an electric button connecting to a saloon and restaurant from which the girls could order food and drinks. Each prostitute paid from $1 to $5 daily for rent, in advance. The belongings of those who could not pay were promptly thrown into the street. From this sordid way of business, the landlords made thousands of dollars a month from which they could pay off the police and still make a healthy profit. And many of them, said Josie, were prominent men, including members of the local churches.

Josie Washburn was clearly appalled by the system: the way the male landlords of the cribs and houses were never punished for allowing women to live in squalid conditions. How sickly and hungry many crib girls were. How raids by police made further victims of the women, who were abused both physically and verbally. The way, in court, that the women's money was thoughtlessly taken from them in the way of fees and fines while those in control of the system looked the other way. And how the real fiends, the men, languished in money and fine houses at the prostitutes' expense. Josie had no problem singling out every one of them—city councilmen and mayors, male landlords, newspapers, police, saloon owners, and others.

Josie Washburn was not the only one to notice how the male landlords in the demimonde easily controlled vice while women suffered. Beginning in 1908, reformers were slowly edging in, trying to regain control over Omaha. They were in for a long haul; by 1910, there were still some 2,500 prostitutes working in the city. Tom Dennison, meanwhile, continued reigning over Omaha. They say that following the First World War, a veteran soldier was hired to write for the *Omaha Bee*. One of his first assignments was to interview a local businessman who was quite friendly with Dennison. There was, however, a caveat: "Mr. Dennison is interested in this story," the young writer was warned, "and it is the policy of this paper to print whatever Mr. Dennison . . . wants."[21] Challenges against Dennison lay ahead, however, as a new mayor was elected and, along with a new police commissioner, set about taking Dennison down. But he wasn't going without a fight.

In 1919, the *Omaha Bee* suddenly began reporting that there were Black men violating white women, and that police were doing nothing about the situation. The public outcry was spurred on by Dennison in an attempt to create an issue bigger than the accusations against him. Most unfortunately, the plan worked to the effect that a Black man named Will Brown was accused of raping a white woman who never did positively identify him as her attacker. Brown was arrested, but the general public was so enraged that a mob numbering around five thousand people descended upon the county jail, nearly lynched Mayor Edward Smith, and took Brown from the jail. He was hanged before the crowd "mutilated and riddled his body with bullets, dragged it through the streets of the city at the end of a rope, and burned it." Fortunately, the police had wisely released the other Black prisoners in the jail to prevent them from suffering the same fate.[22]

Racial tensions in Omaha would continue many more years as Tom Dennison continued controlling the city's underworld. Not until 1932 did Attorney General C. A. Sorenson take Dennison on by trying him in a federal court for "conspiracy to violate Prohibition." The case ended in a mistrial, but the jig was up; at last, Dennison and fifty-eight of his buddies were exposed for what they were, and the group lost their public support. The trial was especially hard on the now-elderly Dennison, who moved to California. He died in 1934 from injuries sustained in a car accident. Also gone was Omaha's bawdy frontier past.[23]

CHAPTER ELEVEN

Anna Wilson, Queen of the Underworld

NO OTHER BUSINESSWOMAN IN OMAHA COULD MATCH ANNA "ANNIE" Wilson. The lady was not just the city's only wealthy longtime madam, but also remained generous and dedicated to those less fortunate. She was an ideal madam, befriending and caring for the many women who worked for her over time. And toward the end of her life, she tried her best to make large donations to the city of Omaha. These traits, along with her love for philanthropy, aptly earned Annie the moniker of "Queen of the Underworld."[1]

Annie's beginnings are quite mysterious. Born on May 27, 1835, she told others she was from a Baptist minister's family, or perhaps a wealthy family, and born in Louisiana, Georgia, or New York. Nobody ever did know where the lady was really from, or her real name. When Annie's parents died, she is believed to have been taken in by an uncle. Other glimpses into her past were things the lady told to Reverend C. W. Savidge of Omaha. Savidge said that Annie recalled how she was "mistreated as a child, how she ran away from school and how she fell into the hands of a man who led her into evil ways."[2] Later, she is said to have married a military captain, but left him when her life became too mundane.

In about 1867, Annie arrived in Omaha. The city was already quite rowdy with plenty of men's entertainment. Annie's first job was as a performer in a music hall. Audiences were quite keen on the seemingly educated, pretty lady. When the music hall closed, Annie could only turn to someone she trusted. His name was Dan Allen, and he was a professional gambler and former steamboat owner. Allen was well familiar with the riverboats offering games of chance sailing up and down the Missouri River, as well as the gambling houses of Omaha. He made good money at both.

As Annie's relationship with Allen warmed, plans were made for her to operate a series of classy brothels in Omaha's demimonde. The first of these was noted in the 1870 census, which shows Annie residing with Allen, two Black servants identified as ten-year-old John Robinson and seventeen-year-old Violet Lewethers, and two women, Jennie McDonald and Emma Williams. The latter two were in their twenties, and their occupations were discreetly listed as "shirt maker." Annie's closest competition was Madam Emma Davis, who employed eight female "shirtmakers," two servants, and was worth a cool $27,000. Annie's property was worth a little less than half of that.

Not to be outdone by her competitors, Annie eventually became noted for her balls, which lasted all night as champagne flowed and the madam sailed through her parlor bedecked in beautiful gowns and fine jewelry. But she also was known for her motherly instincts toward her employees, treating them with respect and providing medical care while they worked for her—and financial assistance even when they could no longer work for her. Much like the celebrated Dora Topham of Ogden and Salt Lake City, Utah, it was Annie's goal to encourage and help her girls leave the profession and live respectable lives.[3] When one of her employees married, Annie arranged an elegant and elaborate wedding reception for them. She also gave the newlyweds financial assistance to start their lives together, and willingly took back any disenchanted bride to help her pursue the career of her choice.

Annie Wilson, it seemed, was more than able when it came to controlling her queendom in the demimonde. Only one exception is known, when on a night in 1875, the madam drank a bit too much champagne during one of her soirees and passed out. When some cur made off with some $10,000 of the madam's jewelry, officers caught the thief and "saw that he was sent to prison."[4] That one scathing incident aside, Annie Wilson and Dan Allen continued living contentedly at 136-138 Douglas Street, a sizeable property located in the midst of the Burnt District. Annie ran a clean house, to the extent that she was seldom mentioned in newspapers. She paid her fines and her taxes—and did not hesitate to go after anyone who tried to cheat her. In 1877, for instance, she sued one Samuel Colburn over some property in block 100 on Douglas Street, and won.

By June of 1880, Annie had relocated to 914–916 Douglas Street. The census documents nine young ladies at Annie's, as well as a Black cook. Annie truly had it made, as her only competition was a house next door, run by Clara Dillon who had had only three girls and her eight-year-old sister who was in school, besides.

Annie Wilson and Her Girls in 1880

Annie Willson [*sic*], age 37, born in Louisiana, parents born in England, landlady, single, occupation "Keeping young ladies boarding house"
Mollie Scott, age 30, born in Ohio, single, dressmaker
Lillie Gibson, age 23, born in Canada, single, dressmaker
Pearl McLellan, age 29, born in Texas, married, milliner
Jenna Bartlett, age 22, born in Maryland, single, milliner
Alice Burton, age 19, born in Illinois, single, dressmaker
Francis Reed, age 35, born in Massachusetts, single, dressmaker
Jessie Grey, age 18, born in Canada, single, milliner
Jessie Reynolds, age 18, born in Michigan, single, milliner
May Coleman, age 21, born in Michigan, single, dressmaker
Mary Lee, age 25, Black, born in Missouri, single, cook[5]

Annie continued purchasing property. In July, she bought lots 7 and 8 in block 100 from Downing & Bemis Brewing Company for just $100. The following year, she bought more property in the exclusive Kountz subdivision. This was most likely 2018 Wirt Street, where Annie would eventually retire, but it is quite possible that she made the beautiful mansion there her private home at the time of her purchase. All was well in her world save for Dan Allen, who had contracted kidney disease in about 1876, and often left town in search of medical treatments for his ailment. This could explain why Allen did not appear in the 1880 census.

And in 1883, it was reported that he had returned from such a trip in such bad shape that he was confined to his bed. Finally, on April 28, 1884, Allen died at the Douglas Street house. He was buried the same day, in an ornate casket with hundreds of flowers as numerous friends were in attendance. He also left a $30,000 estate and bequeathed $1,000 to each of his brothers and sisters and their children. The rest, $10,000, went to Annie with the stipulation that when she died, the remaining money would go to Allen's heirs.

Annie wisely continued investing Allen's money, as well as her own. By the time of the 1885 Nebraska census in June, she had built an all-new mansion at 912 Douglas Street. Two imposing buildings, connected within, were built of brick and spanned two lots, each towering three stories high with a basement. One source says there were twenty-six rooms in all, and various tunnels from the basements led to saloons and cigar stores for the convenience of clients who did not wish to be seen entering the brothel. Because the house was located close to the Territorial Legislature, discreetness would have been mighty important. The census also reflects that Annie had twenty-five girls, as well as a housekeeper, cook, and waiter. Curiously, although the birthplaces of Annie's girls and their parents were documented, their ethnicities were marked "U" for "unknown." It is entirely possible that the genteel madam simply provided a list of what the census taker was requesting, rather than allowing him to interview each woman.

In December, Annie added another story to a house she owned on 12th Street near Capitol Avenue. But her brothel on Douglas Street was her castle, and she conducted her lavish parlor house with very little trouble. An exception was the time, in June of 1886, when some garbage piled in one wing of the house caught fire. But the fire occurred in the early evening and only burned the window shutters before being extinguished by a bucket brigade. It was out in its entirety by the time the fire department arrived.

The madam was still purchasing property when, in 1891, she made a most extraordinary gesture: she offered up her fabulous house on Douglas Street to the city, for lease as a city hospital. The building was ideal, with thirty-seven rooms with bathrooms "and other accommodations on each floor," according to the *Daily Bee*. The city mulled her offer for several weeks, however, before ultimately declining the offer.[6] But why would a successful madam offer up her most lucrative property for lease to the city? It can only be surmised that Madam Annie, after hearing or even witnessing various suicides and cases of venereal disease in the Burnt District for some time, decided to assist the city in abating such problems. The lady may have in fact been attempting to retire, for the *Daily Bee* reported in August that Annie's residence at 1609 California Street also caught fire but was put out with minimal damage. A few weeks later, the madam again made an offer to the city to donate a large bronze fountain from her well-manicured yard, to be installed in Hanscom Park. The gift was initially accepted, only to be denied a few weeks later (not until a few weeks before Annie died in 1911 did the city finally accept the fountain). Omaha officials, it seemed, were ever too eager to accept Annie's kindnesses, only to rebuff those kindnesses after considering who the offers were coming from.

Annie carried on. Between 1893 and 1896, she purchased even more properties along Douglas Street and was frequently listed in city directories at those properties. She weathered the attacks against the demimonde during 1897, when her property at 110–112 North Ninth was included in a list of "dives" where liquor was being sold illegally, each of them a brothel. And, she made considerable money along with many other women in the flesh trade during the Trans-Mississippi and International Exposition in 1898. But what the madam really wanted to do, apparently, was retire from her profession.

By 1900, Annie appears to have finally got her wish. The 1900 census reveals that the madam now lived at her California Street home, with just a servant and a couple of roomers. Some of her houses were now leased to other women as she continued buying properties. A stink was raised when it was reported that Annie looked at some property that had formerly housed "the old Omaha city mission property" on Tenth Street, between Dodge Street and Capitol Avenue. Annie explained that she had indeed looked at the property, but decided to buy a different parcel across the street. Ever a reminder that Annie was a madam, the *Daily Bee* complained immediately about how the Christian work the mission had accomplished in the past would now be desecrated.[7] A few months later, Annie also added a second story to another house at 112 North 9th Street for $4,500. Clearly, the lady wasn't going anywhere no matter what the newspaper said, and she was continuing to make gobs of money in a variety of ways.

In 1901, Annie moved again, this time to her mansion on Wirt Street. It is guessed that, in 1891, Annie hired Omaha pioneer Alfred D. Jones to construct the house. It was quite grand, towering three stories tall with a "fine parlor" and over a dozen rooms inside containing expensive furniture, fine art, and Annie's private library of over a thousand books. The lawn around the house was well maintained with beautiful gardens. Annie's neighbors were now well-to-do, upstanding citizens and there were several churches in the area. Surprisingly, Annie was a welcome addition to the neighborhood, often delivering tea to the "Old People's Home" nearby and visiting with its residents. On the side, Annie did continue visiting at least one of her brothels, as evidenced on a night in January of 1909 when a man named Jack Curtain, also known as Albert Clark, killed patrolman Lafayette Smith.

Annie was at the brothel when Curtain burst in. He was ordered to leave, but pulled a gun instead and snatched a "gold and diamond-set locket" from Annie as he backed toward the door. One of the girls in the house, Anna Cardot, tried to stop Curtain, but he trained his gun on her and forced her to stand against a wall as he fled. Another girl, identified as Betsy or Jennie Smith, followed Curtain into the street and chased him until he whacked her on the head with the butt of his gun. The injury was bad enough that later, the girl was still too bedridden to testify against the thief. Other women in the street began hollering for the police. The jail was only two blocks away, and Curtain was finally arrested. Annie later testified against him.

Back in the comfort of her Wirt Street home, Annie tried to resume her respectable life. In April, she donated $300 to a building fund for the "Child Saving Institute."[8] And in August, she also began selling off her many properties—one of them sold for $25,000. Annie must have known her health was frail, for in 1910, the elderly madam suffered a stroke. She recovered, but fulfilling her philanthropic wishes became more important to her than ever. Even so, Annie's name was published on a list of known brothels after Governor Chester Hardy Aldrich commanded district attorney James English to begin filing complaints against such places in 1911. How Annie responded is unknown, but she did continue selling off her properties. Yet she also yearned to continue helping the city.

In August, Annie again offered to donate her three-story brothel on Douglas Street for the city to use as an emergency hospital. It was a sweet deal: Annie wanted $125 in rent each month, and also wanted to be exempt from paying property taxes for the house. In return, she offered $500 toward needed repairs and said that, when she died, the property would be bequeathed to the city. When asked why she was donating her property, Annie simply answered that "she wanted to help humanity."[9] Omaha's health commissioner, Connell, jumped at the deal. "Omaha is sadly in need of such an institute," he said, "and this building is in an ideal location."[10]

Times had changed from the first time Annie made such an offer. This time, as the city mulled over Annie's offer, letters began pouring in from all over the country asking the madam for money. Meantime, someone who was clearly against the city taking Annie's deal actually tried to set fire to the Douglas Street brothel. The flames were quickly extinguished, although the arsonist was never caught. Determined to make a deal, Annie lowered the rent to $100 per month and offered an additional $500 for repairs. This time, the city accepted, and none too soon, for on October 27, Annie Wilson died at her home on Wirt Street.

Annie's many kindnesses brought out the best in memories of her, including the fact that she often encouraged prostitutes to "leave the life of the red light." Many of those women, now leading respectable lives, came to her funeral. Flowers flowed all around her casket, and her pallbearers were chosen by friends of Dan Allen.[11] Annie was buried next to Allen in Prospect Hill Cemetery. Local legend claims that her decision did not go down without a fight; Prospect Hill had initially declined to sell her a burial plot when she was still alive. The determined madam purchased a couple of plots at Forest Lawn Cemetery instead, and informed Prospect Hill Cemetery that she had planned to donate money to them. Should she be forced to use her Forest Lawn plot instead, she said, her money would be donated there instead. In the end, Annie was indeed buried at Prospect Hill Cemetery—under nine feet of concrete, lest anyone change their mind about where her final resting place should be. "An immense polished stone in the dimensions of a king-size bed with four posts" was installed over her grave and that of Allen.[12]

Naturally, everyone wanted to see what happened when the wealthy madam's will was finally read a few days after her funeral. Claiming no living heirs, Annie had indeed bequeathed $10,000 apiece to several charities and made sure that $9,000 of the $10,000 Dan Allen left her went back to his heirs. The Wirt Street mansion was left to the Old People's Home Association, as well as $10,000 for improvements and maintenance. Other recipients included the Associated Church, a "child protective home" called The Creche, the Child's Saving Institute, the Omaha City Mission, the Bishop Clarkson Hospital, and the Wise Hospital. And, it seemed most fitting that the hospital in Annie's former brothel in the red-light district would eventually be used to treat venereal diseases.[13]

Anna Wilson's likeness as it appeared in the *Tensas Gazette* in 1912. COURTESY LIBRARY OF CONGRESS

Not everyone was happy with Annie's choices. In January of 1912, an attorney from Sacramento, California, Albert Pait, placed an ad in the *Daily Bee* claiming Annie was really Margaret Alice Pait and that she had four long-lost brothers. Meanwhile, the use of Annie's home on Wirt Street was still being debated by the Old People's Home Association when

Joseph Nelson, who still occupied the home, was found dead under mysterious circumstances. Some said the man committed suicide, depressed because Annie left him nothing. The *Daily Bee*, however, told a different story, reporting that Nelson took a spill in the alley behind the house one night due to a stroke. Witnesses saw a young man with him, who said he would take the elderly Nelson inside and summon help. The next day Nelson was found dead in his bed and the gas in the kitchen stove had been left on. The strange young man had disappeared. Although the death was ruled a suicide, Nelson's death remains highly suspicious. Notable is that the house had also been broken into previously.

In the end, Annie's mansion on Wirt Street never was used by the Old People's Home Association. The house was described as a "very attractive, large brick house, having large reception hall, parlor, living room, dining room, kitchen, den on the first floor; six fine sleeping rooms on the second floor; large, completely finished third floor. House is in excellent condition, newly decorated throughout; fine hardwood floors all through; beautiful plumbing, tiled bath, lavatories on first floor and in bed rooms. Hot water heat. Nice south front yard; fine shade, large porch, good brick garage." But the Association wanted an all-new facility and claimed there was not enough money to run the house at its proposed location.[14] The Association was eventually granted permission to sell the property in 1913, and the beautiful mansion was eventually torn down—as was Annie's palatial parlor house on Douglas Street.

Today, Annie Wilson is remembered each Memorial Day due to the kindness of Mrs. Thomas Kimball, founder of The Creche. During Memorial Day festivities in 1912, Mrs. Kimball, in a gesture of solidarity, placed a yellow rose on Annie's grave. She continued the tradition, which did not go unnoticed, up until she died in 1930. After that, Mrs. Kimball's son, architect Thomas Kimball, took up the annual ritual until he, too, died in 1934. Another woman, Eloise McNichols, carried on the tradition for a few more years. But the tribute had ceased by 1979 when some cemetery officials were seen once again gracing Annie Wilson's grave with a yellow rose. The tradition was revived, and, hopefully, continues to this day. Meanwhile, Wilson & Washburn, a neighborhood pub in the former Burnt District, pays tribute to Annie Wilson and Josie Washburn, who worked for Annie before becoming a prominent madam herself in Lincoln, and later wrote the scathing truth about life in the demimonde.

CHAPTER TWELVE

Awful Annie Cook

ANNA WILSON OF OMAHA WAS CLEARLY EXEMPLARY IN EVERYTHING A madam should have been. She was an astute businesswoman who worked with city officials to run a clean palace of pleasure. She looked after her many employees like a mother. She managed her money to the extent that she died wealthy. She was a philanthropist who donated her time, property, and money to assist local charities. Anna remains well known for the good she did even while working in a profession that was considered bad. But there also were, unfortunately, a healthy handful of madams who were not good women, not angelic, not unappreciated contributors to their communities, and not people that fans of the prostitution industry would admire today. While a good madam took care of her girls and made sure they stayed fed, healthy and safe, there were those who were known to abuse their employees, sometimes beating them, locking them in their rooms, or worse. Annie Cook was one such woman.

Annie was Anna Maria Petzke when she was born in Denver, Colorado, circa 1873. Her parents were Russian immigrants who owned a livery stable, but only her divorced mother, Emilie, was head of the household by the time of the 1880 census. The family at that time consisted of Anna's brothers, Albert and Charles, an older sister named Bertha, and a young sister named Elisa. Emilie took in laundry while sixteen-year-old Albert, her oldest child, toiled as a cigar maker. The rest of the children are documented as being in school.

In about 1893, Annie met Frank Cook, a farmer from Hershey, Nebraska, who was in Denver purchasing supplies. Cook, who was some fifteen years older than Annie, proposed marriage. Annie accepted, and the newlyweds soon made their way to Frank's eighty-acre farm in Nebraska. The following year, Annie gave birth to her only child, a daughter named Clara, at North Platte. But Annie does not appear to have been satisfied to settle down as a wife and mother. Instead, she gradually grew greedy and downright meaner than a snake. They say that if Clara displeased her, Annie beat the child and/or starved her. Then, on a trip to see a physician about a kidney infection in Omaha, Annie somehow fell in with a local madam and decided to pursue the brothel business. For the next several years, Annie, apparently on the sly, made several trips to Omaha under the guise of needing medical treatment. Instead, she spent her time there in a brothel, presumably as the madam of the house.

By 1900, there were two Annie Cooks: the wife and mother at a farm in Hershey, and the discreet madam who reigned over a place on bawdy Douglas Street in Omaha. Now living at the Cook farm were Frank and Annie, little Clara, and Annie's older sister, Elise (nee Elizabeth Louise Petske), now called Louise and sometimes known as Lizzie. Annie's sister, who has been described as "feeble minded," must have depended on her sister for support.[1] The story of how Lizzie came to live with Annie is most interesting. Like Annie, Lizzie was born in Denver. Although Lizzie was seemingly a normal, happy child, Annie was able to eventually convince the family that her sister was mentally incompetent and would likely never marry. Annie offered to take care of Lizzie, who was duly sent to the Cook farm during the summer of 1900.

Annie's plan to keep her sister a virtual slave on the Cook farm backfired, at first. Unbeknownst to her, Lizzie had met a man back in Denver. His name was Joe Knox, and he too hailed from Nebraska. Soon after her arrival at Annie's, Lizzie managed to send several letters to Knox telling of the abuse she suffered at her sister's hands. In 1901, Knox proposed marriage, and the couple eloped to North Platte before moving to the groom's property at Hyannis. A daughter, Mary, was born in 1902. For the next three years, Annie plied the gullible Lizzie with letters, asking her to bring Mary for a visit. When Lizzie finally gave in and returned to the Cook farm in 1905, Annie was just as ruthless as before and even managed to chase off Joe Knox whenever he tried to intervene. Eventually Knox gave up. Lizzie, and now Mary, were left at the mercy of the cruel Annie Cook.

Although Annie had enrolled Clara in high school in Omaha in about 1909, she pulled the girl from her classes after a year or so and moved her to North Platte. There, Clara was made to balance her homework from her new school with playing piano in another brothel Annie operated. The North Platte bordello was large enough to employ a number of girls. As with other houses of prostitution, certain officials were known to visit Annie's place for pleasure. Unlike many madams who utilized their friendships with officials to stay in business and maintain their houses, however, Annie seems to have used her prominent clients for personal gain. Instead of working with these men, Annie used them "as a means of extortion," although how she did this remains unclear.[2] Before long too, some of Annie's clients took an interest in young Clara. Thus, the girl was forced into prostitution as part of her duties at the brothel and dropped out of school altogether.

Stories about Annie Cook's ruthlessness have been told time and time again, perhaps to the extent that her tale has lost some of the more intricate and more truthful details. In spite of Clara moving to North Platte in about 1909, for instance, the 1910 census reveals she and her mother still living at the farm with Frank in Hershey. Clara, however, is documented as the wife of William H. Vanlue, a farmer who was ten years older than she. The two had married in North Platte the previous October. The union lasted less than two years; in August of 1911, Clara filed for divorce from Vanlue "on the grounds of cruelty and improper attention to other women during the greater part of their two years of married life."[3] Did Clara meet Vanlue while working at her mother's bordello in North Platte? It is hard to say, but by the time of the 1920 census, she was back at the Hershey farm with her parents. Also living there were Annie's sister, now identified as Elizabeth Knox, and sixteen-year-old Mary. Years later, author Nellie Snyder Yost interviewed Mary Knox about her time at the Cook farm. It seems Annie had grown extremely abusive toward her family, especially Mary, who told of the "torture and starvation" she experienced over the course of some sixteen years.[4]

Annie's abuse toward others would spread like wildfire. Using the money from her North Platte brothel, she was able to purchase some land adjacent to the Cook farm and, in 1923, established the Lincoln County Poor Farm there. The Poor Farm had previously been run by a woman who treated the inmates "with dignity, respect, and favorable conditions." That ended under Annie's reign, as the woman turned the poor farm residents, most of them men, into virtual slaves, brandishing a buggy whip and spewing forth epithets to coerce them into doing as she commanded. Locals whispered about some of the inmates dying "under mysterious circumstances, some floating in irrigation ditches." For some reason, nobody ever investigated the deaths. Annie's deadly secrets were apparently kept by the authorities, over whom the woman had some sort of power, or form of bribery, or threat. Meanwhile, Clara, Lizzie, and Mary were "virtual slaves" at the Cook farm next door and were also in charge of keeping the North Platte brothel clean.[5]

All this time, Annie's faithful husband, Frank, stood by helplessly. Although he disapproved of the way Annie treated the inmates of the Poor Farm and his family, he apparently did nothing more than keep the residents entertained with songs and stories. He also dared not cross Annie, possibly fearing for his own life. The authorities looked the other way too, even when county clerk Theo Lowe suggested, in February of 1924, that the land on which the poor farm was located was too large. He also noted that "As a rule, the patients at the Poor Farm are old people not able to work."[6] There was more: in March, a new report came out in the North Platte *Daily Telegram* that the Poor Farm, said to be run by Clara Cook, "was not what it should have been."[7]

It is interesting that Clara is recorded as being in charge of the Poor Farm, since most stories about her family focus on Annie being at the helm. The report mentioning Clara was made under J. H. Van Cleave, a spokesman for the City Welfare Board, the Women's Christian Temperance Union, the Woman's Club, and the "Committee of Five Hundred." Van Cleave declined to give details and only said, twice, that no charges had been filed against Clara (leading to speculation that some sort of wrongdoing had been committed). The spokesman only recommended that "other bidders" should be allowed to take over the Poor Farm. The trouble was, there were no other bidders in the running. To complicate matters more, a separate inspection of the place, reported the same day in the same newspaper, found it was "clean and well heated," its inmates "contented and well fed." A payment to Clara Cook in the amount of $410.95 was duly paid for their care. Notably, however, the county commissioners had voted "to take lady and small boy from County Poor Farm and put her on train for Lexington" on March 16.[8]

The "small boy" may very well have been Joseph Martin, whom the Cooks wound up taking in as a foster son. His mother, Sarah, was a deaf-mute and one of the first inmates to come live at the Poor Farm in 1923. In one version of the story, the mother was worked to death and the Cooks adopted little Joe. All that is known is that Sarah did die at the Poor Farm in 1925, and is today interred in the North Platte Cemetery. Yet if that is true, she would not have been put on a train out of town in 1924, and whether the unnamed woman and boy did board a train remains unknown. Nellie Snyder Yost would eventually interview Joe and "marveled that his experiences had not turned him bitter, or emotionally twisted."[9] One time, for example, Clara had been working in Omaha, presumably at Annie's brothel, and purchased two pair of overalls for Joe as a Christmas present. When Annie came in the room and saw the boy enjoying his new clothes, she snatched them up and threw them into a burning stove. Another time, after starving Joe, Clara, and Lizzie as some sort of punishment, Annie discovered Frank had made everyone pancakes in her absence. The furious woman put a lock on the kitchen cupboards. Fed up and frustrated, Frank moved into the barn.

Little by little, Annie's victims began escaping her clutches. In 1924, Annie tried to force Mary into working at one of her brothels. The girl outright refused, a fight started, and Annie came after her with a butcher knife, stabbing her. Mary was able to flee into the dark and rainy night in search of help and finally caught a ride to North Platte. She never returned to the Cook farm but led a sad life: all three of her husbands died early, and Mary spent the rest of her life trying to come up with a plan to rescue her mother.

After Mary Knox escaped her sadistic aunt, life went on at the Poor Farm. Clara continued to be identified as being in charge. Behind her was Annie, forcing her daughter to run the place, as well as the brothels in North Platte and Omaha. The family was making good money in both places, and one writer surmises that Clara "eventually grew to like the things that money could buy and joined with Annie in taking pleasure in the money that was coming into the family." It was also Annie, however, who routinely coerced her neighbors to help out on the Cook farm, with the assurance that a piece of the family's property would eventually be willed to them. That, apparently, was a lie.

The 1930 census records Clara, Frank, Joe, and Lizzie as continuing to live with Annie, as well as three "roomers" who were no doubt residents of the Poor Farm. Although Clara still ran the farm, at least on paper, she and the rest of the family continued to be the victims of Annie's wrath. The Sunday church services that began at the Poor Farm in about 1932 were likely Clara's idea, but the conditions there were again questioned in 1934, just after Clara successfully signed another year-long contract to run the place. The contract came with several stipulations which were printed in the *North Platte Daily Transcript*: the grounds were to be kept "clean, orderly and quiet." The housing was to provide adequate heat and lighting, and the inmates were to receive adequate care and supervision, proper food, and such diversions as books, magazines, and tobacco. Visiting hours were to be maintained for friends and family.[10]

The rules seemed standard enough, but something didn't set well with a man named Herman Kerr. Apparently, Kerr wrote the county commissioners with several concerns about what was going on at the Poor Farm just a short time after Clara received her contract in January. If the many stories of Annie Cook bribing and threatening the authorities to get her way are true, the evidence may lie in a curious letter to the editor in the *North Platte Daily Bulletin*. Penned in part by Reverend Chester Tulga, the note explained that Kerr "wrote his letter with the best of intentions and to commend the improved situation of the Poor Farm instead of condemning it." The note ended with a statement by Kerr himself, expressing "regret that the misunderstanding occurred."[11] After that, all seemed well at the Poor Farm until May, when Clara Cook suddenly died.

According to legend and local rumor, Clara and Annie were in the kitchen, fighting yet again. The argument escalated. Clara bolted out of the back door with Annie hot on her trail, a "lid lifter" (a heavy metal handle for prying up the round lids from the woodstove) in her hand. Lizzie would later say that Annie threw the lifter at Clara, hitting her in the head. Next, Clara "ran around a tree several times, then dropped dead."[12] That's one version of the story. Another comes from the *North Platte Daily Telegraph*'s May 29 edition, whose article bore the headline, "Clara Cook, Poisoned by Mistake and Dies." The article went on to explain that Clara mistook some disinfectant in a glass for medicine and downed it, dying soon afterward. The paper said the incident was "purely accidental," also that no investigation would be performed.[13]

In 1936, Frank Cook died, too. He was still living in the barn on the Cook farm, and at least one source says that Joe Martin was with him when Frank died in his sleep. Now, the only victims remaining at the Cook farm with Annie were Joe and Lizzie; the 1940 census does not show any boarders remaining at the Poor Farm. A few years later, Joe finally left the Cook farm. He is said to have eventually enrolled in the army, served during World War II, and went to work as an engineer for the Union Pacific Railroad.

At last, only Annie and Lizzie were left at the Cook farm. Annie remained a "player in the town that was 'Little Chicago,' North Platte, until she finally died in 1952—much to the relief of so many who knew her and still feared her."[14] Almost immediately, Mary, who had remarried, blazed a trail to the Cook farm, rescued her mother at last, and took her to live in North Platte. She was there by the time Annie's simple and unrevealing obituary was published in the *Hershey Enterprise* on May 29. The article only said that Annie died at the local hospital, named a few surviving relatives, and announced that the woman would be buried in North Platte. Later, however, local newspapers would at last publish the stories that had been heard for years about Annie's deadly wrath against those at the Poor Farm, and especially, her own family. At least six of her neighbors claimed she had promised to leave her land to them, but without proof they received nothing.

Lizzie Knox only lived six more years after Annie died. The day before she died in 1958, Lizzie specifically told Mary, "When I die, don't bury me next to Annie." Mary made sure to grant her mother's wish.[15] Joe Martin presumably never returned to the Cook farm either, and passed away in 1991. Surprisingly, the Cook farm and the Poor House remain today, although they have been renovated. Supposedly the ghost of Annie Cook haunts them, along with those she terrorized or killed. The place not only draws ghost seekers, but also caught the attention of Hollywood executives in 2017. A new film, *Annie Cook*, was set to star actress Kelly McGillis portraying the "infamous Midwest crime queen." As of this writing, however, the film is still in development.[16]

CHAPTER THIRTEEN

The Naughty Nymphs of North Platte

NORTH PLATTE OWED ITS EXISTENCE TO THE FLEDGLING OREGON Trail, but also General G. M. Dodge, who surveyed the area in 1853 with several other engineers and determined to construct a road through the region. The city of North Platte was duly laid out in November of 1866 as the Union Pacific Railroad made plans to roll into town. William S. Peniston and A. J. Miller began construction on North Platte's first building, a general store made from logs, at Locust and Front streets. Next, John Burke moved a hotel over from nearby Cottonwood Springs. The structures came just in time, for a tent city consisting of three thousand railroad workers, as well as barracks for soldiers, followed. North Platte soon contained over 300 buildings as the population quickly swelled to 5,000 residents. With such rapid growth, the city founders had little chance to establish anything in the way of local law and order. Numerous saloons, gambling houses, and North Platte's first brothel were soon in place, and the violence in town ranged from drunken fights to murder. Sometimes, local residents were forced to handle outlaws and lawbreakers on their own terms. Only when the Union Pacific completed its work and moved on toward Julesburg, Colorado, was the violence abated somewhat.

In 1868, General William Tecumseh Sherman visited North Platte as county commissioners made plans for constructing an official county jail. William Peniston was put in charge of the project, and the resulting structure on Front Street between Vine and Locust streets cost a whopping $2,500. The price reflected the materials comprising the log structure, but it was so poorly built that it was easy for prisoners to escape. Thus, lawmen had a difficult time wrangling outlaws, and the idea of prosecuting any wanton women who had drifted into town was not yet an issue. But the women were definitely there: General Sherman later commented that "There were not enough women in North Platte to make a heaven, but there were enough to raise hell."[1]

One of the earliest madams in North Platte was Hattie Jones, who boldly opened her first brothel right next to the county jail. Later, in the 1870s, she moved to Front Street. There was plenty of business to be had, but not all of it was good; in May 1880, Hattie complained to the police about a woman who had stolen a gold chain from her. In 1885, Hattie also had issues with another woman, Catharine McLaughlin. Beginning in March, Hattie sued Catharine for foreclosure and was awarded $295.55. Later that year, the state census recorded Hattie as a "bawdy house keeper" who employed only one woman, nineteen-year-old Electa Hostetter.

Directly around the corner from Hattie was competition in the way of a larger brothel headed by saloonkeeper George Smith, who employed a housekeeper named Margaret Perry. There were also five girls working for Smith: Katie Bush, Bessie Johnson, Margaret Mustard, Jane Simpson, and Nina Spencer. Hattie, meanwhile, may have been experiencing financial issues, since her troubles with Catharine McLaughlin went on until December. Nothing else was reported about Hattie until 1888, when she was fined for selling liquor without a license in Omaha. And around 1896, the State of Nebraska officially filed charges against her. Hattie, apparently, decided she had enough of North Platte and moved on.

By 1888, lawbreaking was so prevalent in North Platte that the county jail was abandoned in favor of an all-new, two-story brick affair on Locust Street—the location of the red-light district. City officials also took measures to make North Platte one of the first "dry" cities in the state. But wily bootleggers of the town simply began labeling their beer as "buttermilk."[2] In 1890, women were officially banned from entering saloons. That, however, did little to stop more women from opening more brothels after the dawn of the twentieth century.

Notorious Houses of North Platte During the 1900s

Acme Rooms (also known as the Home Rooms), 610 ½ North Dewey

Atlas Rooms, 611 ½ North Locust

Broadmoor Rooms (also known as the Broadmoor Hotel), 105 ½ W. 6th and 107 ½ West Street

Como Rooms, 611 ½ N. Locust

Elks Rooms, 106 ½ E. 6th

Glendale Rooms, 104 ½ and 106 ½ E. 5th

Gosney Rooms, 513 ½ N. Dewey

Hinman Rooms, 108 ½ E. Front

Ideal Rooms, 801 ½ N. Locust

The LeMaster, 215 ½ East 6th Street

The LeMonte

Lotus Rooms, 605 N. Locust and 610 ½ N. Locust

Madison Rooms, 511 ½ N. Dewey

Mayflower Rooms, 723 ½ N. Locust

Modern Rooms, 723 ½ N. Dewey

The Oakdale (aka the Squaretop), 400 East Front

Oxford Rooms, 717 ½ N. Locust

The Rest, 100 ½ East Front

The Rex

The Savoy

The Star, 614 ½ N. Dewey[3]

Some of the women in these brothels, such as Josephine Oyen Johnston, remained in business for over thirty years. Josephine was born in Holland on October 26, 1886. She was in North Platte by about 1906, and in about 1907, she married Charles "Charlie" Johnston. Her new husband ran a saloon, and it wasn't long before Josephine was involved in the business as well. The 1910 census finds the Johnstons living at 615 East 2nd Street with Charles's brother, Lee. Two years later, Josephine gave birth to her only child, a daughter. But the baby lived only a short time. "The infant daughter which was born to Mr. and Mrs. Charles Johnson last week, died," reported the *North Platte Semi-Weekly Tribune*, "and was buried in the North Platte cemetery."[4]

By 1920, the Johnstons owned the Ritz Bar, a saloon and pool hall, at 605 Locust Street. The address was popularly known for the "Lotus Rooms," upstairs, which offered men's entertainment. Prohibition was now in full swing, but that did not seem to affect the Ritz nor Josephine, who now ran the Lotus Rooms with a number of women in her employ. At least that is what local folks said. The census tells a different tale, documenting only three male boarders. It is quite possible that Josephine had no girls living with her, renting her rooms out in shifts instead for the best profit. The Johnstons likely lived on the premises as well. By the following year, however, the couple—or at least Josephine—had relocated to a private residence at 614 Dewey.

Josephine's profits enabled her to buy more property. In February of 1928, she purchased the York Feed Store, a two-story building on Locust between Sixth and Front streets, for $15,000. The following year the name of Locust was changed to Jeffers Street, but the Johnstons' business at the Ritz remained the same. Notable, however, is that the upstairs bordello was now called the Como Rooms. When Charles died in 1936, he left all of his property, worth $4,000 to Josephine. The madam hired a man named Verne Austin to run the Ritz as she continued her own business upstairs. From all appearances, Josephine intended to stay in business as long as she was able; when her building was damaged in June as a viaduct was built on Jeffers Street, she was one of several business owners to file a claim against the city.

In November of 1938, after thirty-two years in business, Josephine Johnston died at the young age of fifty-two years while still living above the Ritz. The *North Platte Daily Bulletin* noted she was in the hospital and had been ill for some time. In life, Josephine had done quite well for herself. The Ritz Saloon went to Verne Austin, while each of Josephine's brothers received $1,000 per her will. Her jewelry collection went to a sister-in-law, Clara Owen, and Clara's three daughters. The rest of her money, as well as some land and several postal bonds, was left to Sister Mary Barbara, Josephine's own sister who was living as a nun in Iowa. Notable is that St. Patrick's Church held services for her, an unusual kindness to women of the demimonde.

During Josephine's time in North Platte, many of the ladies of the town had worked out a system with city officials. Few sources mention any fines, but surely the women paid high rents, as well as hefty property and income taxes to stay above the law. The finer houses did require their girls to submit to medical exams once a week. Anyone found to be infected, or pregnant, was ordered to stop working until they were certified as healthy by their physician. Officials likely knew that many of the women in the demimonde were in their profession in order to make money to support their families and make sure their children received a college education. One source puts the average price of time with a lady at $5, with $3 going to the girl and $2 to her madam. On the busiest nights, a madam could rake in between $500 and $1,500.

Unlike Josephine Johnston, other madams only spent a short amount of time in North Platte before moving on. Maud Mathews, for instance, was arrested for prostitution in June of 1911. In court, Maud protested that she had been arrested before, had left town, and returned "a reformed woman." She also said she was just passing through North Platte on her way to Colorado when an Officer Troutman arrested her and "made ungentleman [*sic*] like advances toward her."[5] But Maud's testimony was refuted by her landlady, Mrs. Starkey of the Travelers' Lodging House, who said Officer Troutman had conducted himself properly. In the end, Police Judge Warren declared there was not enough evidence to charge Maud with prostitution. She apparently stuck around for at least another month; in July, she and prostitute Vivian DeVere filed an official complaint against Cecil O'Hara because Cecil too was working in the skin trade. After that, Maud apparently left town.

Cecil O'Hara was still in North Platte in July, when she brazenly asked permission of two county commissioners, reported as Streitz and Walters, to open a brothel south of town. Cecil wanted to operate "under the protection of the law," explaining that her place would be less of an issue to the public than those women operating in downtown hotels. She also wanted to buy a liquor license. In answer, and possibly due to the prior complaints of Maud Mathews and Vivian DeVere, Cecil and a man named Curt Weimer were immediately arrested for running a house of prostitution. Vivian even testified that Cecil had asked her to come work for her, but she had refused. In the end, the case was dismissed. Several months later, however, Cecil, Weimer, and one Leona Scott were arrested for "the sale and unlawful keeping of intoxicating liquor without a license."[6] This time, Weimer's case was dismissed and Scott's case was deferred. Cecil, however, was fined $300.

In January of 1912, Cecil was arrested yet again, this time along with M. F. Boquette. The latter was likely Millard Boquette, the well-known bordello owner of Grand Island. A permanent injunction was filed against Cecil that prohibited her from running a bawdy house, while Boquette was ordered to pay $300 and remain closed for one year. He was also prohibited from ever leasing the property for use as a brothel. Furthermore, the sheriff was instructed to "seize all the furniture and personal property in or about the house and sell it." The profit would be absorbed by the court to pay for prior costs Cecil did not pay, and Boquette did not offer to pay them for her.[7] Sure enough, a sheriff's sale was announced in the *North Platte Telegraph* for February 24 at the jailhouse. Up for grabs, however, were just a hack worth $60, and a double harness worth $8. Cecil, or Millard Boquette, must have executed a tremendously quick packing job before leaving town.

Although Vivian DeVere must have felt some satisfaction at testifying against Cecil O'Hara in 1911, she had her own troubles. In court, she had testified that her husband in Iowa owned a ranch—but she also had just recently been seen purchasing beer at a local hotel. Two railroad switchmen, who knew Vivian, verified that they knew the hotel, knew that it sold beer, and also knew that fast women frequented the place. Luckily, the charges against Vivian for purchasing beer were dropped, but she was not so lucky in 1912. In March, the *North Platte Semi-Weekly Tribune* tattled that the husband in Iowa was not the only spouse Vivian claimed. "Vivian DeVere, who at one time hobnobbed with some of North Platte's swift young men, is now accused of having a corner on husbands and the court up at Valentine will proceed to unravel Vivian's tangle," said the paper. "Three living and one dead husband attest [to] Vivian's winsomeness, and all these were accumulated within a few years. The only reason she did not allow a North Platte man to carry her away was because she could not find one possessing sufficient 'dough' for her to keep up her Paris model gait."[8]

The scandal in the paper didn't stop Vivian. Two years later, the lady married yet again, to Charles Reynoldson. The newlyweds moved to

Roone County. But Reynoldson soon discovered that his blushing bride was not all she seemed to be. Not only was Vivian dead broke but she had recently been the traveling companion of one James Royer—whom she met while in jail in McCook. Vivian claimed she had not married Royer, but the *Frontier*, a newspaper in O'Neill, claimed the man had filed for divorce in Cherry County. The *Frontier* also verified that Reynoldson also was seeking a divorce as a means to prevent Vivian from getting her hands on his property.[9]

Other madams also had a tough time of it. In September of 1911, just a few months after Cecil O'Hara's arrest, Madam Emma Wilson was sued by one J. C. Vermilyea for $167.20. What the tiff was about is unknown, but Emma countersued for $207. Vermilyea was awarded $79.50 as Emma's attorney vowed to appeal. But he apparently never did. Emma underwent further troubles in 1914, when Myrtle and Alfred Ring were arrested at her bordello. With them was their three-year-old son whom Emma, "charged with leading an immoral life," was accused of abusing and neglecting. Also, the *North Platte Semi-Weekly Tribune* reported, she had "been associating with Greeks." The charges against Myrtle were levied by a woman named Mrs. Ada Kelley, and a Mrs. Campbell and Mrs. Etherton testified against her as well. Miss Kyle of the Nebraska Child Saving Institute was going to take the Rings' child.[10]

Emma's run-ins with the law continued. She was alternately known as "Seventy Six" in 1915, when she was arrested for running a brothel. A temporary injunction was filed against her. Emma pleaded guilty, but hastened to clarify that she was not running a house of prostitution. Furthermore, her arrest was actually the result of a complaint against three men who were "being disorderly near her house," and had themselves been arrested. Emma testified that one of the men was "beastly drunk," and that when she refused them admittance, the men began to destroy her property. The three perpetrators countered and claimed Emma had invited them in. They were each fined a dollar. The subsequent decision to arrest Emma was actually part of a "cleanup campaign" the city was engaging in. Several of Emma's neighbors had recently filed a complaint against her. Emma pleaded guilty and was fined $10 and costs. When she complained about the fine versus what the men had paid, she only received a stern lecture from Judge Miltonberger, who told her that "if she continued to break the laws of the city in the future her case would come before a higher court with a correspondingly severe penalty."[11]

Just five days later, Emma was in trouble again. This time, her neighbors again charged her with "conducting an immoral house." Emma patiently explained once more that she was not running a disorderly house but a house of prostitution. She apparently believed there was a difference between the two euphemisms.[12] But she also refused to put up with those who took advantage of her. Just three days after her trial, Emma filed her own complaint against John Pitts. Emma claimed that Pitts had sold a horse she owned for $300 and refused to pay her. For once, the court had mercy on Emma Wilson. "The defendant pleaded not guilty and represented that he had ever been a faithful Sunday school boy with his golden text always on his tongues end," chuckled the *Semi-Weekly Tribune*. Pitts was unable to furnish bail and remained behind bars.[13] Whether Emma got her money is unknown, but in May, she packed her bags for Chicago to live with her brother.

Even with Emma Wilson's departure, plenty of scarlet women remained in North Platte. Although the city had its share of troublesome women, others, like Madam Mable Kaufman, were actually upstanding businesswomen. Born in Grand Island on Valentine's Day in 1893, Mable moved to North Platte in 1913. By 1919, she was listed in the local *Traveler's Directory* as the proprietress of the Broadmoor Hotel at 107 ½ West Street. The *Traveler's Directory* was no doubt a guide to the nightlife of North Platte, especially designed for businessmen and other revelers who visited the city and were looking for a place to kick up their heels. Such directories were usually pocket-sized and typically included bars, gentlemen's clubs, hotels, restaurants, and, of course, houses of prostitution.[14]

Mable had also married and resided with her husband, William, in a respectable lodging house at 220 East 4th Street as of the 1920 census. A year later, the couple moved to 605 Locust, where Mable also took over as madam at the Lotus Rooms. She would eventually run many more supposed rooming houses which discreetly operated as brothels. By now, North Platte was commonly referred to as "Little Chicago," largely due to so many gambling joints and bootlegging operations there. But Mable was different from many of the bawdy ladies in North Platte. For one thing, she hired only the best, most refined women to work for her. Her employees numbered as few as eight, or up to twenty during Nebraska's fall harvest season. Her customers ranged from cowboys, farmers, and railroad men to professional doctors, lawyers, and politicians. In time, Mable would expand her operations to include the Atlas rooms at 611 ½ North Jeffers. The madam's many business enterprises may have had something to do with the eventual departure of William from her life, for in 1929, Mable appears to have been the sole proprietor at the Broadmoor Hotel. And, the 1930 census confirmed she was divorced.

Mable soon found another man. His name was Harold "Jack" Vosburg, and for a time the couple was happy. In the 1932 city directory, Mable appears twice: once as the illustrious madam and again as Mrs. Harold J. Vosburg. Both addresses were at the Broadmoor Hotel. Now, Mable dabbled in philanthropy, mostly as a member of the Red Cross. When she took a couple of weeks off to see her family and friends in San Francisco, Jack likely went with her. The two did not marry, however, until 1946. Notable too was that Jack did not work for or with Mable. Rather, he held a separate job as the head of the meat department at the local Piggly-Wiggly grocery store. Life, it seemed, was good until 1957, when Mable and Jack called it quits and divorced in January. Mable's life of discontent was still evident in February, when she took an advertisement out in the *Telegraph-Bulletin*: "Party is known who picked up two packages in Woolworth's Friday," the ad read. "Please return to Woolworth's. Mable Kaufman."[15]

Little else was reported about Mable in the local papers until she passed away in 1969. She was buried in Grand Island. Because she had no children, her estate was sold at a public auction. Only then did some interesting details about her personal belongings give some clue as to how wealthy she was. The auction listed, among other things, Mable's 1951 Cadillac Coupe, some diamond rings and platinum jewelry, beautiful mahogany furniture, two mink coats, a Stradivarius violin made in 1736, an 1897 model 12 Winchester rifle, and several more valuable items.

Mable was one of many demimonde women who weathered military efforts to crack down on red-light houses across the nation during World War I and National Prohibition beginning in 1920. Church folk, reformers, respectable citizens, and especially the Nebraska Department of Public Welfare, began urging the city to do something about their shady ladies—especially their health standards. City officials, unwilling to give up the profits they made from North Platte's skin trade, instead came up with a series of new ordinances in an effort to control the red-light district's health issues as much as possible. Most of them made sense; for instance, women who contracted social diseases were not permitted to work. Furthermore, infected women were to burn "any and all dressings, cloths, cotton, tape and other materials used in treatment and upon or about the person afflicted." Also, such victims were not allowed to run or work at any brothel and were ordered to get medical treatment. Anyone violating the ordinances could be fined up to $100 or spend three months in jail.[16]

Proper madams of the demimonde likely agreed with the new ordinances. A sick, diseased, or pregnant prostitute gave a house a bad reputation and caused loss of income, besides. There is little doubt that Mable Kaufman had no problem adhering to the rules because she ran a clean, upstanding house. And when Madam Lucile Calder arrived in North Platte around the same time the new ordinances were published, she too likely followed the edicts in order to run a healthy, successful business. In fact, Lucile and her husband, Robert, were living on Locust Street during 1920 before partnering with Mable at the Lotus Rooms in 1921. Both were arrested there in February.

After Mable moved on to her Broadmoor Hotel in 1929, Lucile remained at the Lotus Rooms. In the 1930 census she said she was a widow, and the census recorded only one couple, Clint and Marie Groves, as well as a man named Steve Brown, living with Lucile. The madam was, however, still in business. Later that year, the *Daily Telegraph* reported that "Lucile Calder, proprietress of the Lotus Rooms, was fined $104.80 in police court this morning upon a charge of riotous conduct and disturbing the peace." Lucile, it turned out, had a problem with her "ex-husband," presumably Robert. She resolved it by hurling a brick

The caption for this image in North Platte reads, "Palace Hotel where Mildred Irwin lives. She entertains in the saloon on the corner. Taken 1938." COURTESY LIBRARY OF CONGRESS

through the window at his place of business. Exactly what the issue was is unknown, but Lucile also announced loud and clear that she would be selling her palace of pleasure and would vacate North Platte within ten days.[17] It appears that Lucile did give up selling sex at the Lotus Rooms, but she did not leave North Platte. City directories and newspapers indicate she still lived in North Platte during 1932 and served as a witness for the court in 1940. She seems to have gone respectable, as it were. In September of 1941, the *North Platte Daily Bulletin* published a blurb in the society section about Mrs. William Flynn, who threw an elegant party for a friend. Guests were served "luncheon at the close of the evening, buffet style." The lists of guests included Mrs. Lucile Calder.[18]

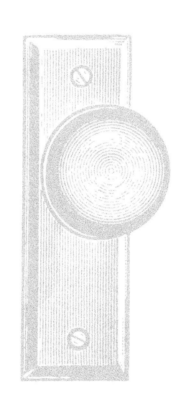

CHAPTER FOURTEEN

The Shady Ladies of Lincoln

IN 1856, LINCOLN WAS JUST A SMALL VILLAGE, CALLED LANCASTER, IN Nebraska Territory when area settlers realized there was much to be made of the natural salt basin in the area. Lancaster was the county seat by 1867, when the name was changed to Lincoln and the city was made the capital of newly formed Nebraska. Soon, cattle and other industries were making a name for themselves in what became known as the Haymarket District. And within a year, a simple, wooden brothel was built at 124 South 9th Street. More would follow as the Burlington and Missouri River Railroad rolled into town, followed by the Atchison and Nebraska Railroad and the Midland Pacific Railroad. A depot was constructed just blocks from that first brothel, and before long a red-light district had grown south of O Street between 7th and 12th Streets. Like so many towns throughout Nebraska, the new demimonde was called the "Burnt District."

Lincoln's first real madam of note was Josie Washburn, and for good reason: not only did she brave the often tumultuous and dangerous prostitution industry for several decades but she also dared to reveal everything she knew about the institution upon leaving the sordid life behind. It was tough enough to turn respectable after years of being looked down upon as just another soiled dove, but Josie desired to write about those portions of her life and profession that would most give a true understanding to what went on in the demimonde. Her book, *The Underworld Sewer: A Prostitute Reflects on Life in the Trade, 1871–1909* gave daring insight into the prostitution industry and how she approached her life,

Lincoln's State Fair Program in 1887 set the standard for how ladies in attendance should dress. COURTESY LIBRARY OF CONGRESS.

although she naturally did not give away all of her secrets. That would have been against the prostitute's code.

Nobody seems to know exactly where, when, or under what name Josie was born. The best guess by scholars is that she was born circa 1853 either in Maine, Rhode Island, or Wisconsin; that her parents were of foreign descent, and that her given name might have been Helena. The only truth about her comes from the woman herself, who said she "stumbled into Omaha in August 1871" at the age of seventeen years and went to work for Madam Anna Wilson.[1] Josie remained in Anna's employ for eight years, learning everything she could in preparation for running her own house. When she left Anna's in 1879, however, Josie worked on her own for only a short time (during which she accidentally shot herself with a revolver) before marrying in 1880.

Josie described her chosen mate as "the only son of a distinguished college professor" who may have been named Frank Stone. For the next fifteen years, life was blissful—until Stone left her in 1895, leaving her without a means of support. Josie decided to do the only thing she knew how to do. She moved to Lincoln and became a madam of her own house at 226 South 9th Street. The competing houses, she said, numbered between six and twelve bordellos and were "not of the extremely fashionable kind with costly furniture, nor of the lowest grade as you will find in larger cities."[2]

Josie appears to have aspired to run a parlor house that was a cut above the others in Lincoln. Her clients ranged from politicians to businessmen, from church-going men to wealthy travelers. When monthly fines were required of the red-light ladies beginning in 1885, she dutifully paid between $14.70 and $29.70 each month, with her girls paying between $5.70 and $9.70. Although she was sometimes allowed to simply send a list with the names of her employees and the required fines to city hall, other times Josie and each of her girls were required to appear in court personally, so that "they might see us and know us and keep tabs on us." Raids were sometimes staged, and Josie clearly remembered how embarrassing the wagon ride to court was, with some of the women crying and trying to hide their faces. Other times, Lincoln's brothels were forbidden from selling the beer on which they were able to make a decent profit. Those caught selling it anyway were fined between $50 and $100. Any woman who defended herself or talked back received an additional $50 fine or jail time ranging from one to three months.[3]

Josie was sometimes picked on in other ways. In 1896, the Lincoln *Evening Call* revealed that another paper, which the writer called the "Morning Discrepancy," had written "one of its semi-occasional lurid fairy tales." The story concerned a young woman named May, a domestic for a respectable family in Omaha. Her cousin, "Four Eyes," was a prostitute and talked May into moving to Lincoln and taking up the life. May found work at Josie's for a time but eventually went to the police station and turned herself in. She was supposedly taken in by the "Rescue society," but the whole story, said the *Evening Call*, was a fabrication "to besmirch the fair name of Lincoln with untrue scandals."[4]

Newspaper tales aside, it is true that the occasional disturbance took place at Josie's. Once, also in 1896, a young man identified as Raymond Hall sent his friend, Russell Harrold, to visit the madam with the story that one of her girls, "Gypsy," was in jail and needed to pay a fine of $5.70 to get out. Josie gave Harrold the money, but in truth, there was no fine. Instead, Harrold, Hale, and Gypsy took off to Omaha. Josie immediately filed a complaint and the boys were brought back to Lincoln. The *Nebraska State Journal* guessed that if money was repaid to Josie, the charges would be dismissed. Josie apparently forgave Gypsy; a year later, the girl's name appeared below Josie's in a published list of fines paid by prostitutes. In October of 1897, another of her girls fell asleep while smoking in bed and caught the linens on fire. By the time two policemen happened to notice smoke coming from the house, the madam herself had doused the flames.

Josie also had her fair share of romance troubles. Sometime in 1897 she lent money to Fred Nagel, who had just recently purchased a newspaper, the *Freie Presse*. Over the next three years, Nagel used some $4,000 in loan money from Josie to build the newspaper up and was hoping to go national with it. But when the man suddenly married someone else in 1900, the spurned madam sued Nagel for breaching his promise to marry her. Most unfortunately, she lost her case.

The 1900 census documents Josie and five other women who were listed as "boarders." Josie told the census taker she was born in 1860 in Rhode Island, was married, had no children, and that her parents were natives of Scotland. Of her five boarders, four of them—Grace Gay, Flossie LaBlanch, Jenette Freman, and Eva West—ranged in age between nineteen and twenty-five years. A fifth boarder, Fritzin Hill, was forty-three years old and likely was employed as a servant. All of these occupants were likely on hand in August, when the *Nebraska State Journal* reported that Josie was caught serving beer to her customers. The madam, along with some of her girls and two clients were taken to the police station along with "several cases of beer." The men were forced to serve as witnesses, but Josie willingly pleaded guilty. She was quite frank when she explained that she "had been selling beer for some time, and had expected to get caught sooner or later."[5] In the end, Josie was only fined a dollar for selling liquor without a license—but paid $20 for keeping a "resort of ill repute." Three of her seven girls were fined $5 plus costs. Two others were dismissed because they had already recently paid a fine. The last two girls failed to appear in court.

By 1903, Josie said, the monthly fines required of her and other women had risen to $29.70, nearly a thousand dollars in today's money, which very well left her and many other women without anything "to live on." Police were sympathetic, or so they would have the madams believe, and told the ladies they could sell beer without a license to help their income. Two months later, however, the men retracted their offer, refused to admit they had allowed selling beer at all, and warned the women that anyone caught doing so would be fined $500. Gone were the days of paying a dollar fine for selling libations to her customers; Josie quickly learned to avoid being caught selling beer by hiding all bottles and glasses anytime there was a "ring" at the door. The ploy worked most of the time, although if everything looked too "intensely serene and harmless," the police hauled the women to court "on general principle and suspicion."[6]

A year or so after the beer debacle, some churches began questioning why the women were being required to pay their monthly fine in advance. Doing so, they said, made it appear that prostitution was perfectly legal when money was paid ahead of time. The authorities switched dates to reflect payment at the end of the month, but the complaints continued. The fining system was finally withdrawn altogether, but now police conducted raids instead. The fines levied for various infractions were as much as $100, with threats to impose fines as high as $500 or jail time. To Josie, the lecture served as a warning to the women of the red-light to "agree to whatever the police proposed" or suffer the consequences.[7]

At least the police apologized to Josie when they raided her house during the state fair in September of 1904. Everyone in the demimonde was making good money from the fair, but the chief of police explained to Josie that the city was in arrears. It had also been some time since she paid any fines. Josie duly paid and continued to do so each month. Some months later, the city administrators dared to ask her to work for them on an upcoming reelection campaign "in a political way." But the madam had no interest in plying politicians, and politely declined the offer.[8]

The city was clearly in the wrong by asking Josie for political favors. By 1905, city hall was so corrupt that the general public began demanding change. The city administration's efforts to be reelected not only failed, but the former police chief and city detective were also indicted for various crimes. Notably, five women of the red-light were called to testify against them. The men were found not guilty, but they were publicly shamed. Tired of the shenanigans going on in city hall, Josie closed her brothel in 1907. Soon after, she began working on her book and exposing the truth about how the demimonde in Lincoln operated.

Why did Josie, after working for so many years in the skin trade, decide to lambast the business she herself helped propagate? For one thing, Josie entered the trade as a desperate teenager in need of shelter and money. And although she was able to leave the profession for a time, she was forced to return to it when her husband left her. There was no agency or kind person to help her do otherwise. In many ways, Josie had the last word by publishing her book and exposing the prostitution industry along with the sordid, crooked politics of it all as it really was. "It is not my intention to condemn good men and women," she wrote, "but to awaken them to some awful facts."[9]

As of 1909, Josie had returned to Omaha where she lived in a respectable neighborhood as she penned her book. The former madam also wanted reform in the prostitution industry, including helping other women who wanted to leave the profession. She began by proposing a bill to Nebraska's legislature for a grant of $100,000 to build a reform home for the women. She also engaged the help of Hester Tuttle Griffith, an activist for the Women's Christian Temperance Union in Hollywood, California. Neither panned out, but Josie did publish two pamphlets in 1913 and 1914 warning against social diseases and the evils of saloons and dance halls.

In 1920, Josie left Omaha and moved to Minneapolis, Minnesota—the home state of Hester Griffith—and opened a boarding house for elderly ladies. Five years later, she wrote to A. E. Sheldon at the Nebraska State Historical Society that she was moving to Spokane, Washington. After that, however, Josie Washburn disappeared from the public eye altogether, and what became of her remains unknown. Not until 1997 was her book shared with the rest of the world in a newly published format. At last, Josie Washburn's voice was heard.

When Josie was in Lincoln during 1880, only a few prostitutes were identified in the census. But there were many more than that. They included Lydia Stewart, who would reign as a madam in Lincoln for two decades. Lydia was born Mary Elizabeth Wallace in 1847, in Ireland. By 1873, she was in Lincoln, with enough money to purchase some property in the red-light district. There is a good chance that Lydia made her money at the Midland Precinct in Colfax County, where the 1878 Nebraska state census found her working as a prostitute with four other women. Soon after, Lydia moved into 124 South 9th Street, Lincoln's oldest brothel. The first time newspapers mentioned her, however, was in 1886 when she was arrested for running a brothel and selling liquor without a license.

Like many madams, Lydia's heart could be one of gold, or one of steel depending on the situation. She once adopted an orphan named Margaret Klotz, for instance. Anxious to keep the girl unaware of her profession, Lydia sent Margaret to live with neighbors and later enrolled her in a far-away Catholic convent school. The following year, Lydia made the papers after an unruly customer, W. E. Pfenning, attempted to shoot one of her girls, Frankie Moore. The furious madam bodily "threw him into the street," and he was later arrested.[10] Lydia was arrested too, in 1893, in a room above the Columbia National Bank. One Henry Christopher filed a complaint against the madam, alleging that she "made the night hideous in that vicinity." Apparently, the room was being rented by a "young man who has captured the courtesan's veteran affections," but he was gone when Lydia was found there.[11] She was ordered to pay bail of $100 and appeared in court the following day.

Nothing more was heard of Lydia until August 8, when the madam died of some "disease." Her funeral services were held at St. Theresa's Church. Lydia's will directed she be buried beside her mother in Chicago, and her body was taken to the train immediately after the service. The rest of Lydia's will was quite interesting: she left $200 to one Mary Fox for caring for her while she was sick. James Elinor, identified as Lydia's "reigning favorite," received $1,000. Another $500 was given to Lydia's executor, William McLaughlin, to assist "unfortunate girls of the Catholic faith." Surprisingly, the rest of Lydia's estate—her "clothing, jewelry and household furnishings," as well as pretty much everything else—was left to Lydia's sister, Anna Bailey of Chicago. McLaughlin was directed to sell Lydia's property on lots 13 and 14 in block 54 in Lincoln, and that money would also go to Anna.[12]

Lydia's will naturally did not sit well with Margaret Klotz. Litigation almost immediately began regarding Lydia's estate, which was estimated to be around $30,000. Margaret Klotz had a copy of a different will that was penned some four years before Lydia died. In that will, Margaret was to receive the bulk of her mother's estate. In court, Margaret charged that Lydia had been forced by Anna, who cared for her during her last days, to sign the new will just before she died. Margaret won her case. Had Lydia's body remained in Lincoln, it likely would have been buried in a special section of Wyuka Cemetery, established in 1885 specifically for prostitutes. One of the occupants in January of 1885 was Pearl Forcade, a teenage prostitute who was murdered by a drunk at a place identified as "Mollie's Hall."[13] Pearl was buried as her family was notified, but when her brothers arrived to claim the girl's body, it was inexplicably missing from the grave. Accusing eyes turned to Lincoln's University of Nebraska medical school, because it had just recently been noted that the school was running short of cadavers.

Rumors were soon rampant that the medical school had stolen Pearl's body, and perhaps others as well. But the *Nebraska State Journal* defended the institution, stating flat-out on January 11 that "the alleged resurrection of bodies of persons in the cemetery here for the use of the medical college has no basis in fact."[14] In the same issue, however, the *Journal* reported that Pearl's body suddenly reappeared, but there was no development on how or why her body was taken. The article ended by stating that Pearl's relatives were just happy to have her body back. The state legislature, however, heard the story and cut the funding for the medical school, which closed in 1887.

In the wake of Pearl Forcade's demise, the city of Lincoln put forth ordinances forbidding prostitution for the first time in 1885. But the news did not sit well with police judge Alfred Parsons, who had his own ideas about how lucrative the prostitution industry could be for the city. Parsons decided to accept fines for prostitution as a means to ignore the ordinances even as others suspected the fines were merely a way to extort money from the women of the demimonde. The latter group was correct; in 1887, madams Molly Hall, Rose Howard, and Lydia Stewart staged a protest against Parsons after they, thirteen of their employees, and four male clients were arrested. The ladies claimed Parsons pocketed their fines in the amount of $329, resulting in their arrest for not paying the money. The city council investigated and discovered that the women were speaking the truth.

When he appeared before the council, Parsons tried to claim that he misunderstood the law. When that didn't fly, he "challenged the council's authority to remove him from his position." Mayor Andrew Sawyer responded that Parson's "wanton disregard of duty, this shameless violation of law, this private barter and sale of justice to the gamblers, pimps, and prostitutes of Lincoln were enough to arouse the righteous indignation of every citizen possessing the slightest regard for law, order or decency."[15] A few months later, city council passed a new ordinance permitting them to fire Parsons. In turn, Parsons filed a successful appeal with the US circuit court in St. Louis, Missouri. The fight was on: the city council removed Parsons from office anyway and he was subsequently incarcerated in an Omaha hotel for a time until the courts gave way and allowed Parsons to be terminated. Although this did not put an end to the extortion of money from wayward women, madams Molly, Rose, and Lydia had at least had their say in the matter.

Hypocrisy in government reared its ugly head again in 1890, when the *McCook Tribune* published a list of brothels in Lincoln with a "high license." A "high license," it was revealed, meant that the madams of these houses were allowed to sell liquor, but did not have to purchase a city license or contribute money to the school fund.

High License Houses in 1890

Fannie Chapman (no address given)
Jessie Disbrow, 227 S. 6th
Dora Frazier, 720 North Street
Sadie Freeman, 716 L Street
Hattie Hoover, 137 S. 6th
Jennie Kingon, 135 S. 10th
Nellie Roberts, 1028 M Street
Lydia Stewart, 124 S. 9th
Anna Tripp, 800 North Street
Lincoln Turnverein, 909 O Street[16]

The list of "high license" houses identified in the *McCook Tribune* were but a small portion of the actual brothels operating in the Burnt District. The 1891 Sanborn Fire Insurance map identifies a number of houses as "female boarding" or "ill fame" on South 6th Street between M and N streets, in an area south of O Street between 6th and 11th streets, and another area in the vicinity of 7th and 9th streets. For Lincoln reformers, the number of brothels in the demimonde was clearly becoming a problem—especially after the Silver Panic of 1893 caused a depression in the larger cities across America. Four years later, however, Lincoln had rebounded to the point of collecting several fines from its shady ladies and blatantly listed their names in the *Lincoln Evening Call*. Twenty-five women were named in all. It is unknown if all of them were madams, but certain of them—Rae Cameron, Georgia Wade, and Josie Washburn—were known to run brothels during their time in Lincoln. Most of the women paid $4.70 in fines and court costs, the exception being "Florence Perkins, et al.," who paid $12.25. Also, four men—A. Johnson, Charles Smith, J. A. Stevens, and Perry Swanson—were fined between $5 and $6.20 for allowing a prostitute to visit their rooms.

While the newspapers had no problem publishing the names of women who paid fines, they were often equally sympathetic to the ladies. In 1900, Ludell McMahon (also known as Della McMahon, aka Lorene Smith) committed suicide at Josie Washburn's brothel. The *Lincoln Star Journal* published a truly moving and descriptive account of the girl's fall from grace and ultimate death. Ludell, it was reported, was from a respectable family but chose the brothel life—until she met Hugh Tiffany, who vowed to keep his lady fair respectable. The pair made a nice couple for about a year, during which Tiffany took the girl with him on a business trip to Nebraska City and deposited her at her parents' home in Beatrice. From there, Tiffany went on another business trip to Denver, with the promise to marry Ludell when he returned.

In Tiffany's absence, he and Ludell dutifully exchanged letters and photographs. All was well until Ludell's friend from the old days, prostitute Susan Kent, came for a visit and convinced the girl to return to Josie's. When Tiffany found out, the broken-hearted suitor bundled up Ludell's letters and photos and returned them to her, along with a note "renouncing her love forever." Later that day, Ludell purchased some arsenic, consumed it, and "died in agony." She was only eighteen years old. Broken-hearted over Ludell's life and loss, Josie and her girls threw the fanciest funeral for the girl they could manage, and "a more affecting drama will never be witnessed," said the *Lincoln Star Journal*.[17] The mourners wore black, while six of Josie's girls wore beautiful white gowns and served as pallbearers. Even outsiders were moved to tears as Reverend Fletcher Wharton presided over services. Although he was careful not to lecture the madam or her girls, Wharton's words about Ludell stirred Josie and her girls so deeply that they could be seen visibly sobbing. Ludell was buried in the area for "unfortunates" in Wyuka Cemetery.

Ludell McMahon's death may have been a sobering event for Lincoln's wayward women, but it did not deter them. As of 1903, there were still fifteen or more brothels operating in the Burnt District. A few years later, the district came under the scrutiny of County Attorney Frank Tyrell and others who wanted it closed altogether. Beginning in 1907, the houses of prostitution began facing charges that they were operating against the law more than ever before. Citizens, meanwhile, hatched a new plan of attack as respectable companies began purchasing various bordellos and either tore them down or turned them into legitimate businesses. The urban renewal of sorts included the historic brothel at 124 South 9th, which Madam Rose Kirkwood had purchased after Lydia Stewart's death in 1893. Madam Rae Cameron leased the house for a time, but Rose had it back by 1900 when she, seven prostitutes, and a Black servant occupied the rooms during the census.

In 1903, Rose replaced the wooden house in its entirety with a larger, two-story brick building. She also made sure to build a more discreet side entrance on the south side of her new brothel, as well as a basement. Inside, the business remained the same until about 1908, evidenced by the arrest of a "state official" there.[18] By the time of the arrest, the People's Mission had saved enough money to purchase Rose's property. Later, it was revealed that Rose also went by Rose Dillon, but also Mrs. Grace M. Sterns, wife of Jacob M. Sterns, who sold the building to the mission in 1910. The People's Mission remodeled the former brothel to provide religious services and temporary shelter to men, and, later, women and children. The old beer garden was turned into a playground. Thus ended North Platte's long and illustrious reign of prostitution. Today, Rose Kirkwood's former brothel, the last remaining remnant of the demimonde, is on the National Register of Historic Places.

CHAPTER FIFTEEN

Outrageous Oklahoma

THE SOONER STATE OWES ITS EXISTENCE TO THE LOUISIANA PURCHASE of 1803, when a portion of the area known today as Oklahoma was added to the United States. More land would be acquired in 1819, 1825, 1828, and 1850. By the latter year, the territory had long been designated as "Indian Territory," so-named when the federal government began relocating Indigenous people of the "Five Civilized Nations" to live there.[1] Following the Civil War, white settlers began taking an interest in the territory. The cattle industry, along with farming, mining, railroads, and oil, would fuel the settlement of the land for the next several decades.

Although alcohol was legal in other parts of Oklahoma Territory, it remained highly illegal in Indian Territory. This resulted in the establishment of a number of "wet" towns on the other side of the boundary where alcohol sales flourished—at least until the Oklahoma Constitution added a Blue Law section, which made alcohol illegal statewide in 1907, when Oklahoma became a state. Long before that, however, small towns began springing up along the railroad tracks and cattle trails, and many of them were remote. Meanwhile, Oklahoma remained divided; parts of the Territory were open for settlement, while parts of the "Indian Lands" remained virtually unsettled until the Dawes Act of 1887 allowed for private ownership of land by qualifying Natives.

There was another, even more remote portion of Oklahoma too: an area known as the "Public Land Strip" in the Oklahoma panhandle. This patch of land was a virtual no-man's land near the Kansas border in 1888, and law enforcement rarely wandered through. Despite Prohibition laws in the adjoining state of Kansas, those across the border knew they could imbibe freely in the Public Land Strip and get away with it. A small area south of Liberal, Kansas, and Tyrone, Oklahoma, proved to be just the ticket. Between the two towns, a new community called White City was established and quickly earned the nickname of Beer City. There was no church, no post office, no school, nor any other entity that would attract city or government officials. Beer City was soon rife with dance halls, a busy red-light district, and enough saloons to satisfy the cowboys ambling through the area.

To say Beer City was a "wide-open" town is an understatement. Advertisements for White City in area newspapers brazenly let prospective residents know that the community was "the only town of its kind in the civilized world where they is absolutely no law [*sic*]." Boxing matches, horse racing, wrestling, and traveling wild west shows added to the fun. Like other cattle towns, Beer City's soiled doves were of the itinerant variety, flying in when cattle were being shipped to appease the many cowboys about town and then flying out to greener pastures afterward. Some of them divided their time between Beer City and Liberal, since there was a hack service between the two. The best-known madam at Beer City was known as "Pussy Cat Nell," who operated above the Yellow Snake Saloon. Once, they say, Nell fired a passel of buckshot at the one town marshal recorded in Beer City's history. She was not without reason, since it turned out the man was "an active rustler" to boot. Beer City's debauchery lasted only two years; after the panhandle was made part of Oklahoma Territory in 1890, the law began paying much closer attention to the Public Land Strip.[2]

Early Anglo settlers were prohibited from owning land in Oklahoma until 1889. Even then, land purchases were limited to an area in the middle of the territory referred to as "Unassigned Lands."[3] But Americans were chomping at the bit to score sizeable chunks of farmable property within Oklahoma Territory. The United States government finally gave in, and came up with an ingenious plan to sell off surplus lands in Indian Territory: land runs. Between 1889 and 1901, a series of land runs permitted thousands of settlers to sign up, line up in a designated area, wait for the signal, and rush like mad to snatch up their own 160–acre piece of land.

Oklahoma's first land run took place on April 22, 1889. What a sight it must have been, with folks on foot, horseback, and in wagons waiting for a gunshot to signify that the race was on. Their goal was to scramble as quickly as possible and claim a homestead somewhere on some 1,887,796 acres of land. Similar runs would be staged in 1891, 1893, 1895, and 1901, as well as a land auction in 1906. Men, women, and even children from all walks of life took part in Oklahoma's land runs, including at least two prostitutes—if not more. As a boy of just nine years, William Patton Brooks was commanding a wagon full of dry goods with which to open a store as he awaited the gunshot to ring out. But those around him were so excited and restless in the moments before the gunshot sounded that the cavalry set a prairie fire to stave them off. Both the fire and the shot spooked the boy's horses, which bolted directly toward the flames. Fortunately for Brooks, two wayward women had climbed into his wagon right before the gun sounded. "Sonny, move over," one of them said, "we need a ride." As the horses bolted, the ladies each grabbed a rein and were able to steer the wagon clear of the fire.[4]

Those bawdy women who missed out on the land runs needn't have worried. In at least one instance, the tent city of Tacola, later known as Cloud Chief, was settled within hours in anticipation of the 1892 land rush. The temporary town quickly erupted into a wide-open tent city complete with saloons and gambling joints. There were also a number of growing cattle and railroad towns in place, with plenty of railroad men, business travelers, and cowboys who were willing to pay for time with a lady. These included Avard, whose post office opened in Woods County during 1895, and whose saloons remained open all night long.

The presence of shady ladies in Oklahoma Territory soon caught the attention of authorities who had outlawed prostitution in certain areas. As early as 1893, newspapers were reporting on arrests and proceedings of women who dared ply their trade. In January, for instance, the *Kingfisher Free Press* noted that prostitutes Della Fiddler and Minnie Fenshaw were each fined $5 for "keeping a house of ill-fame." Interesting is that May McAfee, "a colored lady of the same stripe," was fined only $3.[5] Several months later, the *Guthrie Daily Leader* warned men "to be more careful when they go to a city" after one Judge Honstin James was somehow "badly mixed up with the demimonde" of Caldwell. In October, the *Purcell Register* published news of a "bitter, unrelenting war" against the "sirens of easy virtue." And in November, another newspaper reported that Enid's "Midway Plaisance" was officially moved from E Street to an area on B Street, where a dance hall was already in place.[6]

Enid officials appear to have been the exception when it came to accepting the members of the demimonde within their city and even established an official district for them. On the flip side were towns like Muskogee, which chased their good time girls out of town in January of 1894. "But like the famous cat," the *Muskogee Phoenix* commented, "they have come back."[7] The town of Vinita, which was overseen by Cherokee law, also drove their prostitutes away, in May. A little over a year later, the *Chickasaw Chieftain* in Ardmore noted that scrappy Ida Writer, "the queen of the Gainesville demi-monde," was successfully forced to "pack up her doll rags" and leave town after several court appearances.[8]

Newspapers also frequently reported on women of the red-light who were victims of violence and even murder. When Belle Foster was found dead in a hut outside the city limits of Perry, Oklahoma City's *Oklahoma State* newspaper cried foul. The woman was supposed to have died from "dissipation" or, rather, her own debauchery. An autopsy, however, revealed that Belle had been poisoned. The newspaper said that the woman was once a "highly educated" daughter of one of the leading families of Alabama and had married well. Some months earlier, however, Belle inexplicably left her husband, ran off with a man named McDonald, and traveled with him through Tennessee and Arkansas. The two were in Oklahoma by the time the "Cherokee Strip" was opened for settlement, whereupon McDonald left the woman. She apparently was forced to a "life of shame" in order to survive.[9] Other newspapers claimed Belle left McDonald and took up with another man. It was he who discovered her body and summoned police. The coroner found a large amount of opium "administered by unknown parties" in Belle's system, as well as an excessive amount of alcohol. Belle was interred in the potter's field as police continued looking for her killer.[10] He or she was never found.

In the case of the shooting of Annie Malloden in Muskogee during March 1895, police were able to identify her attacker. He was a troublemaker named Frank Carver, one of Annie's customers who sought to make the woman his own and shot her for "being on too intimate terms with another party."[11] Annie was able to flee and get help, but died soon afterward. Carver was sentenced to hang. Another time, prostitute Alice Sharpe of Silver City was robbed at gunpoint after a customer saw her put the money he gave her into a small purse she kept in "her bosom (which also contained her watch)." The thief was never caught. Sometimes the perpetrator was another prostitute. In 1895, two women were fined for "engaging in a slugging match."[12]

In spite of the obvious presence of women working in red-light districts throughout Oklahoma, they appear curiously absent during the 1900 census. Census takers in only a few cities and towns—Enid, Judkins, Oklahoma City, Perry, and Ponca City—enumerated women who said they were prostitutes. Presumably, the women themselves cared not to be identified as such, and gave more respectable-seeming occupations. Notable too is that in Judkins, only one woman, May Higgenbotham, told the census taker her true occupation. But an all-new industry was coming to the Sooner State: oil, which would boost Oklahoma's economy considerably. Between 1904 and 1906, over thirty oil boomtowns were established in Oklahoma Territory. The men who worked in the oilfields were generally referred to as "roughnecks," largely due to the heavy manual labor they performed on a daily basis. After a hard day's work, these tough men sought out the soft bosoms of women who were willing to entertain them. The prostitution industry remained very much alive and well in Oklahoma Territory. So did accompanying violence among women in the demimonde.

One of the strangest incidents involving a prostitute revolved around one Katie DeWitt James in 1905. The day after filing for divorce from her husband on the grounds of "cruelty," Katie and her fourteen-month-old daughter, Lulu Belle, boarded a train at Custer City. The plan was to go see the lady's cousin in Ripley. Katie's father, Henry DeWitt, delivered her to the train station himself. Several weeks later, however, DeWitt became worried. He had received no word from Katie, who was in the habit of writing him often. DeWitt soon rode to Oklahoma City, voiced his concerns to a Sheriff Garrison, and hired detective Sam Bartell.

Garrison and Bartell tracked Katie to Clinton, where they learned she had left the train and stayed the night at the house of William Moore outside of town. The invitation has been extended by Moore's sister-in-law, a prostitute named Fannie Norton, who for some reason introduced Katie as "Mrs. Smith." The two women had met on the train and shared a common bond: both were having trouble with their husbands. Their camaraderie was believed to be why Katie veered off course on her trip. The next morning, Fannie told Katie she would take her to Hydro, where she could resume her trip. But Katie never made it. Two hours after the women left, Fannie returned home alone and soon left for Clinton.

Bartell checked around and discovered that on the way to Clinton, Fannie's buggy had been seen detouring into a field, but when it returned to the road, only Fannie was in it. A short time later, Fannie had pulled up to the farm of Peter Bierscheid, where she handed Lulu to a boy and asked him to give the child to his mother to care for until she returned. But Lulu's dress was covered with blood, and as she drove away, Fannie tossed out a blanket full of baby clothes. Next, Fannie appeared in Guthrie, where she enrolled four of her own children at a private school and left for Shawnee. In both places, Fannie asked those she encountered to keep her presence a secret.

Officials searched the field Fannie drove into but found nothing. Bartell finally caught up with her, and took her in for questioning. She was "very nervous" but claimed that Katie had appeared to have recognized a male acquaintance on the road. She had, Fannie said, jumped from the buggy, climbed into the man's wagon, and went on. When Bartell accused Fannie of killing Katie, the woman denied it while "crying bitterly." Later that night, the woman managed to ingest some poison and died.

Not until August 31 was Katie James's body found in the field where she met her end. She had died from a bullet to the head. A gold ring worth $5 remained on one finger. Nearby was Fannie's revolver, identified as such because she had once used it "to shoot a Weatherford bartender in the back." Attorney G. W. Cornell, who found the body, wrote to Governor Ferguson and asked for the reward money that had previously been advertised regarding Katie's disappearance and death. Although the money was originally intended for whoever apprehended Katie's killer,

Cornell was given $80 anyway. Still, Fannie's motive remained unknown. It was ascertained that she had seen $23 in Katie's purse at some point, but the idea of robbery was questioned since Fannie would have seen the valuable ring on Katie's hand.

During the inquest over Katie's death, Martin James was questioned. The man, referred to by newspapers as "a cad," exhibited no grief for his murdered wife and did not help look for her body. He also had several witnesses who provided an alibi for him during the time Katie was killed. In the end, only Fannie could be held responsible for Katie's death. Martin James successfully petitioned for custody of Lulu, remarried, and disappeared. Today, Fannie is buried in Shawnee. Katie is buried in Weatherford. Nearby, a bridge across Big Deer Creek is named "Dead Woman's Crossing" after the incident.[13]

As the murder of Katie James faded from memory, the Oklahoma Enabling Act was signed in 1906 for Oklahoma to begin the process of becoming a state. Indian Territory was no more, and the forty-sixth state immediately enacted its own Prohibition throughout the land. One would think that statehood, combined with statewide Prohibition, would have quelled Oklahoma's naughty ladies. It didn't. According to one newspaper statistic, some "60,000 girls were made prostitutes in 1909, through drink."[14] Further evidence of prostitution remaining in Oklahoma came the following year, when Governor Charles Haskell proposed a law prohibiting bootleggers, gamblers, and prostitutes from contributing to campaign funds.

Now, prostitutes needed to mask their true professions even more than before. During the 1910 census, nearly every prostitute in the state listed her occupation as something else. The one exception was Bartlesville, where the ladies evidently didn't get that memo and identified themselves as prostitutes.

Other prostitutes were identified through newspapers. One of them, Ruby Darby, worked in the lively town of Shamrock and was known to hop up on a pool table so her admirers could watch her dance. And in Ragtown, later known as Wirt, brothels were known to function on the second floors of certain buildings. These and other clues remained as proof of ongoing prostitution in Oklahoma for several more years. The

The 1910 Census, Bartlesville

Name	Birthdate	Birthplace
Nellie Bary	1885	Kansas
Lulu Battles	1885	Texas
Maud Brown	1884	Kansas
Eva Fair	1877	Kansas
Lizzie Koontz	1887	Texas
Daisy Kuntz	1889	Missouri
Rae Pennett	1887	Missouri
Bessie Robinson	1892	Missouri
Elsie Staedin	1887	Germany
Grace Vernon	1885	Illinois[15]

once largely rural state was growing, and 30 percent of its land fell into urban cities and towns by 1920. The larger the city, the more chances there were for bootleggers, gamblers, and good time girls to set up shop. In rural areas, small towns located between respectable communities sometimes harbored red-light ladies and other forms of vice. One such place was Smackover, a community situated between Three Sands and Salt Fork River where "every other store" functioned as a saloon. Oilfield employees from Three Sands routinely visited Smackover for access to games of chance, illegal hooch, and a bevy of working girls.[16]

The law did occasionally intervene. During the early 1920s, for example, the number of prostitutes, drinking holes, and gambling houses had grown out of control at the oil boomtown of Cromwell. There was little that respectable folks could do, since no local law enforcement had been established and only the Seminole County sheriff could enforce the law. He did, one time, travel to Cromwell where he promptly rounded up the women, handcuffed and shackled them, and made them walk the entire fifteen miles to the county jail at Wewoka. Yet citizens in general were unhappy that the sheriff refused to hire a deputy to patrol the town. There was a reason for that: both the sheriff and the county attorney were routinely receiving payoffs between $40 and $2,500 from wayward women and gamblers.

At last, frustrated citizens wrote to retired US marshal Bill Tilgh-man, a seasoned and well-liked lawman in Kansas and Oklahoma (where he had once run a gambling house in Guthrie). Tilghman was asked to serve as the chief of police. They also wrote to Governor Martin Trapp about the matter. Although he was seventy-one years old, Tilghman took the job and soon rooted out the problem in the way of one Wiley Lynn. Tilghman was fairly sure that Lynn, a federal Prohibition officer, had been taking bribes from lawbreakers. One night in 1926, an inebriated Lynn began "shooting up the town." Tilghman managed to get his gun from him, but Lynn had a second gun on him and fatally shot the mar-shal. Then he fled town, along with a number of Cromwell's gamblers and bad girls who feared retribution. Although Lynn was later captured, tried for Tilghman's death, and acquitted, he himself was killed a short time later during a scuffle in southern Oklahoma. Wiley Lynn was not the only crooked lawman in Oklahoma during the 1920s. There was also Bert Bryant, also known as Jose Alvarado, who was once accused of taking $2,500 from a madam in Denoya in Osage County. Bryant was made to return the money in the presence of two bankers before being arrested for stealing the money. The court decided that since he had given the money back, Bryant should be acquitted.[17]

The last real troublesome boomtown in Oklahoma was Roxana, which took full advantage of the lack of law enforcement. The story goes that, in 1927, a "huge gusher made a poor farmer a millionaire over-night," and the town was platted in July.[18] Roxana was built very quickly as laborers came looking for work from miles around. The town soon had a reputation as a rough and tumble oil boomtown. There were no police to oversee knife fights, car thefts, and even one store that dealt only in stolen goods. At the oil derricks, fancily dressed prostitutes routinely met workers right at the plant gate at paydays each Friday. The town only lasted a little over a decade, ending with a refinery fire. Roxana was vacated in 1939.

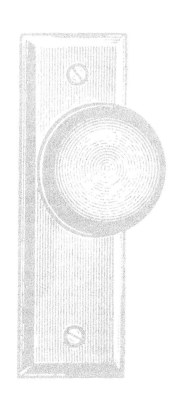

Chapter Sixteen

Ardmore's Wild Women

ONE OF OKLAHOMA'S EARLY TOWNS, ARDMORE, WAS THE SCENE OF ONE of the first red-light districts in Indian Territory. Located between the Arbuckle Mountains and the Red River in the Chickasaw Nation, Ardmore was formed when the Atchison, Topeka, and Santa Fe Railroad ran through a local ranch in 1887. The new town quickly became a well-known center for trade and cotton production. By 1890, there were already 2,500 residents. Some of them were of the red-light variety, for in 1894, the *Daily Ardmoreite* reported that one John Horn was arrested for assaulting "the person of a dusky demimonde."[1]

At first, Ardmore exhibited support and sympathy for their fallen women. When Vivia Gale, also known as Rose Welch, committed suicide in 1894, the *Daily Ardmoreite* explained that local citizens made sure she received a "decent burial." As Vivia Gale, the woman had once been married to John Gale of Butte, Montana. Why they were no longer together was not revealed, but apparently Vivia had received an angry letter from her brother-in-law, J. M. Barton of Texas. She had written to both men before doing herself in with chloroform. In reporting the story, the writer described Vivia as "a fine example of womanhood and [she] did not appear as [a prostitute]."[2] That same year, Ardmore's *Chickasaw Chieftain* noted that in spite of offers to help her, another woman living in "the most abject and squalid poverty" died and was buried at Ardmore, her real name unknown.[3]

Like many towns, Ardmore did eventually grow weary of its wayward women, perhaps because most of them refused offers to help them reform. Also at risk were people associated with the demimonde. In May of 1894, a man who rented some residential property for he and his family was lambasted in the newspaper when it was discovered he was actually subletting the property to some prostitutes. And shortly after much of Ardmore burned during a fire in 1895, the respectable women of the town worked to keep the local working girls from rebuilding. "Give such people a foothold," warned the *Chickasaw Chieftain*, "and they are as hard to get rid of as a heavy crop of weeds."[4]

Although the good women of Ardmore were resolute in their desire to rid the town of its undesirable element, it was a tough battle. When a woman thought to be a prostitute named Irish Nora attempted suicide via morphine in 1896, the *Daily Ardmoreite* expressed gentle hope that she would reform. But local sympathies were countered by the burning of several buildings near the red-light district in the east part of town, including the newly built Biggars building which functioned as a brothel. The arsonist was never caught. When Ardmore finally incorporated in 1898, the new city government began trying to squelch the prostitution industry in its midst.

One of the first acts of officials at Ardmore was to vote in its first law against prostitution. As the new city council mulled over the new ordinance, J. T. Brown was charged with renting rooms to prostitutes. He was fined $5 plus costs, and when he couldn't pay, was sent to jail. That happened on August 18; just four days later, the *Daily Ardmoreite* published Ordinance 38 which, rather than outlawing prostitution itself, simply forbade men from associating with bad girls—namely being seen with them on any street, in any alley, or in any other public place. Offenders could be fined up to $25. The new ordinance worked, at least for a little while. During 1899, two men caught "associating with prostitutes" were fined $10.65 each.[5] Another young man was assigned to perform "street work" for the city in lieu of a fine. Similar charges continued throughout 1899. In November, one Josie James was fined for prostitution. Also, a "colored" prostitute was fined $10 after she falsely accused a "colored" man of robbing her.[6]

By 1901, prostitutes were rampant in Ardmore. Among those arrested and fined that year were three other Black women, Mary Angelina

Brown, Malinda Jane Jones, and Berlina Sophia Smith. Each paid a fine of $10.90. A year later, however, the *Daily Ardmoreite* reported that prostitutes were scattered all over the city. Respectable citizens didn't like it, and took especial issue with a local judge who, like so many others across the country, had instilled a system wherein ladies of the lamplight were allowed to operate as long as they paid their fines. But he was also accused of "furnishing money to bring prostitutes into the city."[7] Naturally the judge denied any wrongdoing. Now too, the local ladies' Benevolent Society was doing their best to aid unfortunate women and convince them to reform. Those who refused, like prostitute Ada Ray, continued paying fines hovering around $10.

[ORDINANCE No. 38.]

ASSOCIATING WITH PROSTITUTES.

AN ORDINANCE Prohibiting Walking and Driving With Prostitutes in the City of Ardmore.

Be it Ordained by the City Council of the City of Ardmore:

SECTION 1. That it shall be unlawful for any male person over the age of 14 years to walk or drive with any prostitute, in or upon any street, alley or other public place within the corporate limits of the city.

SEC. 2. Every person violating the provisions of section one of this ordinance shall be deemed guilty of a misdemeanor, and upon conviction thereof in the mayor's court, be fined in any sum not more than $25.

SEC. 3. The provisions of this ordinance shall become operative and in full force from and after passage and publication.

Passed and approved this, 22d day of August, 1898.   JNO L. GALT,
DAVE BEST,   Mayor.
City Recorder.

Ardmore's prostitution ordinance in 1898. COURTESY LIBRARY OF CONGRESS

Like other places in Oklahoma, Prohibition had an effect on the demimonde of Ardmore beginning in 1907. Two Black prostitutes were convicted in September, and two more women were taken to court in December. There were likely more, but after 1907, charges against working girls began occurring less and less—that is, until 1913 when an oil boom hit Ardmore. Shortly after the Healdton Oil Field was established, the city experienced a marked population boom that included workers and their families, but also a bevy of hard-drinking gamblers and prostitutes. By now, however, debauchery was well known as an unsavory characteristic of oil towns. Fortunately, the many churches in Ardmore were on hand to "assume a more active role in stabilizing social conditions and providing an atmosphere conducive to raising families."[8] Before any positive results could be reported, a gasoline tank car exploded in the railroad yard at Ardmore in September of 1915. Much of the downtown area was blown to pieces as forty-three people were killed and hundreds of others were injured. Although the city eventually recovered, national Prohibition was looming in the near future, and besides, pioneer prostitution as it was known in the nineteenth century was fading to nothing more than memories. Ardmore's wicked women soon moved on, and disappeared forever.

CHAPTER SEVENTEEN

The Giddy Girls of Guthrie

LIKE ARDMORE, GUTHRIE'S BEGINNINGS ALSO ARE LINKED TO THE Atchison, Topeka, and Santa Fe Railroad. The fledgling town owed its existence to the land run of 1889, which took place on April 22. It was indeed one of the wildest days Oklahoma would ever see. Journalist Frederick Barde of the *Kansas City Star* was on the scene and reported on a huge tent where upward of 1,500 men and women drank and gambled. The proprietors, brothers Dick and Bill Reeves, were highly successful and went on to run their business, which was often fraught with violence, for another twenty years. During the land run, the Reeves brothers watched as people flowed into the area during that day. By nightfall, some ten thousand people had settled in the new town. Within four months there were some three hundred businesses in Guthrie, which became the territorial capital in 1890. When Oklahoma was made a state in 1907, Guthrie continued as the first state capital. As the new city of Guthrie found its roots, officials set about creating laws against prostitution. These were in place by May, when fines were being collected from prostitutes, as well as the local gambling joints.

Why did Guthrie allow for fines against prostitution instead of shutting their brothels down? The answer was simple: local authorities had learned from other cities that a fining system could prove quite lucrative versus closing houses. It was no secret that other cities' coffers were filled on a regular basis from the fines and license fees paid by women of the demimonde. In addition, fining prostitutes on a regular basis allowed the city to keep track of their wayward women. Anyone unable to pay was

Arrests Related to Prostitution in Guthrie, 1889–1900

Year	Running Brothel	Prostitution	Fines Paid
1889	2	46	Between $8.50 and $36.00
1890	9	43	Average fine $7.50
1891	9	148	Between $7.50 and $10.00
1892	0	202	Between $7.50 and $10.00
1893	0	337	Between $10.15 and $13.65
1894	0	270	Between $10.15 and $13.65
1895	0	219	Between $11.65 and $31.65
1896	0	152	Between $11.65 and $31.65
1897	0	207	
1898	0	169	
1899	0	136	
1900	0	142[1]	

likely sent to jail, where they could work off their fine or wait for someone else to pay their bond.

Guthrie's most notable prostitute in 1890 was Ada Blanche Miller, also known as Crystal Earle, who occupied a house on Perkins Avenue between Division and South First Streets. Crystal was bound to become well known in Guthrie. In March, a woman described as "that character known as Miss Norma" had brought some sort of charge up against Crystal, who was referred to as "the White Elephant Siren."[2] The White Elephant was a notorious dance hall and sporting house which, allegedly, featured "fifteen blondes and fifteen brunettes." The girls were known to ride around town in wagons to drum up business.[3] Commissioner Allison had apparently found Crystal guilty, and she was "bound over in the amount of $500." Instead of appearing in court, however, Crystal wisely hired two attorneys, Dale and Thomas, to show up in her stead. The men explained to Allison that the lady was "confined to her bed under the physician's care," and they were allowed to sign her bond for her. This annoyed the *Oklahoma State Capital*, which reported the story and questioned the commissioner's motives.[4]

Hell's Half Acre in Guthrie as it appeared in 1889. COURTESY OKLAHOMA HISTORICAL
SOCIETY

Crystal was soon in the newspapers again. This time she, along with
fellow prostitute Pearl Smith and a man named Al Bass, was arrested
for the alleged assault on one Felix G. Ott. The *Oklahoma State Capital*'s
reporter had great fun writing the article, which was headlined, "Fresh,
Festive and Funny—He is Finally Foiled from Fighting Featherweight."
Apparently, Ott, the postmaster at the small town of Elm, was visiting
Guthrie with some friends. The group was at a place known as the Parlor
House, where "they matched a fight with the inmates and got the worst
of it." The group was rounded up and went to court, where Ott was fined
for contempt. Later, at the gambling house of William Tilghman, the
man was drunk when "someone put a bump on his head." Ott returned
to the courthouse the following morning and pressed charges against
Crystal and her friends.[5]

A month after the incident at the Parlor House, Crystal was again
in the papers. This time, one George Lipe sued her for some unknown
infraction. The case was dismissed. That wasn't the only time Lipe
appeared in court; in fact, the man was actually the son of millionaire
Clark Lipe, in Colorado, and had recently embezzled money from his
own mother. Also, documents filed in Guthrie throughout 1890 and
1891 show he was involved in several other disputes. But Crystal Earle

was a special case. In fact, just two months after appearing in court with her, George Lipe married the woman on October 11. In reporting the union, the *Oklahoma State Capital* dedicated a little ditty to Crystal:

> No more to tread of patron feet
> The Elephant will resound—
> For Crystal Earle, no longer sport—
> In wifehood troth is bound.[6]

Whether Crystal was aware of her new husband's legal issues when she married him is unclear. It is known that even she had lent him money with which to buy property before the marriage. Afterward, however, when it became clear that George Lipe was an embezzler, an incensed Crystal demanded that her new husband sign his property over to her in order to keep debtors and the courts from taking it. And when Lipe was indeed convicted in March of 1891 in Colorado, Crystal left him. But it wasn't until 1893 that she filed for divorce—and seized Lipe's property. In court, she said she was just a housekeeper and was duly awarded both the property and her divorce. Soon after that, Crystal dropped her old pseudonym and became known simply as Blanche Lipe.

The newspapers, which had enjoyed expounding on the charges against George Lipe, his subsequent prison time, and the tug of war between he and Blanche over property, just couldn't leave the lady alone. In August, the *Guthrie Daily News* begged its readers for information as to whether Blanche was in Guthrie or visiting Colorado with her friend, Hazel Kirke. It turned out that Blanche was indeed in Colorado. When she returned to Guthrie, she had a letter from George Lipe exempting her from all blame in his imprisonment, as well as their property issues. He also was due to inherit a great deal of wealth when his mother died.

One of the properties Blanche retained was her former workplace, the White Elephant, which she now ran as a madam. Under her ownership, there was little trouble save for one incident in 1897, when the ladies of the club went "to a rival establishment and proceeded to make a 'rough house' on a thorough plan." The women were subsequently arrested, but

Blanche's name was not mentioned.[7] The last time she appeared in the newspapers was in 1900, when she sold the White Elephant, as well as everything in it, for $2,000. After that she disappeared and was never heard from again.

During the years Blanche Lipe remained in Guthrie, the city continued grappling with its growing prostitution industry. "Gamblers are increasing," noted the *Guthrie Daily Leader* in September of 1893, "also the demi-monde." A month later, the *Guthrie Daily News* announced that "the most salacious of the demi-monde of Guthrie have migrated to Perry, where there is a fine market for their peculiar wares." The newspaper also expressed that some of the ladies' well-paying customers had left for Perry too, "and will give the new comers a ringing and joyous welcome." Several months later, in May of 1894, the *News* also proudly reported that many wicked women and their cohorts had "folded their tents mostly and disappeared, or been forgotten." Just weeks after that, city officials succeeded in producing a new ordinance ordering all saloons to close at midnight. The *Guthrie Daily Leader*, however, voiced its opinion that doing so only enhanced "good beer trade" for the city's brothels since they could technically continue selling the stuff after midnight.[8]

The wily women of Guthrie clearly, were not gone after all. In July, prostitutes May Young and Della Tyler were arrested for stealing a diamond worth $50 from another woman of the demimonde, Jess Bohn. Their court case made the papers mainly because the proceedings took an entire day that lasted until seven o'clock that evening. To top it off, attorneys J. J. Boles and Mr. Decker of Decker, Jones & Devereux got into a heated argument that resulted in Boles being fined $50 for contempt of court. In the end, the case was dismissed.

May Young especially was quite adept at making a mockery of the court system. In August of 1897, the *Oklahoma State Capital* reported that May, who had left her respectable Guthrie family in 1891 to take up life as a prostitute, married a well-known saloonkeeper named George Stroeble. The union lasted only two weeks before May took umbrage with her new husband. In a very public display, the "young thing" suddenly sold Stroeble's team of horses, wagons, and other items for $150 before giving her husband "a licking on the street." Then she took whatever cash she could find on the man and beat a hasty retreat to Texas. What Stroeble had done to set May off in such a manner was not explained, although it was insinuated that the only reason the girl married him in the first place was to get his money. A thoroughly ashamed Stroeble left Guthrie soon afterward for Leavenworth, Kansas, where he became a permanent resident of the "soldier's home."[9]

For several more years, prostitution continued to flourish in Guthrie. Although the fines against the industry were diminishing beginning in 1900, prostitution and gambling arrests remained a priority in the local law books. Now, however, the ladies of the night were ambling off to other, greener, pastures as mining and oil industries began appearing all over Oklahoma as well as the west. The authorities were still willing to let the ladies slide, to a degree. In August of 1900, Flossie Nelson, who had purchased the White Elephant from Blanche Lipe, was taken to court on charges of prostitution. Her case was dismissed, but several of her employees were in court by the coming week. The following October, White Elephant employee Pearl Christian was arrested for the theft of jewelry, pillow cases, sheets, and a skirt. Pearl pleaded guilty and paid a $15 fine. Her male cohort also was fined. The White Elephant finally closed for good after two thousand residents signed a petition against the place in 1901. Three months later, the Choctaw Railroad Company purchased the property and planned to move the White Elephant to a new address in East Guthrie. Instead, the structure was moved to Kingfisher to start a new life as a sporting house.

By 1904, citizens in the capital city were downright sick of the remaining prostitutes in town, as well as city authorities who allowed the brothels to remain open so long as their monthly fines were paid. Things escalated as far as the grand jury, which agreed that allowing bawdy houses, as well as gambling joints, to continue operating was illegal. The findings were published in a report, and the court instructed the clerk to send a copy to the county commissioners. Judge Burford, who presided over the matter, stated that the statutes expressly forbid taking in money in exchange for allowing such places to run, and threatened any city official who continued taking in fines. That was pretty much the end of frontier prostitution in Guthrie, except for one hold-out: the Blue Belle Saloon.

Guthrie's history would not be complete without paying homage to the Blue Belle, which was located on West Harrison Street. This tidy brick building with the fancy entryway still survives on Harrison at the corner of 2nd Street, and remains an iconic representation of Guthrie's bawdy history today. Unfortunately, however, the Blue Belle has been subject to legendary rumors and enough fiction that the truth about what happened there has mostly been lost to history. Fortunately, a few writers have made a valiant attempt to document the building, and there are enough news articles and more solid stories to give a semi-solid glimpse into the Blue Belle's bawdy past.

The story of the Blue Belle Saloon goes that, on the day of the 1889 land run, one John Sempsel was able to purchase the property, erected a tent, and began selling libations and tobacco. Who built the original building on the property is fuzzy, but at some point early on, two men, John Selstrom and Jack Tearney, purchased the property. In 1893, the original structure is believed to have burned. By 1894, a second, two-story brick structure stood on the site at the corner of Harrison and Second streets, and continued to offer alcohol and gambling. In quick succession, a barber, office and restaurant, and finally a gaming room occupied a small structure in back of the building. The first time the new Blue Belle Saloon was mentioned in newspapers was in January of 1899, when the *Oklahoma State Capital* newspaper announced the saloon would soon receive some money from the Sharkey-McCoy boxing match. A year later, the Blue Belle was robbed in the dead of night. Two men, James Richards and Charles Eads, were arrested for the deed, but were later acquitted. By 1901 only gambling, not prostitution, was taking place on the second floor.

In July of 1903, the *Oklahoma State Register* announced that the Blue Belle was closing, and the building was being relocated to South Vine Street. In its place, the Heim brothers would be building an all new, three-story affair. The Fred Heim Brewing Company directed the Freemont Land and Improvement Company to construct the new building, although the third story was never built. A "C-11" crest atop the front door signified Ned Cheadle, Heim's agent and bottler for the brewery. The all-new Blue Belle Saloon premiered in January of 1904. Three years later, however, the business was forced to stop all gaming and liquor activity after Oklahoma became a state.

Between 1908 and 1930, the Blue Belle was connected by hallways to the building next to it and was occupied by a furniture store, a grocery, a restaurant, and a music store. On the bottom floor, silent screen actor Tom Mix is said to have bartended prior to his illustrious career, although that is debatable since there is no record of a saloon operating in the Blue Belle during this time. Upstairs, however, were seventeen rooms that construed what "was probably a bordello. It was connected in early days by an iron sky-walk to the Elks Hotel across the alleyway."[10] It was most likely during this time that a woman known only as "Miss Lizzie" ran the brothel. Folk tales of epic proportions are told about Lizzie. One source says she was "a highly intelligent business lady and a devout Christian."[11] Others state that government employees and businessmen constituted many of Lizzie's customers, and that a tunnel system from the building allegedly kept their visits secret from the public. The sky-walk likely also served this purpose.

The worst stories about Lizzie concern her habit of purchasing young girls from, or at least taking them as collateral, when she loaned money to needy families. One of her girls, for instance, was supposedly a young teen named Claudia who was forced to work for Lizzie after the madam loaned her parents money to save their farm. The girl was naturally sad and frightened. One day a customer became fed up with her depressing demeanor, they say, and beat her to death. Lizzie covered the crime by burying Claudia next to the coal chute. Another of Lizzie's girls was known only as "Estelle B." and also was "sold" to the madam at the young age of fifteen years. Estelle also is believed to have "died an untimely death at the cruel hands of Miss Lizzie or her customers."[12] The upper floor of the Blue Belle is believed to have operated until as late as World War II.

When the state of Oklahoma finally repealed its Prohibition laws in 1959, a whole new generation of drinking holes slowly but surely opened up in Guthrie. In 1977, the old Blue Belle Saloon's name was restored, and has remained so pretty much ever since. The building still sports much of its original interior in the way of the original tin ceiling, woodwork, and even a bar dating back to 1899. A staircase in the back leads to what is thought to have been a speakeasy in the basement. The building has, in the last several decades, served as a variety of different restaurants and bars. And as new generations of customers enjoy the historic surroundings, the spirits of Madam Lizzie and some of her girls are said to roam the building to this day. They are, in their own way, the last vestige of Guthrie's once colorful nightlife.

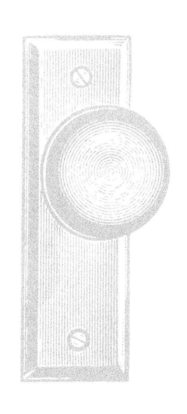

CHAPTER EIGHTEEN

Hell's Half Acre in Oklahoma City

THERE'S A REASON THEY CALLED OKLAHOMA CITY'S RED-LIGHT DIStrict "Hell's Half Acre." For quite some years, the area bordered between Broadway Avenue (aka "Battle Row"), Front Street (today's Santa Fe Street), Grand Avenue, and California Avenue was home to a number of wicked brothels, saloons, and gambling houses. Hop Boulevard, also known as Bunco Alley and located within Hell's Half Acre, was said to be the worst street in the entire neighborhood.[1] Other avenues were known as Maidens Lane and Alabaster Avenue. Around the corner from Alabaster Avenue was an area on Front Street where "dives in plaster-board shacks" accommodated Black prostitutes and their customers. Throughout Hell's Half Acre, women plied their trade, scrapped with each other and their customers, and kept the police on their toes. But Hell's Half Acre was somewhat unregulated, supported by corrupt businessmen and even newspapers who rallied for a "wide-open town" where madams, saloon owners, and gamblers called the shots and strong-armed local politicians and officials.[2]

Oklahoma City was born on April 22, 1889, during one of the territorial land runs. What a sight it must have been to see people coming in swarms to set up their tents right in the middle of what would become the downtown area. By nightfall, the city was settled and government officials had been elected. But although laws and a police department were soon formed, Oklahoma City's demimonde, gamblers, and tipplers would remain largely unregulated, untouched by the law. Back then, the red-light district also included certain places along 2nd Street and other nearby roads. The district was not official; rather, business owners simply chose their own location because they liked it and it was lucrative. And although churches, Prohibitionists, and reformers complained to the city on a regular basis, there wasn't a thing to be done about Hell's Half Acre.

By August, just over three months after Oklahoma City was established, there were nine billiard halls, eighteen "club houses," and countless bordellos flourishing in Hell's Half Acre. Some of the saloons—Black and Rogers, Turf Club, and Two Johns—were very well known. That the city condoned them is evidenced by the location of Black and Rogers, directly below the city council chambers and police court on the second floor of the same building.[3] Various sources provide snippets of information about the brothels of Hell's Half Acre, which fairly squirmed with activity day and night. Writer Albert Mcrill describes a typical scene along Battle Row: "A hundred horses tethered on either side of the street pawed and snorted to the whistling of bullets, the cracking of heads, and the blatant carousing of a weltering, fighting mass of cowboys, liquor-soaked tramps, tin-horn gamblers, and excited city men" who drank themselves silly and "came tumbling out of a dozen saloons, shouting and smashing beer bottles over each other's heads and engaging in a hilarious free-for-all celebration."[4] For the ladies of Hell's Half Acre, these men were ripe for the picking.

By 1891, Oklahoma City had at last established some ordinances regarding the demimonde. An article in Oklahoma City's *Evening Gazette* confirmed that previously, the bagnios, and each woman within them paid a monthly fine of $5. Now, the city raised those fines to $15 per house and $10 per inmate. In addition, women were no longer allowed in saloons, and those tippling houses found in violation would be fined between $5 and $25. For a time, citizens were content with this system, although Prohibitionists regularly lectured about the evils of vice to anyone who would listen. "A Dialouge [*sic*] in Hell! The Saloon Keeper and the Assassin! The Libistinex and the Demimonde!" cried one advertisement in the *Oklahoma Daily Times Journal*. "Come and hear Elder Goodrich at the court house on Broadway."[5] Since the courthouse was actually located within Hell's Half Acre, however, it is questionable whether anyone attended the lecture.

Hell's Half Acre was more settled by the 1900s. Gone, for the most part, were the transient prostitutes who drifted in and out of town so quickly that their names were never recorded in history. Gone too were the rougher, rowdier days when a man took his life into his own hands when exploring the neighborhood. Also, Oklahoma City officials somehow managed to move the demimonde to an area along West Second Street. Now, more demure women ran finer houses in the red-light district, and dutifully dealt with law enforcement and city officials as a means to remain open with the least amount of trouble. But only sixteen prostitutes and two houses of prostitution were recorded in the 1900 census.

Oklahoma City Harlots in the 1900 Census

Name	Residence	Birthdate	Birthplace
Gertie Anderson	Oklahoma City	1889	Illinois
Laura Evans	Oklahoma City	1872	Kansas
Susie Fields	Oklahoma City	1872	Kentucky
Effie Fisher	Oklahoma City	1873	Illinois
Dora Goodwin	Oklahoma City	1877	Illinois
Viola Harris	Oklahoma City	1874	Illinois
Girtie Hodge	Oklahoma City	1882	Kentucky
Lulu Little	Oklahoma City	1882	Kentucky
Gracie Maxwell	Oklahoma City	1887	Illinois
Bessie Moore	Oklahoma City	1875	Texas
Myrtle Moore	Oklahoma City	1873	Texas
Mattie Probo	Oklahoma City	1867	Kentucky
Fannie Richards	Oklahoma City	1873	New Mexico
Maggie Roberts	Oklahoma City	1880	Illinois
Gertie Sawyer	Oklahoma City	1880	Illinois
Annie Wynn	Oklahoma City	1865	Illinois

Surely, there were many more women than the census listed, since an amazing amount of vice, crime, prostitution, and violence was still present in Hell's Half Acre by 1901. There was also a new system in place: brothels and gambling houses were occasionally raided. Attorneys for the proprietors and prostitutes would already be at the jail by the time the law breakers were brought in. Bail and fines were readily paid, after which the perpetrators were free to go back to work. Bribes and protection money also were part of the proceedings, which is likely why the raids did not take place on a regular basis.

Newspapers scrambled to keep up with the happenings in Oklahoma City's demimonde. During 1902, news accounts included that of a "colored female preacher" who was seen lecturing at the corner of Broadway and California avenues.[6] But the lady's efforts were largely overshadowed by the goings-on at the Vendome, the fanciest parlor house in town that was located across from the city hall on Broadway Avenue. Brussels carpets, fine furniture, and other luxuries made the Vendome "a very high-toned joint of its class."[7] Just one night's stay—which included dinner and entertainment—could cost as much as $40. But even the Vendome could not escape the occasional scandal. On a summer's evening in June of 1902, the parlor house made the papers after one of its inmates, Lizzie Long, fired a gun at a customer. Alternately known as "Sporting Lizzie," the woman had already been identified as a "notorious pilferer" in St. Louis, Missouri, back in 1890. At the Vendome, they say, she had once "sent a houseful of customers tumbling down two flights of stairs."[8] This time, Lizzie and W. E. Monehan, a professional gambler, were in the reception room of the Vendome. Apparently, Lizzie took umbrage with Monehan over his attentions to another woman and fired a gun in his direction. The noise was heard on Broadway Avenue and the police were summoned. Lizzie was arrested, and bonded out in anticipation of her trial. Soon afterward, she was taken to El Reno some thirty miles away, where she was wanted for forgery.

The articles about Lizzie did not sit well with Mrs. Annie L. Brown, madam of the Vendome, who filed a defamation suit against the *Daily Oklahoman*. The Vendome, said the madam, was a "lodging house" that "was run in a respectable and orderly manner." Furthermore, said Annie, her house "was a house of fair fame and good repute." She was also very upset that the *Daily Oklahoman* circulated all over Oklahoma Territory, thereby spreading the story. Annie claimed her reputation had been destroyed, and she wanted $1,000 in restitution.[9] According to the local *Weekly Times-Journal*, Annie appeared to have especially objected to the blaring headline which proclaimed in all capital letters, "MISSED HER MAN. DENIZEN OF THE VENDOME SHOT AT LOCAL GAMBLER. IN THE CITY'S HEART A HIGH-TONED HOUSE OF ILL-FAME HAS BEEN CONDUCTED OPENLY." Annie claimed the paper "falsely, wickedly and maliciously libeled her." And unfortunately, the *Journal* also decided to re-run the original article so that anybody who had not already read it could see it.[10]

It is unknown whether Annie won her suit or received the $1,000 to smooth her ruffled feathers. Now, the Vendome became the target of ridicule, and when an El Reno woman and her paramour were arrested on charges of adultery there in July, the *Daily Oklahoman* reported on that incident, too. Oklahoma City police had received a call from J. B. D. Mulkey, who told them he suspected his wife of being with another man at the Vendome. Police duly arrived at the place, were admitted by a hesitant Madam Brown, and opened the door to a room to find Mulkey's wife and one Charles Pemberton inside. Mrs. Mulkey had managed to put on a robe, but Pemberton had yet to pull up his pants. The two were hauled into court, where the furious wife burst into a rage. "You d____d cowardly cur!" she screeched at her husband. "It's a good thing I haven't a knife here, or I would cut your heart out. If I get out of this trouble, I will kill you if it's the last thing I ever do!" Mrs. Mulkey also began to "claw and hit" her husband until he was rescued by officers. She, and Pemberton, paid a fine.[11]

The Vendome made the newspaper one last time in 1903 when two girls from there, Minnie Thompson and Mollie Lind, were found drunk on the street and arrested. The Vendome may have closed for good soon afterward; three months after Minnie and Mollie were jailed, the *Daily Oklahoman* noted that Annie Brown had recently purchased some $1,700 in new furniture and supposed she was "probably contemplating re-engaging in the rooming house business." In her prime, Annie may have aspired to make the Vendome one of the most elite parlor houses in town, and it worked after a fashion. The Red Onion, run by Madam Daisy Clayton, however, made no such effort.

Indeed, the Red Onion was allegedly known as one of the worst brothels in town. The only known news item concerning the place serves as commentary on the depressingly sad conditions there. In October 1902, twenty-seven-year-old Gertie Nye committed suicide via morphine at the Red Onion. She had previously spent time at the insane asylum in Norman after separating from her husband, John Nye. A letter found with Gertie was addressed to a man named Jesse, and told him she was "at Birdie's house." The note also told Jesse that he should not "forget the one that loved you better than her own life . . . I have no friend but you in the wide world and we cannot be together." But a photograph of the man was also left for Gertie's friend, Nellie. A note was included for her as well, telling her it was Jesse's fault that Gertie was in a bawdy house. The authorities tried to contact John Nye to no avail. They also found Gertie's father, who merely responded that he "had had enough trouble with the girl."[12]

On the opposite end of the spectrum, Madam Ethel Clopton managed to survive quite nicely in Oklahoma City for roughly two decades before losing everything dear to her. Going by the 1910 Oklahoma City census, the lady was born Ethel Hoag in 1873, in Tennessee. But she also was documented at the home of her parents in Tennessee that year, where it was stated that she was born in Mississippi in 1871. She was known as Ethel Clopton when she first appeared in the Oklahoma City Directory during 1902, when she lived at 413 West 2nd Street. Around this time, one John Holzapfel filed a petition against Ethel and C. W. Bunn and alleged that Bunn was renting property to Ethel "for use as an immoral resort."[13] The lady acquiesced and had moved to 24 ½ Grand Avenue by 1903, likely operating on the second floor. By 1905, Ethel had apparently commandeered the entire building.

As of the 1910 census, Ethel had moved again. This time she was found living at 1700 West Reno, a roadhouse in a remote area of town. The census taker recorded her as single and noted that she rented her brothel. Also in the house was Ethel's sister, Eva Hoag. The only prostitute documented at the house that day was Beba Delore, but the presence of four Black servants—Lulu Baker, Charles Wash, and Will and Lena West—indicates that Ethel might have employed other women as well. Lack of news articles about Ethel during this time would seem to indicate she ran a clean house, paid her fines, and stayed out of the eyes of the law. Later, the same census also documented Ethel and Eva at the home of their family in Memphis, Tennessee, where they must have been visiting. No occupation was listed for Eva—likely in order to keep her parents from knowing what she really did for a living.

In May of 1911, Ethel married Harry Scott at Britton, a small community north of Oklahoma City. Just over a year later, Ethel's mother, Sarah Hoag, came to Oklahoma City after her husband died. If she didn't know the occupations of her daughters before, Sarah must have become aware of it now. But she was actually in town to file a lawsuit against attorney Charles Ruth. What the issue was is unknown, but Sarah was back in Memphis when she too died, on November 1. She left no will, only some property in Doffings Addition, in Oklahoma City.

Ethel was still reeling from her mother's death when the law raided her roadhouse in April of 1913. Although Ethel was not doing business that night and there were no prostitutes in the house, deputies found a gallon of illegal whiskey, as well as dozens of bottles of beer. Ethel was arrested for bootlegging, hauled to jail, and posted $500 for bail. At her trial in May, it was noted that Ethel had weathered the same charge the previous summer but had been acquitted. This time, however, she made history as the first woman to be indicted by a grand jury. She likely paid a hefty fine in lieu of jail time, since she was back at her West Reno house when she was arrested yet again. The charges this time included running a house of prostitution. Three of Ethel's girls also were arrested, as well as a customer who was charged with "loitering around a disorderly house."[14]

There may have been something more to Ethel's second arrest. Two days after the *Daily Oklahoman* published the news, attorney Charles Hunt filed papers to become the administrator of Sarah Hoag's estate. His interest was in her sole piece of property, which was worth some $3,000. Hunt claimed he was "a judgement creditor of the said Ethel Clopton, the only known heir" to Sarah. Notices of Hunt's intentions were publicly posted at the corner of Main and Hudson and the corner of Grand and Hudson, and were also posted in Oklahoma City newspapers.[15] Perhaps fearing prejudice, Ethel requested a change of venue for her trial. This was apparently granted and, after paying another $2,000 bond, Ethel was freed pending her trial. In the end, "Mother Clopton," as the *Oklahoma City Times* now referred to her, made a deal with the court. She would leave Oklahoma City, and would stay gone for three years. The judge agreed, and within a day or two Ethel departed for Wichita Falls, Texas.[16]

Despite her sudden move, Ethel was not done battling with Charles Hunt. She was able to file a suit against the man, even as he was awarded "possession of a Haddorf Piano and . . . damages for [the case's] unlawful detention and for costs of this action."[17] Ethel and her husband, now identified as Claude Scott, landed in Shawnee as the woman continued her suit, which went on for years. At issue by March 1915, for instance, was an accusation by Ethel and Eva that Hunt had hidden certain documents relevant to the case. Just a month later, however, an entirely different judgement against Ethel cost her most of her furnishings, including an iron safe, which were auctioned off to settle a suit by the firm of McAdams and Haskell. The company had apparently won a judgement of $116.01, which was never paid. Ethel had officially lost both of her battles, as well as her marriage. In November of 1916, she divorced from Harry Scott. After that, Ethel disappeared for good.

Ethel Clopton was not the only madam to eventually lose her place in Oklahoma City's demimonde. Far away, on the other side of Hell's Half Acre, was a woman identified as "Etta Woods and Her Creole Girls."[18] A native of Tennessee, thirty-one-year-old Etta (nee Etta Watkins) was a widow when she first appeared in 1903 at a house at 409 West Second Street, where she would remain for many years. Although the listing for her in the Oklahoma City Directory during 1905 said her occupation was "laundry," it was glaringly apparent to others that Etta's services had nothing to do with washing shirts. By the time of the 1910 census, Etta had achieved what most women of color would never see: she could read and write, owned her own house, and was quite successful. Working for her were Bertha McNeal, Pearl Thompson, and Deona Whatley, as well as servant Emma Dudley. Also in the house when the census taker came by were two men, Ed Harrison and Jim Johnson.

Johnson's name would appear in Oklahoma City's *Daily Pointer* newspaper as an "inmate," perhaps a bouncer, in May 1911, when there was a disturbance at Etta's. According to the paper two women, Anna Thomas and Marie McFadden, got into a fight. The police were summoned and the women, along with Etta, Johnson, and another prostitute, Stella Glover, were arrested. Stella was fined $5. Anna and Marie were each fined $10 for fighting. Johnson also was fined $10. As for Etta, she paid a $25 fine for running a house of prostitution. She also paid a $50 fine in November. Yet in spite of her arrests, Etta continued doing well for a time. In 1914, the *Daily Law Journal-Record* noted she sold a piano to one Paul Valentine for $60, worth nearly $1,700 today.

Although Etta and her girls did well during the early 1900s, that all changed as World War I appeared on the horizon and the military began working in earnest to shut down red-light districts across the country. Desperate to make better money, Etta turned to a new vocation: selling drugs. In 1918, Oklahoma City's *Daily Oklahoman* reported that Etta, along with Edgar Humphrey, had indeed been busted for selling narcotics. "An outlay of needles which police testified were used by dope fiends" were found, and the twosome were fined $19.[19] A similar charge was made in 1920. "Any service she may have given the community is small in comparison with the disgrace she had brought upon it through her nefarious operations," the *Oklahoma City Times* said of Etta. Notably someone from the "federal narcotic department" was present when Etta's house was raided, and actually objected to her arrest.[20] Afterward, Etta moved a final time, to 511 South Broadway, where she was arrested in 1934. This time she was sent to prison.

One of the most unique madams in Hell's Half Acre was a woman identified only as Madam McDonald, who named her place on 2nd Street "the Arlington" after a notorious brothel in New Orleans's legendary red-light district, Storyville. The madam kept only one girl on hand, gently explaining to the authorities that "My house is especially conducted to accommodate married ladies, who want to meet their gentlemen friends when their husbands are away from home, and for young men and women who may be out for a stroll in the evening and desire a secluded place where they will not be recognized."[21] Those who did not desire the services of Madam McDonald could amble across the street to Noah's Ark, called by one source as "the wildest of the wild dens" where "bawds and toughs, of all shades, sizes, and shapes" were available.[22]

In 1903, democrat Robert Lee Van Winkle was elected mayor of Oklahoma City. He was supported by several business owners in the demimonde, including a madam known as "Big Anne," who hoped the mayor sided with them. Soon after a young lady was drugged at Big Anne's, however, public sentiment began turning on the demimonde more than ever before. "The moral conditions of the city are becoming unbearable," pointed out Chief Justice John Henry Burford, "because the officers of the law will not perform their sworn duties and enforce the law." Burford's statement was echoed by a number of citizens, and Van Winkle was pressured into ordering arrests of the very members of the underworld who had supported his election.[23] Among the many new ordinances passed during 1904, city officials proclaimed that anyone leasing a saloon or bawdy house could not renew their lease when it expired. As of January, several saloons and bawdy houses along Alabaster Avenue had been closed. By spring, Van Winkle had stepped down from his office.

Newspapers continued their tirade against the red-light district. In 1905, the *Daily Oklahoman* published an article about Mary and Anna Brentlinger whose mother, Jean LaMonte, ran the Red Star brothel at 431 West Second Street. The girls, ages thirteen years and fifteen years, respectively, were attending St. Joseph's Academy, a convent school in Abilene, Kansas. One day, an unidentified gentleman arrived at the McKibben Hotel in Oklahoma City and explained to Mrs. McKibben that the girls were coming to visit their mother. At issue was a proper place for the children to stay. Neither girl had any idea what her mother did for a living, said the man, and visiting Jean at a brothel was certainly out of the question. Mrs. McKibben agreed to keep the girls at her hotel for the duration of the visit.

Two weeks later, Mary and Anna arrived at the McKibben place. They were able to visit with their mother over the course of two months, after which they were next sent to another convent in Guthrie. While there, Anna became deathly ill with typhoid fever and was sent to the hospital. She was still recovering when Jean LaMonte suddenly appeared and took her daughter to the Red Star and began inviting some of her male friends over to meet the girl. To Anna's horror, her own mother "turned her over to them to be brought out." Jean took the terrified teen back to Mrs. McKibben for a few days to calm her down. But when she returned and attempted to take Anna with her again, the girl refused to go.

An impatient Jean soon "began a system of persecution" as a means to get Anna to go back to the Red Star. After several attempts, during which the McKibbens refused to let Jean coerce the girl, the madam showed up one day while Anna was at church and waited in the McKibben Hotel lobby. When Anna appeared, she was told to "get on your wraps, as I intend to take you home with me." Jean also assured Anna that living and working in a brothel was great fun. Anna, however, had already seen the "fun" her mother intended for her and became hysterical. Mr. McKibben forcibly intervened and told Jean that Anna wasn't going anywhere. The angry madam defiantly filed a complaint at the police station, but when the police chief visited the McKibben Hotel himself, he personally took charge of Anna until she was safely returned to Abilene.[24] That was the last anyone heard of Jean LaMonte.

Oklahoma's statehood and accompanying Prohibition in 1907 marked the end of Oklahoma City's demimonde. New city officials were elected and duly sent out groups of officers called "flying squadrons" to raid any saloons and bawdy houses they might find. The raids continued with a vengeance for many more years. In 1917, Oklahoma City authorities announced, "There is no room in this city for loafers, thieves, gamblers, bootleggers and prostitutes. They shall be forced into war, into work, or into jail."[25] They meant it, too. Within a few more years, frontier prostitution as it was known in Oklahoma City had come to an end.

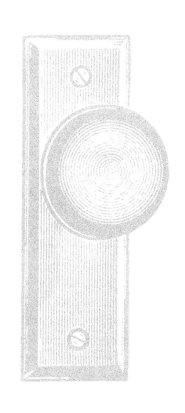

CHAPTER NINETEEN

Big Anne Wynn

MUCH HAS BEEN WRITTEN ABOUT "BIG ANNE WYNN," BETTER KNOWN
as Annie Wynn when she ran a series of brothels in Oklahoma City. The
seemingly brazen woman has been described as "the most influential
force in the city's underworld, issuing orders to county and city authorities, laughing at enforcement officers, wrecking city administrations
right and left, and snapping her fingers at the courts."[1] It is true that, like
many madams, Annie skated along a narrow path through the compli-
cated streets of Hell's Half Acre, evading the law as much as possible and
doing what she had to in order to survive even as newspapers focused
on her escapades. In doing so, she did exhibit her share of power within
Oklahoma City's demimonde. It is also true that the woman towered six
feet tall, and was sizeable in girth besides. But did Annie Wynn deserve
the raucous reputation bestowed upon her by historians in the modern
century?

Annie was Mary Anne McLaughlin when she was born, circa 1865, to
James and Mary McLaughlin in Illinois. Although some sources say there
were eighteen members of her immediate family, only four other children
had been born by the time Annie came along. That's just one of many
misconceptions about the woman who, according to one 1908 account in
the *Daily Oklahoman*, was sent to live with an uncle when she was still a
girl. There she worked for a merchant and, later, as a domestic servant for
a different family. After about three years, she moved to Colorado.

From all appearances, Annie was initially on the straight and narrow,
working and sending money home when she could—until she met up

with a friend identified only as "a young woman from Kansas." She also somehow got mixed up with "a rich ranchman." The *Daily Oklahoman* pinpointed him as the one who, through "money, promises and influences," somehow "ruined her." That Annie lost her virginity to the man is almost certain. Desperate and ashamed, the girl next traveled to Leadville, Colorado, at the age of seventeen years. Most accounts say she was with a friend, perhaps the girl from Kansas. There have been a number of claims about just what Annie did in Leadville. One source says that she ran "a fashionable bagnio on Main Street."[2] Others say she married a saloonkeeper and became a madam.

It is true that Leadville's dance halls were once referred to by a newspaper as "breathing holes of hell, where customers imbibe torchlight whiskey and indulge in the quadrille and the whirling sinuosity's [*sic*] of the waltz." But there is no sign of Annie in Leadville's 1880 census.[3] Nor is there any other documentation proving Annie was even in Leadville at all, save for a Mrs. Ann McLaughlin in the 1883 directory. That woman, however, resided with her miner husband, John, on East 4th Street, which is not identified as part of Leadville's red-light district. All that is certain is that Annie was in Rawlins, Wyoming, during 1887 when she married Edwin Ruthren Wynn on August 5. Wyoming's *Carbon County Journal* said Annie came from Lander.

Although the *Daily Oklahoman* would later claim that Ed Wynn was a saloonkeeper, a different source identifies him as the associate editor of the *Fremont Clipper*, Lander's local newspaper. The *Daily Oklahoman* also claimed that Annie had a falling out with Wynn, who gave her money to go to Chicago. There, she "met her present husband," but he remained unidentified.[4] Most sources believe that it was actually Ed Wynn who accompanied Annie to Oklahoma City, just before the land run of 1889. All that is known for sure is that Annie, along with several others, pitched her tent on Front Street on April 22 in anticipation of the run to "provide female companionship for the overwhelmingly male population."[5] Annie Wynn had arrived in Oklahoma City.

Annie's first official brothel was at the corner of today's North Walker Avenue and West 2nd Street (now Robert S. Kerr Avenue). It was the first of many she would own or run. She was "associated with" the

Arlington, the "boarding house" next door to her, where perhaps she sent erring wives and young couples to Madam McDonald. But "Big Anne's Place" offered a standard combination dance hall, saloon, and brothel.[6] Curiously, a 1908 *Daily Oklahoman* article made mention that, early on, one of Annie's girls "left a little child in her hands. She has reared it and cared for it like one of her own."[7] Who the child was, however, and what became of it, remains a mystery; only Annie, her girls, and four male boarders who were probably guests were documented in the Oklahoma state census for 1890. Notably, Edwin Wynn was not present, and in 1892, Annie returned to Lander long enough to file for a divorce from him.

By 1896, Annie had managed to amass a lot of property on West Second Street, including five lots on which one or more of her brothels sat. Now, the madam dressed "elegantly and in fashion," and conducted herself with "poise and dignity." Her "fat wallet" was her ticket to Oklahoma City's elite financial circles that equaled the status of prominent businessmen in town.[8] She was not, however, exempt from the occasional raid or arrest. "Annie Wynn, better known as 'Big Anna,' was brought up before Judge Harper, yesterday evening, for conducting a house of ill fame," reported the *Daily Republican* in February of 1896. "She asked for a change of venue and was transferred to the district court."[9] Two months later, Annie and another woman, Kitty Nelson, were "found guilty of keeping bawdy houses" and were given the option of thirty days in a jail "or a fine of not more than $500."[10] It is highly likely that wealthy Annie opted to pay the fine.

Annie also had her share of troubles with others. In July of 1896, for instance, one C. G. Frost sued her and won, resulting in the public announcement that her properties in block 64 of Hell's Half Acre would be auctioned off the following month. Annie's attorney, J. A. Wilson, successfully intervened. Annie paid Frost $500 instead, thereby retaining ownership of her property. By 1899, the wealthy madam was well back on top, and purchased more property along 2nd Street in Hell's Half Acre. By 1900, Annie's parlor house at 422 West 2nd Street (alternatively known as Harlot's Lane) in block 36 was doing quite well. Ten bedrooms were occupied by her girls, who entertained a virtual bouquet of various men, including business and property owners, politicians, and other influential figures in Oklahoma City. Interesting is that the census taker listed Annie as a prostitute, not as a madam, landlady, proprietress, or any of the other euphemisms normally assigned to the lady of the house. Also notable is that most of Annie's employees came from her native state of Illinois. Ed Roberts, a machinist, was likely a client who was at the house the day the census was taken.

Annie Wynn's Employees in 1900

Name	Birthdate	Birthplace	Occupation
Annie Wynn	July 1865	Illinois	Prostitute
Girtie Anderson	January 1889	Illinois	Prostitute
Gracie Maxwell	May 1887	Illinois	Prostitute
Lulu Little	March 1882	Kentucky	Prostitute
Dora Goodwin	December 1887	Illinois	Prostitute
Mattie Probo	February 1867	Kentucky	Prostitute
Maggie Roberts	April 1880	Illinois	Prostitute
Viola Harris	November 1874	Illinois	Prostitute
Girtie Hodge	February 1882	Kentucky	Prostitute
Effie Fisher	March 1873	Illinois	Prostitute
Harry Anderson	October 1877	Kansas	Musician
Ed Roberts	April 1879	Illinois	Machinist

At the time of the census, Annie's only close competition was Madam Susie Fields, who had six girls working for her. On the other side of her brothel was Asher Bailey, a "speculator" whose three sons lived with him, as well as two Black servants. Annie and Bailey soon found something more in common than just being neighbors: they also were entangled in their own private love affair. Bailey likely provided some moral support for Annie when, in 1901, Oklahoma City's respectable citizens began lodging more and more complaints about the red-light district, as well as the city's willingness to permit brothels and gambling joints to remain open as long as they paid fines. But raids on these places only took place "periodically," and the fines (construed as "bribes") were minimal when compared to the income made by selling sex, and games of chance.[11] For women like Annie Wynn, control over the demimonde lay in purchasing as much property as possible for use as a brothel. The more brothels, the more money was made. The more money was made, the more fines the ladies could pay to keep officials out of their hair. With that in mind, Annie bought two more lots in block 64 in February.

With the election of county attorney Ralph Ramer in 1902, Annie's empire was soon in jeopardy. The madam now appeared in city directories as "Annie Bailey," perhaps as a means to divert attention away from her demimonde moniker. She still owned her palace of pleasure at 422 West Second Street, and had a vested interest in the Arlington. Down on the corner of West Second and Walker was "Big Anne's Place 444," which was run by the same Effie Fisher who appeared at Annie's in the 1900 census. Annie may also have owned another property in an area referred to as "Old Zulu's."[12] One of Ramer's first moves was to charge Annie with prostitution in 1903, and a temporary injunction was imposed on her brothel—because two young ladies were reportedly raped there in January of 1903.

The victims were twenty-two-year-old Annie Patt and her eighteen-year-old sister Lucy. Both were natives of Holland who had been in the United States for two years. The girls lived with their mother and step-father. Annie had learned to speak English and had secured a job at the respectable Windsor Hotel. According to Annie's testimony, when she and Lucy were invited by an uncle to have a drink at Charley's Saloon on January 26, they readily accepted. Drinking at beer gardens in Holland, said Annie, was quite common and she thought nothing of the invitation. After a few glasses of beer and wine, Annie and Lucy were walking home with their uncle when they happened to pass Annie Wynn's place. From outside, the threesome observed some people dancing; the girls' uncle suggested they go inside "and see how the Americans dance." The girls agreed, and all three went in and sat down together on a lounge.

It was not long before "Big Anne" spotted the newcomers in her par-lor. She accommodated them by bringing them small glasses of beer. But the beverage "was very bitter and tasted unusual," and before long, Annie and Lucy felt ill. When their uncle tried to escort them from the parlor house, he was himself pushed outside by several men who locked the door behind him. Then, two of the men present "dragged Lucy up stairs to her defilement," while sister Annie was taken by three other men into a downstairs room. No amount of protest and screams for help brought anyone to the aid of either girl. Later, in the early morning hours, Lucy was found "wandering about in a half-dazed condition" on the street. The policeman who spotted her said she wore no hat, that her hair was down, and that her clothing was partially unbuttoned. The girl denied she had been with any man earlier. When she described where she had been the night before, however, the officer recognized it as Big Anne's. Upon visiting there he retrieved Lucy's hat.[13]

On February 6, Lucy Patt filed a $20,000 lawsuit against Anne Wynn for damages caused her, including being drugged, wrongful imprisonment, and unlawful intercourse which caused her "shame and irreparable damage."[14] But it was soon very clear that a crime was committed, and charges were filed against Annie Wynn and those involved. Of the five collective men who commandeered Annie and Lucy to the rooms where the crimes occurred, only three—George C. Garrison, John Harmon (aka "Butterfly Kid"), and "Arkansas Kid"—were positively identified. The defendants would later deny that the girls' uncle was pushed out of the brothel or that the doors were locked, and also claimed that neither Lucy or Annie had showed any resistance as they were taken into the rooms where the rapes occurred. No screams were heard, they said. Three witnesses, identified as Jessup, Underwood, and Cassidy, testified that they also did not observe the girls resisting as they were led away. Harmon also claimed that he only followed a group of men taking Lucy upstairs as far as the first landing. Other witnesses would say that, after spending time with the men, Annie and Lucy came back to the parlor and immediately left Big Anne's brothel.

The trial of George Garrison began as authorities searched for Harmon, who fled. The case went on for months, and experienced its share of mistrials and changes of venue. One witness would claim he saw Annie Patt lying on a bed with Garrison, and Lucy lying on another bed with an unidentified man. Neither girl, he said, was unclothed and neither was resisting the men. He did testify, however, that he saw the girls arguing with Garrison a short time later, over how much money they should receive for services. The girls wanted $5; Garrison was willing to pay only $2. Countering this testimony was Lucy's explanation that she was too ashamed to tell the officer on the street what had really happened and, at the time, just wanted to go home.

As the trial dragged on through May, the authorities finally apprehended Harmon in Montana. A day later, George Garrison was convicted of raping Annie Patt. He was sentenced to ten years in prison at Lansing, Kansas. The rest of the trial continued as Annie Wynn considered her alternatives. One of them was to marry Asher Bailey, a respectable man who could speak for her, which the madam did on June 4. The very next evening, Annie and prostitute Maud Davis were in court, where the madam may have thrown about her new name as a means to give some weight as a respectable married woman. It didn't work; Annie paid a $50 fine and Maud paid $25 for contempt.

George Garrison bonded out and awaited his jail time, but the trials for Annie Wynn and John Harmon were yet to come. Legal red tape delayed their court dates until December, but before that another tragedy took place in Hell's Half Acre that shook everyone to the core: in November, Effie Fisher, who was still running Annie's place at 444 West Second Street, was murdered. An unidentified assailant had fired a single shot through the window of the house, killing Effie and slightly injuring one of her girls, identified only as "Sadie." Theories as to who killed Effie immediately flew around town: Had the wealthy woman just recently filed a will? Did her ex-husband, Ed Filson, kill her? Was she murdered for gunning for Annie Wynn's place should the madam be found guilty in the Patt case? Nobody knew, and the mystery went unsolved.

John Harmon was finally found guilty in December. Annie Wynn, however, was not. An angry citizenry now demanded that recently elected mayor Lee Van Winkle begin arresting the prostitutes and saloonkeepers of Oklahoma City. For Van Winkle it was a tough and grueling directive, seeing as many people from Hell's Half Acre had helped him get elected to begin with. But Van Winkle did do as he was told, only to be thwarted by the police department "who refused to enforce the mayor's proclamation."[15] Annie, meanwhile, relocated to another house at 507

West Second Street. When the authorities continued to harass her, she moved again in 1907, to 312 East Grand Avenue. Unfortunately, trouble only followed her.

On August 27, at two o'clock in the morning, a big fire broke out at Big Anne's Grand Avenue house. Work had been being performed in the downstairs portion, where some wood was left piled in a corner. The fire began there, and it was some time before the flames awakened the occupants upstairs. Three of Annie's employees, Lillian Raye, Vergie Wallace, and Sadie Ward, as well as Walter Ward, were trying to escape when they were overcome by smoke. All four died. Rose Jones and C. R. Clark were injured. Arson was suspected, but the coroner's jury also found bloodstains in the house. This led them to suspect that a body had been taken from the house before the fire. Later, bloody clothes were found in the possession of Annie's washerwoman, Lois Chaney. And, it turned out, Annie (now identified as Anne Miller) was seen dining at the Southern Club, when the fire broke out. Accusatory eyes were now cast in Annie's direction as newspapers demanded answers.

Annie and witnesses in the case clammed up as newspapers continued speculating about what really happened—and spreading rumors about the madam. She "has been implicated in several murders and several men have been traced to her house—only to disappear," sneered the *Daily Oklahoman*. "Big Anne is living on Main Street," the newspaper tattled a few days later, revealing that living with the madam were Rose Jones and "Commodore Clark," the two survivors from the fire.[16] Next, J. H. "Judge" Peters, Annie's Black porter, was arrested. Finally, Annie herself was arrested, jailed, and put on trial in February of 1908. This time, nobody, not even Asher Bailey, could or would help the madam. Annie's only comfort, apparently, was her pet parrot which she requested to be brought over to keep her company as she sat in her cell. The request was granted—until the bird squawked so loudly it was taken away, screeching "damn it" as it was returned to Annie's Arlington brothel.[17]

Annie's trial began in May. Central to the case was the testimony of Fannie Ritchey, a former employee, who claimed Annie and one of her customers made a deadly plan to murder one of her other patrons

The *Daily Pointer* was clearly disappointed that Annie Wynn had nothing to say about the mysterious fire at her brothel. COURTESY LIBRARY OF CONGRESS.

and dump his body in the North Canadian River snaking through town. Then, Fannie said, Annie scurried to the Southern Club for use as an alibi as Judge Peters set the fire to cover up the murder. Jurors were torn as to who to believe, but in the end, they actually sided with Annie. She was found not guilty. The trial, however, had weighed heavily upon the madam and she was said to have spent some $75,000 for her defense. With most of her wealth gone, Annie Wynn Bailey decided to throw in the towel. For the next several months, Annie sold off furniture from the Arlington as she prepared to take her leave of Oklahoma City.

In the spring of 1909, Annie finally left for Los Angeles, California. Asher Bailey accompanied her, and the 1910 census finds the couple, along with Bailey's son Jerome, living on Maple Avenue near Los Angeles's Fashion District. The couple appears to have moved around a lot over the years, and were still in Los Angeles when Asher died in 1924. As for Annie, one source claims that the retired madam, with no other person to turn to, reconciled with her ex-husband, Edwin Wynn. In the 1930 census, Wynn appears in the Fremont County, Wyoming, census with his wife Annie, who was born in Illinois, circa 1868. Wynn died in Lander in 1936; Annie followed a year later. Today she is buried under the name Annie McLoughlin Wynn in Lander's Mount Hope Cemetery.

CHAPTER TWENTY

Pauline Lambert of Tulsa

Most annals of America's historic demimondes and their women tend to stop at the end of frontier prostitution as it was known circa 1940, when the last of the ladies blew out their red lanterns for a final time. No compendium of the prostitution industry's history is complete, however, without a nod to Pauline Lambert. While she did not open the doors to her bordello until the mid-1930s, Pauline is quite notable as having worked successfully in Tulsa for some forty-three years. That's quite an amazing feat for someone who weathered Prohibition, two world wars, and a plethora of changes in attitudes toward sex to remain a staple of Tulsa's history. And, her story is quite worth the telling.

Long before Pauline set her sights on Tulsa, the city's history began in the 1870s—over thirty years after Natives of the Creek tribe were removed to the area from Georgia and Alabama. A white settler, George Perryman, established his own ranch that covered much of today's Tulsa and eventually opened a post office. By the 1880s, more and more Anglos were moving to Tulsa. Not all of them were good; numerous outlaw gangs found Tulsa a good place to cool their heels while the law looked for them elsewhere. Most unfortunate is that virtually no documentation exists to prove that these men were accompanied or entertained by any wanton women. In Tulsa, there was no land rush to pull in folks from all walks of life, either. Early histories of Tulsa cover interesting aspects of the town's growth, such as the coming of the St. Louis and San Francisco Railroad in 1882, the opening of the first school in 1884, and its incorporation as a city in 1898. But not even Sanborn Fire Insurance maps can verify there were any saloons that might have catered to working girls. The only three hotels during this time were the Tulsa, the St. Elmo, and the Hotel Allen, all quite respectable. The only "cribs" identified on these maps were those made for storing corn.

The 1898 Sanborn map does show two saloons in town, but they must have been no more than small watering holes. Not until 1900, when the population had reached some 1,390 residents, did the *Tulsa Democrat* state for the first time that a new saloon was opening. Certainly, the ears of those renegades still running around Tulsa perked up at the idea of an official place in which to quench their thirst. The idea may have attracted a few shady ladies as well, who were said to be "attracted to the smell of fresh money in a frontier town."[1] Mostly, however, Tulsa remained quiet and a bit sleepy, until oil was discovered at Red Fork in 1901. When another oil field was discovered at nearby Glenpool in 1905, city officials quickly worked to make Tulsa a shipping transfer station.

From that point on Tulsa grew like a weed, taking on the look and feel of a real live city. As oil was shipped through, the city expanded to include a jail, hospital, several hotels, and many restaurants. Plans were also made for the Tulsa Street Railway. Within a few years, Tulsa's population would balloon to over eighteen thousand residents. As the city grew, it soon became glaringly apparent that flocks and flocks of soiled doves had also flown in to take advantage of everything Tulsa had to offer. Before long, Tulsa's newspapers were full of stories regarding prostitutes, and those who supported their workforce. In January of 1907, for instance, the *Tulsa Democrat* tattled on a local democratic committeeman, Tate Brady, who was leasing a building to prostitutes. In the same article, it was reported that a man from the republican committee, Walter Reneau, was leasing the upper floor of his building to prostitutes also, and that just a few nights before, two men shot each other over a woman there.

More trouble was coming: in September, a bootlegger named Frank Glasscock, also known as "Mizzou," was shot and wounded by the member of a posse for selling illegal hooch. Most recently, the outlaw had created a disturbance at "two or three houses of prostitution." After being shot, Glasscock managed to steal a horse and buggy and remained on the lam.[2] The *Tulsa Democrat* also would report on the arrests and subsequent fines of the city's prostitutes as the newly designated state of Oklahoma outlawed both booze and prostitution. Marion Sale and Pearl Moses paid fines for violations in September. Arrest warrants were issued for Lee Robertson, Fannie Bryan, Midget Earnest, Stella Brown, and Pearl Bradley after the girls failed to show up in court during November. And in December, Mandie Linch paid a fine of $10.40 for working as a prostitute. An amazing twenty prostitutes were brought into court in January, as well. Later that month, Tulsa's *Oklahoma Critic* announced that Attorney General Charles West had come to clean up the city, and "scores of women" had been taking the next train out of town for the last day and night.[3]

The women of Tulsa's demimonde stayed gone for only about a year. By February of 1909, Mayor John Mitchell was declaring a new, all-out war against prostitution, bootlegging, and gambling. Mitchell reckoned that if the city could get rid of its gamblers, the women would follow. He also promised to increase the amounts of fines to discourage wrongdoers from continuing in their respective trades. Yet when prostitute Maud Lowe was charged with working in a brothel a month later, she was only fined $15. A December editorial in the *Tulsa Democrat* charged that clearly, not enough was being done by Tulsa authorities to rid the city of its vice.

Throughout the teens, newspapers continued reporting the names of women, and sometimes their customers, who were arrested, fined, and let loose back into the city. As usual, certain prominent businessmen, politicians, and policemen were tagged for permitting the red-light district all around East 1st Street to flourish. Local newspapers covered many incidents as between twenty and seventy-two prostitutes were fined on a monthly basis. Other incidents included luring young girls to work in brothels. Sometimes complaints were filed by the women themselves when they were assaulted or robbed. In 1913, even Police Chief Ed Yoder came under fire for "accepting money from houses of prostitution [and] has compelled a medical examination of these women once monthly and a fee has been collected for said examination."[4] But at least someone was looking after the health and well-being of Tulsa's red-light ladies.

In 1920, Tulsa's population was estimated at 72,075 souls. Vice—bootlegging, gambling, and prostitution—was now considered "extremely bad" in Tulsa. Major hotels and rooming houses now included prostitution as part of their services, where "the bell hops and porters are pimping for women and also selling booze." There was little fear of the police, who appear to have thrown up their hands in exchange for hush money and bribes. In desperation, reformers successfully solicited a "Federal Report on Vice Conditions" in 1921, wherein a special undercover agent identified only as "T. F. G." physically walked Tulsa's expansive red-light area for five days (including a weekend) in April.[5] The agent talked to several prostitutes and gave a full account on the people and brothels he observed.

Tulsa's Brothels in 1921

Address	Notes
102 N. Boulder St.	Entrance in rear. Madam "a well-built woman" with two girls, one of them about thirty years old.
322 E. 1st St. (upstairs)	Madam (possibly Bessie Phillips) was not in. Three girls, one of them about twenty-two years old.
318 ½ E. 1st St.	Madame Nell Russell and two "inmates." Dennis Warner's restaurant was on the bottom floor. That same year, Nell Russell also was at 326 ½ E. 1st Street.
320 ½ E. 1st St.	The madam "told me her girl was out, and instructed to return later and hire a room, and she would have this girl come to the room."
20 ½ [sic] E. 1st St.	One madam and one girl, aged about seventeen years old.

405 ½ E. 1st St.	Rooming house with two floors, run by Madam Maud Fleming with one girl present. Two hours after agent's visit, the house was raided for gambling and two men were shot. One later died.
E. 1st St. near Main	Empress Rooms with one madam and three girls; the madam also offered to rent a room to the agent if he brought a girl in off the street.
110 Detroit near E. 1st St. (above a livery stable)	Queen City Rooms, with a madam and five women. Only one woman there at the time, about thirty years old.
East Archer St., corner of North Boston	Forbes Hotel. No madam present, just four girls "scrubbing floors, cleaning rooms."
15 ½ N. Main St.	Central Hotel. Madam Mrs. Francis Watson and four girls, including one "heavy-set woman" named Bessie. Four men seen gambling in the hallway.
1084 E. 2nd St. (might be 108 ½ E. 2nd St.)	Wisteria Rooms. Three girls and a "colored" porter who "insists upon a fee of one dollar" in addition to the cost for a girl.
505 E. Archer St.	"Old colored woman as the madame" and four girls.
503 E. Archer St.	No madam, just two young Black girls.
420 E. Archer St.	Midway Hotel. Solicited by a "colored girl" outside the building.[6]

The brothels the agent visited charged an average price of $3, with two houses charging only $2, one house charging $4, and one other place (the once opulent Tulsa Hotel) charging $10. The agent also walked around the streets near the "Frisco depot" and observed porters from the Carlton, DeVern, and Imperial hotels openly soliciting men on the street to visit the ladies upstairs. Some of them offered to rent rooms to men with other women if there were no prostitutes available. Another twenty-four hotels offered girls that "could be ordered in for a fee." A number of women also were seen soliciting on East and West First, Second, Third, and Fourth streets, as well as North and South Main. All told, the agent observed a total of sixty-four prostitutes on the streets, in brothels, or at dance halls, and nineteen pimps in the way of Black porters or bell hops.[7]

Tulsa authorities may have better been able to digest the report by Agent "T. F. G." had an incredibly violent event not taken place that is still talked about today. On May 30, 1921, Dick Rowland and Sarah Page happened to be riding together in an elevator at the Drexel Building on Third and Main streets. Rowland was Black; Sarah was white. Within those few minutes, something occurred. Whether it was a comment, an inappropriate gesture, or assault has unfortunately been lost to history, but Rowland was arrested the following day as rumors began circulating among Tulsa's white population. The story "became more exaggerated with each telling," to the extent that an armed mob of both Blacks and whites soon surrounded the courthouse.[8]

As shots rang out to disburse the crowd, most of the Black citizens present retreated to their homes in the Greenwood District, a large and affluent Black neighborhood. But the entire area was looted and burned on June 1. Martial law was declared as the National Guard arrived and upwards of six thousand Blacks were corralled and held at Convention Hall and the Fairgrounds. As many as three-hundred people are believed to have died during the affray. Over eight hundred others were injured. Thousands more, almost all of them Black citizens, were left homeless.

It is little wonder that the vice report was overlooked during this tumultuous time, since various factions began blaming Tulsa's prostitution problems on the Greenwood District. But Agent "T. G. F.'s" report had only recorded seven Black prostitutes versus fifty-seven white prostitutes. That didn't stop a "race riot" grand jury from accusing Police Chief John Gustafson, of, among other things, neglecting his duties where the red-light district was concerned. The "political discontent" continued for years as "city officials made only weak attempts to crack down on brothels, crooked gamblers, and prostitutes."[9] Tulsa's red-light houses, meanwhile, simply continued operating as they always had. In 1926, the concentrated area of the demimonde became known as the "Blue Dome District," so-named after a fancy gas station built nearby that same year. Here, railroad and oilfield workers could visit the upper stories of various buildings containing brothels with such quaint names as the Bliss Hotel, the Dixie Rooms, and the Oklahoma Hotel. And that's the way Clara Palmer, also known as Pauline Lambert, found Tulsa when she moved to town in about 1936.

Pauline was Clara Gillian when she was born to William and Mildren Gillian on March 14, 1890, in Memphis, Tennessee. The 1900 census reflects a total of seven children at the Gillian farm, and the 1910 census verifies the family had moved to Oklahoma and was living in Henryetta. William now worked as a photographer. Clara was still living at home, but in 1911, she married her first husband, a Scottish miner named George Stenhouse. Two sons would follow: George in 1912, and John in 1914. But Clara also lived with her children at least some of the time; WWI draft records indicate Stenhouse was working at a mine in Puerto Rico during 1917. To pass the time, Clara may have taught Sunday school, a job she once claimed to have had in her younger days. Unfortunately, Stenhouse eventually left Clara, remarried, and moved to California where he died in 1962.

Quite possibly with nowhere else to turn, Clara moved in with Jimmie Palmer, a Native American who worked as an oil lease broker. There appears to be no marriage record, although Clara identified herself as Mrs. Palmer during the 1930 census. Palmer was a good choice; he made good money and owned his home. When that relationship also failed, a "railroad man" Clara knew suggested she try running a boarding house in Tulsa to make money. They say that, in addition to her own sons, Clara was trying to help a sister who also had four children. It was worth a shot.

For a couple of years, Clara bounced around Tulsa as she sought a way to fit in. At one point, she did rent seemingly legitimate "hotel beds" to businessmen coming through town, for twenty-five cents per night.[10] By 1935, however, Clara was living upstairs at 18 ½ East 1st Street under the name Pauline Lambert, the pseudonym she would use throughout her career. Although many have speculated that she had remarried to someone named Lambert, there is no documentation to prove it. All that is known for sure is that by the April 8, 1940, census, Pauline Lambert could be found at the Camel Hotel at 326 ½ E. 3rd Street—near the heart of the Blue Dome District. Ruby Farley was identified as head of the household and three other women besides Pauline, ranging in age from twenty-three to twenty-five years, lived there. Pauline, who apparently was not present at the time, was recorded as a forty-three-year-old widow—far too old to work when compared to the ages of Ruby's other girls.

Pauline actually appeared twice in the 1940 census. A second listing for her between April 10 and 11 identifies her as Clara Palmer at 320 ½ East 1st Street. This time the census gave her correct age, fifty years. Living with her were one Cenith [*sic*] Stenhouse, age twenty-five years, as well as another woman named Helen Rose, and even a maid, Edna Navarro. The documentation of Clara/Pauline under both of her known names leads to the assumption that she appears to have been working as a prostitute as early as 1935, and perhaps working as such for Ruby Farley in 1940. But she also was apparently madam of the brothel at 320 ½ East 1st Street. When her son George registered for service during WWII, he gave the latter address as that of his mother. That address also eventually became known as the May Rooms. Over time, the lady would acquire four brothels altogether, all located on the south side of the 300 block of East 1st Street. They included the May Rooms, but also "Charlotte's" and "Big Nose Ruby's."[11]

Pauline Lambert was as efficient and smart as a businesswoman in the 1940s could be. She was careful to hire eight to ten of only the best employees, many of whom came from wealthy families. At the May Rooms, a series of legitimate businesses ran downstairs, but customers wishing to access the second floor could take a narrow staircase to the upper floors. The seventh step on the staircase had a button underneath it that triggered a bell beside Pauline's rocking chair in the "sitting room" upstairs, which included couches on which her girls sat. The room remained locked, so that Pauline could choose which customers to admit and to keep herself and her girls safe from strangers and policemen. Some of her customers were just high school boys who visited the May Rooms as a "ritual of initiation." Other times, according to District Judge

Clifford Hopper, students pursuing sports were given "victory celebrations" at the May Rooms.[12] Whoever Pauline's customers were, they were said to have been given only seventeen minutes to spend time with a girl. Afterward, the men used a separate entrance to exit the building. Pauline's employees paid her 40 percent of the money they made.

Madam Pauline remained very cautious about the way she ran her brothels. If anyone in the businesses below the brothels heard of or saw police coming, Pauline received enough warning to "scatter her girls in the other adjacent hotels, connected by locked hallways or outdoor ladder bridges." If there was no time to do so, the girls simply hopped out the windows and hid behind the rooftop parapets until the coast was clear. No matter what happened, Pauline's girls remained faithful to her and enabled her to make a lot of money. A visiting relative once recalled how pretty and what a "snappy dresser" Pauline was, and also remembered seeing a bed covered in hundred-dollar bills as the madam gave a tour of the rooms.[13]

Although she spent much time at the May Rooms, Pauline also lived elsewhere as a precaution. Taxi driver Jim Wilkerson later recalled how he frequently drove the madam between her brothels and her private home in nearby Red Fork. Her sons sometimes lived with her, and Wilkerson recalled that Pauline had "a very fine family." The citizens of Red Fork, who apparently were none the wiser to what Pauline really did, liked her. "She could have passed for somebody's grandmother," Wilkerson said. He also revealed that Pauline only worked at her brothels three or four days each week, staying in a small apartment in the back of one of her buildings. Naturally, she was also a good tipper. "We'd go to Red Fork from downtown for 60 cents," Wilkerson remembered. "She was always good for a buck, maybe buck-and-a-half."[14]

During 1941, Tulsa authorities declared a "war on prostitutes," during which some two dozen bawdy houses were busted and their employees were given ten days to leave town. Pauline apparently was not on the list, but in time the madam did fall victim to the occasional raid. When that happened, she simply bonded out and continued running her bordellos while awaiting trial. The wily woman was downright difficult to catch, although she was arrested at least twice—"for playing a jukebox

Pauline Lambert as she appeared in 1952. COURTESY LIBRARY OF CONGRESS

in a house of prostitution."[15] Other times, charges were brought against her for "vagrancy" or "using the telephone to bring girls to Tulsa."[16] Once, in 1952, the madam was charged with tax evasion and was fined $3,000. And in 1958, she was also arrested for "procuring twice within four days."[17] Pauline weathered and paid all of the fines levied against her. But she also sometimes stashed bags of money at the home of her son, George Jr., who lived in West Tulsa.

For a time, the authorities left Pauline alone. But times were changing; gone were the days when prostitutes could simply bribe their way out of trouble, and when police let the ladies slide. By the 1960s, a whole new generation of vice cops and commissioners were in place, and they were determined (or ordered) to close down the bawdy houses of Tulsa once and for all. One new vice officer later recalled how he boldly informed Pauline that "There's a new sheriff in town and you're outta business." The demure, elderly madam was hardly fazed. "Sir, let me tell you this," she said in her grandmotherly voice, "I've been in business a long time and I've seen good vice squads come and go and they're gone and I'm still here." In spite of her rebuttal, the officer couldn't help admire the aged madam as "a tremendous woman." And besides, she made generous thousand-dollar donations to the family of police officers who died in the line of duty.[18]

Pauline was arrested twice more for operating a brothel during 1961. Still, the madam refused to give in. "I'm the only family these girls have," she once explained. "I can't let them go."[19] That wasn't the only reason, since Pauline was still making plenty of money at the May Rooms and easily paid the occasional fines levied against her. But the city soon became dissatisfied with Pauline's habit of paying fines and immediately resuming business, and ultimately called in the Federal Bureau of Investigation in 1969. On January 10, special agent Robert Evans Jr. appeared at Pauline's door with a search warrant and began exploring each of the six brothels Pauline owned. All were located between 314 and 328 ½ East 1st Street but only two, the May Rooms and the Dixie Rooms, were identified by signage in front of the building. Signs on the other buildings were made to appear as if more legitimate businesses were being conducted inside. The madam was indeed very discreet.

During his search, Evans also seized quite a bit of evidence. Taken during the raid were "ledgers, books, records, money, names, addresses and telephone numbers of prostitutes, financial records concerning prostitution activities, and telephone records." These were enough, Evans reasoned, to implicate Madam Pauline so justice could be served. But not until September was Pauline even arrested and she immediately posted bond in the amount of $2,000. At her court appearance with her attorney, Ed Goodwin, Pauline initially pleaded not guilty but later changed it to "nolo contendere." In the end, she was fined $1,500 and received two years' probation, but the latter was rescinded just a year later.[20]

For several more years, Pauline remained a burr under the saddle of law enforcement officers. Although prostitution remained illegal, the madam ran a clean and discreet business. Once, in 1971, she even willingly turned in "Dixie Mafia" member Tom Lester Pugh for paying for services with counterfeit bills, and was likely satisfied when the man was sentenced to prison for killing a witness on the grand jury. She also summoned police when an irate customer tried to assault one of her girls. In the latter case, police officer Joe Lester answered the call, and it was he who would eventually see that Pauline was shut down for good.

The year was 1975. Lester was now working undercover and tried to gain access to Pauline's with a fake driver's license, telling her he was looking for "the chicks." But Pauline remembered the man from five years before. "This isn't your name," she said bluntly, "you are with [Tulsa Police Department], and this isn't a henhouse; we don't have any chicks." The defeated Lester posted himself outside instead, and when he saw two elderly customers leave, questioned them to learn the name of the girl they had been with. Using her name, Lester tried to access Pauline's place again with the story that "his daddy sent him." Pauline apparently wasn't present, for this time he gained entrance, was quoted a price, and was able to procure an injunction against Pauline. "Why are you doing this to me?" an exasperated Pauline asked Lester. "I'm only charging $15."[21]

In spite of his determination to close Pauline down, Lester seemed fond of the madam. He later described her to others as a "remarkable, sweet, friendly woman whose appearance belied her profession," who appeared "just like anyone's grandma."[22] But Lester had a job to do, and he was determined to do it. In 1977, another sting was set up to trap Pauline. This time, Officer Janice Beeler called Pauline and posed as a prostitute looking for work. She was told to come to the May Rooms. Beeler arrived wearing a wire, and two detectives outside listened as the job was described, as well as the pay, and Beeler was assigned to a room. Soon after, a client was sent to the officer and "made sexual advances toward her and paid her $15." Beeler then made an excuse to step out, and quickly let the detectives in. Pauline was again arrested, her money confiscated, and she was convicted in court—but with the option to apply for a suspended sentence.[23]

The year 1978 was equally tough for Pauline. In January, her oldest son, George Jr., died at the young age of sixty-six years. His death, no doubt, was hard on Pauline. Countering her grief was an adoring public, who soon learned about Pauline's plight with authorities. Not everyone was happy about it. In 1978, Frances Leach, a "wealthy widow," stepped forward to pay for the madam's lawyers. "She probably has saved more marriages than any minister in Tulsa," Leach declared. Indeed, folks felt sorry for the elderly madam. As for Pauline, she at last decided to set the record straight as she awaited her trial by granting an interview with Mary Hargrove of the *Tulsa Tribune* in June. Pauline talked of her days as a Sunday School teacher and gave an accounting of "her glory days when she had six to eight full-time 'girls.'" She also had something to say about the type of business she ran. "I've had girls here, I don't deny it," she said, "but there has never been a report of venereal disease to come out of the May Rooms, and I'm proud of that. My girls go to the doctor all the time."[24]

Pauline's family would later claim the lady "never drank, smoked, or used coarse language." But if the madam garnered any additional public sympathy from her interview in the *Tulsa Tribune*, it was largely overshadowed by the outcome of her trial. This time, she was convicted for pandering, a felony in Tulsa.[25] She was sentenced to three years in prison, but notably the eighty-eight-year-old madam now used a wheelchair to get around. And, it was no secret that even the judges who saw her in their court called her "a living legend."[26]

In the end, Pauline was never sent to prison. She was, however, finally shut down for good when Joe Lester procured a court order to do so in February of 1979. With her empire closed forever, people got on with their lives and seemed to forget about Tulsa's longest-running madam who had provided some local color for the city for decades. And when Pauline checked herself into a nursing home soon after closing, she did so under her old name, Clara Palmer. By then, nobody remembered that the esteemed madam was once a single mother who originally moved to Tulsa in an effort to support her children. When she died on October 31, nobody recognized Clara Palmer's obituary in the *Tulsa World*.[27]

In the years after Pauline's death, her court case continued to surface in court records now and then. The first time was in April of 1980, when it was argued that the madam "had suffered enough by losing her home and business." In that instance, the presiding judge delayed her sentence to prison "indefinitely."[28] The second time was in December of 1983, when the 1980 appeal expired and a bondsman was ordered to produce the madam in court. It would take many months of searching for her before it was discovered that Pauline had given the authorities the ultimate slip by quietly dying. Judge Graham, who had presided over Pauline's many court cases over the years, likely smirked a bit when he assured the court that she definitely would not be "running a bordello anymore."[29] At last, Madam Pauline Lambert had triumphed over those who would suppress her.

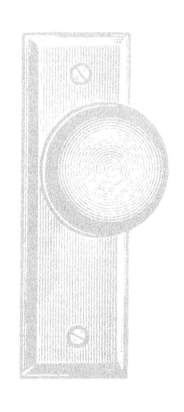

Selected Bibliography

Books

Agnew, Jeremy. *Brides of the Multitude: Prostitution in the Old West.* Lake City, CO: Western Reflections Publishing Company, 2008.

Bloomfield, Susanne George, ed. *Impertinences: Selected Writings of Elia Peattie, a Journalist in the Gilded Age.* Lincoln, NE, and London: University of Nebraska Press, 2005.

Boyer, Glenn G., ed. *I Married Wyatt Earp: The Recollections of Josephine Sarah Marcus Earp.* Tucson, AZ: University of Arizona Press, second printing, 1979.

Bristow, David. *A Dirty, Wicked Town: Tales of 19th Century Omaha.* Caldwell, ID: Caxton Press, 2000.

Buechler, A. F., and R. J. Barr, eds. *History of Hall County, Nebraska.* Lincoln, NE: Western Publishing and Engraving Company, 1920.

Butler, Anne M. *Daughters of Joy, Sisters of Misery: Prostitutes in the American West 1865–90.* Urbana and Chicago: University of Illinois Press, Illini Books Edition 1987.

Cobbey's Annotated Statutes of Nebraska, Vol. II. Beatrice, NE: J. E. Cobbey, 1907 edition.

Colcord, Charles F. *The Autobiography of Charles Francis Colcord.* Tulsa, OK: C.C. Helmerich, 1970.

Coleman, Ruby. *The Wild Years 1868–1951: North Platte and Lincoln County, Nebraska.* North Platte, NE: Ruby Coleman, 2020.

Collins, Jan MacKell. *Good Time Girls of Arizona and New Mexico: A Red-Light History of the American Southwest.* Lanham, MD: TwoDot, A division of Rowman & Littlefield Publishing Group, 2019.

———. *Good Time Girls of California: A Red-Light History of the Golden State.* Lanham, MD: TwoDot, A division of Rowman & Littlefield Publishing Group, 2021.

———. *Good Time Girls of Colorado: A Red-Light History of the Centennial State.* Lanham, MD: TwoDot, A division of Rowman & Littlefield Publishing Group, 2019.

———. *Good Time Girls of the Rocky Mountains: A Red-Light History of Montana, Idaho, and Wyoming.* Lanham, MD: TwoDot, A division of Rowman & Littlefield Publishing Group, 2020.

Cook, Rod. *George and Maggie and the Red Light Saloon: Depravation, Debauchery, Violence and Sundry Cussedness in a Kansas Cowtown.* Lincoln, NE: iUniverse, Inc., 2003.

Directory of Colorado Springs, Colorado City and Manitou for 1892. Colorado Springs, CO: The Republic Publishing Company, 1892.

Dodge, Fred, and Carolyn Lake, *Under Cover for Wells Fargo: The Unvarnished Recollections of Fred Dodge.* Norman: University of Oklahoma Press, 1999.

Drago, Harry Sinclair. *Notorious Ladies of the Frontier.* New York: Ballantine Books, 1969.

Dykstra, Robert. *The Cattle Towns: A Social History of the Kansas Cattle Trading Centers Abilene, Ellsworth, Wichita, Dodge City and Caldwell, 1867–1885.* New York: Atheneum, 1970.

Enss, Chris. *According to Kate: The Legendary Life of Big Nose Kate, Love of Doc Holliday.* Lanham, MD: TwoDot, A division of Rowman & Littlefield Publishing Group, 2019.

Erdoes, Richard. *Saloons of the Old West.* Avenel, NJ: Gramercy Books, a division of Random House Value Publishing, 1979.

Franzwa, Gregory M. *Maps of the Oregon Trail.* Gerald, MO: The Patrice Press, 1982.

Griep, Mark A. *124 South 9th Street Through the Decades: Sporting, Savings Souls, and Making Culture.* Nebraska: no pub., 1998.

Gulliford, Andrew, ed. *Preserving Western History.* Albuquerque: University of New Mexico Press, 2005.

Hightower, Michael J. *Banking in Oklahoma Before Statehood.* Norman, OK: University of Oklahoma Press, 2013.

Jones, Schuyler, ed. *Hunting and Trading on the Great Plains 1859–1875.* Norman: University of Oklahoma Press, 1986.

Keire, Mara L. *For Business & Pleasure: Red-Light Districts and the Regulation of Vice in the United States, 1890–1933.* Baltimore, MD: The Johns Hopkins University Press, 2010.

Kelsey, D. M. *Our Pioneer Heroes and Their Daring Deeds.* Philadelphia: G. O. Pelton, 1883.

Kirschner, Ann. *Lady at the O.K. Corral: The True Story of Josephine Marcus Earp.* New York: HarperCollins, 2013.

Larsen, Lawrence Harold. *The Gate City: A History of Omaha.* Lincoln, NE: University of Nebraska Press, 1997.

Lee, Wayne C. *Wild Towns of Nebraska.* Caldwell, ID: The Caxton Press, 2008.

Lindsay, Arthur. *It Takes a Home: Commemorating 90 Years of Service by Peoples Mission.* Nebraska: Cross Training Publishing, 1997.

MacKell, Jan. *Brothels, Bordellos & Bad Girls: Prostitution in Colorado, 1860–1930.* Albuquerque, NM: University of New Mexico Press, 2003.

———. *Red Light Women of the Rocky Mountains.* Albuquerque: University of New Mexico Press, 2009.

Mackey, Thomas C. *Red Lights Out: A Legal History of Prostitution, Disorderly Houses, and Vice Districts, 1870–1917.* Houston, TX: Rice University Press, 1984.

Marks, Paula Mitchell. *And Die in the West: The Story of O.K. Corral Gunfight.* Norman: University of Oklahoma Press, 1989 [1996].

Martin, George W., ed. *Transactions of the Kansas State Historical Society, 1905–1906*, vol. 9. Topeka, KS: State Printing Office, 1906.

McCoy, Tanya, and Jeff Provine. *Haunted Guthrie, Oklahoma*. Charleston, SC: The History Press, 2015.

Meyers, E. C. (Ted), *Mattie: Wyatt Earp's Secret Second Wife*. Blaine, WA: Hancock House Publishers, 2010.

Monahan, Sherry. *Mrs. Earp: The Wives and Lovers of the Earp Brothers*. Lanham, MD: TwoDot, A division of Rowman & Littlefield Publishing Group, 2013.

Morris, John W. *Ghost Towns of Oklahoma*. Norman, OK: University of Oklahoma Press, 1978.

Moynahan, Jay. *Culinary Delights from the Red Lights: Recipes from the Bordellos and Backstreets of the Frontier West*. Spokane, WA: Chickadee Publishing, 1999.

———. *Forty Fallen Women: Western Doves and Madams, 1885–1920*. Spokane, WA: Chickadee Publishing, 2008.

Oklahoma Reports: Cases Determined in the Supreme Court of the State of Oklahoma, vol. 15. Ann Arbor, MI: Harlow Publishing Company, 1906.

Oneill, Therese. *Unmentionable: The Victorian Lady's Guide to Sex, Marriage, and Manners*. New York, Boston, and London: Little, Brown and Company, 2016.

Reonigk, Adolph, ed. *Pioneer History of Kansas*. Lincoln, KS: A. Reonigk, 1933.

Roenfield, Ryan. *Wicked Omaha*. Charleston, SC: The History Press, 2017.

Rosen, Ruth. *The Lost Sisterhood: Prostitution in America, 1900–1918*. Baltimore, MD: The Johns Hopkins University Press, 1982.

Sawyer, A. J., ed. *Lincoln the Capital City and Lancaster County: The Incarceration of the Lincoln City Council*. Chicago: The S. J. Clarke Publishing Co., 1916.

Shellum, Brian G. *Black Officer in a Buffalo Soldier Regiment: The Military Career of Charles Young*. London and Lincoln, NE: University of Nebraska Press, 2010.

Stratton, Joanna L. *Pioneer Women: Voices from the Kansas Frontier*. New York: Touch-stone Books, 1982.

Tefertiller, Casey. *Wyatt Earp: The Life Behind the Legend*. New York: John Wiley & Sons, 1997.

Washburn, Josie, and Sharon E. Wood. *The Underworld Sewer: A Prostitute Reflects on Life in the Trade, 1871–1909*. Lincoln and London: University of Nebraska Press, 1997.

Waters, Frank. *The Earp Brothers of Tombstone*. Lincoln and London, University of Nebraska Press, Bison Books, 1976 edition.

Wiles, Gary, and Delores Brown. *Femme Fatales, Gamblers, Yankees and Rebels in the Goldfields*. Hemet, CA: Birth of America Books, 2005.

Woods, Pendleton. *Historic Oklahoma County: An Illustrated History*. San Antonio, TX: Historical Publishing Network, 2007.

Documents

"Burials in Evergreen Cemetery, Colorado Springs." Pikes Peak Library District Special Collections, Colorado Springs, Colorado.

"City of Colorado Springs Death Register, 1894 and 1895." Pikes Peak Library District Special Collections, Colorado Springs, Colorado.

INTERNET

"1921 Tulsa Race Massacre." Tulsa Historical Society and Museum. tulsahistory.org/ exhibit/1921-tulsa-race-massacre/.

"A Call to Action: The Past and Future of Historical Archaeology, Conference Abstracts." Society for Historical Archaeology, January 2016. sha.org/wp-content/ uploads/2015/05/Abstract-Book-Final-10116.pdf.

Ancestry.com.

AncientFaces.com.

Anderson, Ethan, "Femme Fatales of the Frontier." *Kansas Memory Blog*. kansasmemory .org/blog/post/358280567.

"Annie Cook's Poor House." Seeks Ghosts, March 25, 2016. seeksghosts.blogspot .com/2016/03/annie-cooks-poor-house.html.

Aron, Nina Renata. "Meet the Sisters Who Ran 'the Most Famous and Luxurious House of Prostitution in the Country.'" *Timeline*, April 16, 2017. timeline.com/ meet-the-sisters-who-ran-the-most-famous-and-luxurious-house-of-prostitution -in-the-country-b2fc0a0d414c.

"Bartell Place." Homestead Kansas, homesteadks.org/bartell-pl-junction-city2.html.

Barton County Chamber of Commerce. "Future Home of The Wyatt Earp Park." bar-toncounty.com/wyatt-earp-park//.

Bureau of Land Management. General Land Office Records. glorecords.blm.gov.

Burton, Laura M. "Ardmore Gas Explosion." Encyclopedia of Oklahoma History and Culture, Wayback Machine. web.archive.org/web/20140630194522/http:/digital .library.okstate.edu/encyclopedia/entries/A/AR009.html.

Campbell, Denel. "Gambling and Prostitution." denelecampbell.com/2017/11/01/ gambling-and-prostitution/.

Cantrell, Charles. "Tulsa Night Life Is Turning Blue and Green." GTR Media Group, 2019. gtrnews.com/tulsa-night-life-is-turning-blue-and-green/.

Carlson, I. Marc. "The Tulsa Race Massacre." May 28, 2014. tulsaraceriot.wordpress .com/tag/brothel/.

Correa, Tom. "Wyatt Earp—The Peoria Bummer." *American Cowboy Chronicles*, August 11, 2016. americancowboychronicles.com/2016/08/wyatt-earp-peoria-bummer .html.

"Crawford." Crawford Historical Society, Crawford, Nebraska. crawfordmuseum.org/ community/.

Criminal Docket, US District Court. "The United States vs Clara Pauline Lambert Palmer." September 1969. oknd.uscourts.gov/sites/default/files/oknd/paper_dock-ets/69cr0112.pdf.

"Dawes Act (1887)." National Archives and Records Administration. ourdocuments .gov.

Dawes, Marta. "Prospect Hill." web.archive.org/web/20130217090426/http://www .steveandmarta.com/graveyards/prospect_hill/prospect_anna_wilson.htm.

"Dennison's Political Machine." Nebraskastudies.org. nebraskastudies.org/en/1900 -1924/racial-tensions/dennisons-political-machine/.

"Department History." Dodge City. dodgecity.org/420/Department-History.

Diffendal, Anne P. "Prostitution in Grand Island, Nebraska, 1870–1913." *Diffendal* 16, no. 3. hdl.handle.net/123456789/767.

Edgar, Joshua. "Scratching the Itch: The Role of Venereal Disease during the Settling of the American Frontier." krex.k-state.edu.

FamilySearch.org.

Farris, David. "Big Anne Wynn and Hell's Half Acre." *Edmond Life and Leisure.* edmondlifeandleisure.com/big-anne-wynn-and-hells-halfacre-p12171-76.htm.

Findagrave.com.

"Founding of Omaha Subject of NET Television's 'Omaha's First Families.'" web .archive.org/web/20070928020439/http:/mynptv.org/nptv/first_families_preview _page.html.

Fox, Courtney. "Wyatt Earp: The Wild West Icon Served as a Consultant on Early Western Films." *Wide Open Country.* wideopencountry.com/wyatt-earp/.

Gunderson, Erica. "Historical Happy Hour: A Toast to the Ever-leigh Sisters." WTTW, July 28, 2017. news.wttw.com/2017/07/28/ historical-happy-hour-toast-everleigh-sisters.

Guthrie, Oklahoma. *1890 Oklahoma Territory Directory.* Logan County (OK) Researchers Home Page. usgennet.org/usa/ok/county/logan/dir/1890guthrie.htm.

Hancock, Joseph. "Thompson, William (Billy)." *Handbook of Texas.* Texas State Historical Association. tshaonline.org/handbook/entries/thompson-william-billy.

Historical Marker Database. hmdb.org.

"Historical Population of the 25 Largest Cities in Kansas." kslib.info/DocumentCenter/ View/1180/City-Populations-1860-2012?bidId=.

History.com.

History Nebraska. history.nebraska.gov.

HistoryNet.com.

"History of Ardmore, Oklahoma." US History. u-s-history.com/pages/h2398.html.

"History of Guthrie." Greater Guthrie Chamber of Commerce. guthriechamber.com.

"History Timeline." Deadwood, South Dakota. deadwood.com/history/ history-timeline/.

Huck, Terri J. "Mattie Blaylock Earp: Hidden from History." terrijhuck.com.

"Important Oklahoma Land Rush Archive—Prostitutes Saved Dad's Life Opening Day." Worthpoint. worthpoint.com/worthopedia/important-oklahoma-land-rush -archive-18505186.

"James H. Kelley." Military Wiki. military.wikia.org/wiki/James_H._Kelley.

"Junction City, Kansas." Legends of Kansas. legendsofkansas.com/junction-city-kansas/.

Kansas State Historical Society. kshs.org.

"Kirkwood Brothel." City of Lincoln, Nebraska Planning Department. app.lincoln.ne .gov/city/plan/long/hp/sites/sitestemplate.htm?site=kirkwood.

"Lambert v. State, Oklahoma Court of Appeals." Case Number F-79-09, 1980. Justia US Law. law.justia.com/cases/oklahoma/court-of-appeals-criminal/1980/5410. html.

"The Lawmen of Dodge City and Ford County, Kansas." Ford County Historical Society. kansashistory.us/fordco/lawmen.html.

Legends of America. legendsofamerica.com.

"The Life of Wyatt Earp." American Experience, PBS. pbs.org/wgbh/americanexperi ence/features/wyatt-earp-life/.

"Lincoln: The New Capital." Historic Haymarket, lincolnhaymarket.org.

"Mike Meagher." Cowley County Historical Society Museum. cchsm.com/resources/ misc/wortman_cc/meagher_mike.html.

National Register of Historic Places. nps.gov/subjects/nationalregister/index.htm.

Nipper, Clara. "Sex in the City." *This Land Press*, October 8, 2011. thislandpress .com/2011/10/08/sex-in-the-city/.

Oklahoma Historical Society, okhistory.org.

"Oklahoma's Most Haunted City Ghost Stories from Guthrie." Wander Wisdom. https://wanderwisdom.com/travel-destinations/ Oklahomas-Most-Haunted-City-Ghost-Stories-from-Guthrie.

Peterson, Lindsey, "Trolley Takes Omahans on 'Gritty City' Stroll." KVNO News, August 9, 2011. olliethetrolley.com/trolley-takes-omahans-on-gritty-city-stroll.

"The Pioneer Spirit." City of Grand Island. grand-island.com/community/ the-pioneer-spirit.

"Publishing History of Newspapers in Nebraska." Nebraska Newspapers. nebnewspa pers.unl.edu/publishing.

"'Queen of the Underworld' Anna Wilson." scribd.com/document/13273842/Queen -of-the-Underworld-Anna-Wilson.

"Richardson County." Nebraska Archives Records, 1855–1979. history.nebraska.gov/ sites/history.nebraska.gov/files/doc/Richardson%20County%20%5BRG245%5D .pdf.

Roberts, Gary L. "Allie's Story: Mrs. Virgil Earp and the 'Tombstone Travesty.'" web .archive.org/web/20160307033040/http://home.earthlink.net/~knuthco1/Trav esty/AlliesStory1source.htm.

"Roxana." Exploring Oklahoma History. blogoklahoma.us/place.aspx?id=266.

"Rushes to Statehood: The Oklahoma Land Runs." Explore the West, National Cowboy Museum. nationalcowboymuseum.org/explore/rushes-statehood -oklahoma-land-runs/.

Rouse, Stephanie. "An Update of the 1984 Haymarket Redevelopment Plan: Lincoln, Nebraska." *Community and Regional Planning Program: Professional Projects* 5 (2012). digitalcommons.unl.edu/arch_crp_profproj/5.

Sanborn Fire Insurance Maps, Library of Congress. loc.gov/collections/sanborn-maps.

Sasse, Adam Fletcher. "A History of Anna Wilson's Mansion in North Omaha." North Omaha History. northomahahistory.com/2016/10/06/north-omaha-mansion-13 -anna-wilsons-home/.

"South Sioux City." City-Data. city-data.com/city/South-Sioux-City-Nebraska.html.

Strike, Karen. "The Indomitable Goldie Williams: The Life and Times of a Defiant Prostitute (1898)." *Flashbak*, October 8, 2019. flashbak.com/the-indomitable-goldie-williams-the-life-and-times-of-a-defiant-prostitute-1898-419879/.

"Sumner County." Sumner County, Kansas. ks-sumner.publicaccessnow.com/AboutSumnerCounty/CountyHistory/RailroadHistory.

"Supreme Court of Oklahoma." Uplaw. webcache.googleusercontent.com/search?q=cache:9SwpoqU6T9wJ:https://uplaw.us/search%3Fkeywords%3Dappealed%26resource_type%3Dsupreme_court_of_oklahoma%26sort%3Dscore_asc+&cd=1&hl=en&ct=clnk&gl=us.

Thomas, Leah M. "Ada Everleigh (1864–1960)." *Dictionary of Virginia Biography*, Library of Virginia (1998–), published 2015. lva.virginia.gov/public/dvb/bio.asp?b=Everleigh_Ada.

Tulsa TV Memories. tulsatvmemories.com/mayrooms.html.

Wertz, Joe. "Hell's Half Acre" (courtesy of the Gazette and Tierco Media), OKC History. okchistory.com.

Women's Cultures. "The Great Sheedy Murder Trial and the Booster Ethos of Lincoln County, Nebraska." Gilded Age Plains City. gildedage.unl.edu/narrative/topics.php?q=women.

"Wyatt Earp Biographical Notes." Wandering Lizard History. web.archive.org/web/20110927225659/http://www.inn-california.com/articles/biographic/earp1.html.

NEWSPAPERS

Arizona:
Arizona Daily Star
Globe Arizona Silver Belt
Tombstone Weekly Epitaph
Weekly Arizona Citizen

California:
Los Angeles Mirror
Oakland Tribune
Sacramento Record-Union

Colorado:
Aspen Daily Leader
Aspen Tribune
Colorado City Iris
Denver Daily Times
Glenwood Springs Avalanche
Pueblo Chieftain
Rocky Mountain News

Georgia:
Savannah Morning News

Illinois:
Chicago Chronicle
Chicago Inter Ocean
Chicago Tribune

Kansas:
Abilene Chronicle
Atchison Champion
Atchison Daily Champion
Caldwell Advance
Caldwell Commercial
Caldwell Post
Dodge City Daily Globe
Dodge City Globe
Dodge City Times
Ellis County Star
Ellsworth Reporter

Ford County Globe
Galena Sentinel
Hays City Sentinel
Junction City Daily Union
Junction City Tribune
Junction City Weekly Union
Kansas Farmer and Mail and Breeze
Leavenworth Times
Ottawa Herald
Tombstone Weekly Epitaph
Topeka Commonwealth
Topeka State Journal
Weekly Kansas State Journal
Wichita Arrow
Wichita Beacon
Wichita City Eagle
Wichita Daily Eagle
Wichita Eagle
Wichita Herald
Wichita Weekly Eagle

Louisiana:
Tensas Gazette

Missouri:
Carthage Banner

Nebraska:
American Omaha
Chadron Democrat
Columbus Journal
Custer County Republican
Dakota County Record
Falls City Daily News
Gothenburg Independent
Grand Island Daily Independent
Grand Island Evening Times
Hershey Times
Lincoln County Tribune
Lincoln Evening Call
Lincoln Evening News
Lincoln Journal Star
Lincoln Nebraska State Journal
McCook Gazette
McCook Tribune

Nebraska City People's Press
North Nebraska Eagle
North Platte Daily Bulletin
North Platte Daily Telegraph
North Platte Daily Transcript
North Platte Semi-Weekly Tribune
North Platte Telegraph
Omaha Daily Bee
Omaha World Herald
O'Neill City Frontier
Platte Valley Democrat
Red Cloud Chief
South Sioux City Press
Stanton Register
Valentine Democrat

North Dakota:
Jamestown Weekly Alert

Oklahoma:
Ardmore Alliance Courier
Ardmore Chickasaw Chieftain
Cordell Herald-Sentinel
Daily Ardmoreite
Daily Oklahoman
Daily Republican
Enid Daily Enterprise
Guthrie Daily Leader
Guthrie Daily News
Guthrie Southwest World
Kingfisher Free Press
Morning Tulsa Daily World
Muskogee Phoenix
Muskogee Phoenix News
Oklahoma City Daily Law Journal-Record
Oklahoma City Evening Gazette
Oklahoma City Times
Oklahoma City Weekly Times-Journal
Oklahoma Critic
Oklahoma Daily Times Journal
Oklahoma Post
Oklahoma News
Oklahoma State
Oklahoma State Capital
Oklahoma Times

Perry Evening Democrat
Perry Morning Sentinel
Pond Creek Tribune
Purcell Register
Tahlequah Telephone
Tulsa Daily Democrat
Tulsa Daily Legal News
Tulsa Daily World
Tulsa Democrat
Tulsa Post
Tulsa Tribune
Tulsa World

South Dakota:
Black Hills Daily Times

Black Hills Weekly Times
Daily Deadwood Pioneer-Times

Texas:
American Statesman
Brenham Weekly Banner
San Antonio Light
Weekly Democratic Statesman

Virginia:
Greene County Record

Wyoming:
Cheyenne Daily Leader

PAMPHLETS

North Platte Library Association. Cemetery Tour brochure, vol. 12, September 2018.
North Platte Public Library Foundation. "The Dirty Thirties Cemetery Tour" booklet, June 2010.
North Platte Public Library. "The Movers and Shakers of Little Chicago," 2008 Cemetery Tour.
"US Public Health Service" pamphlet. Washington DC: Government Printing Office, 1921.

PAPERS

Jeffries, John B. "An Early History of Junction City, Kansas: The First Generation." Master's Thesis, Oklahoma State University, 1963.
Luckett, Matthew S. "Honor among Thieves: Horse Stealing, State-Building, and Culture in Lincoln County, Nebraska, 1860–1890." Dissertation, University of California, Los Angeles, 1914.
Munns, Anna Marie. "Money and Ill Fame: Interpreting a Prostitution Hierarchy in Fargo, North Dakota's Historic Red-Light District." North Dakota State University of Agriculture and Applied Science, November 2017.
Simmons-Rogers, Alexandra L. "Red Light Ladies: Settlement Patterns and Material Culture on the Frontier." Oregon State University, October 28, 1983.
Smith, Jessica K. "Morality and Money: A Look at How the Respectable Community Battled the Sporting Community Over Prostitution in Kansas Cowtowns, 1867–1885." Kansas State University, 2013.
Wolters, Rachel. "Vice and Race: Segregation in Kansas Cattle Towns." Southern Illinois University, Carbondale, May 2013.

PERIODICALS
Chronicles of Oklahoma
Kansas Historical Quarterly
Kansas History
Kansas History: A Journal of the Central Plains
Montana: The Magazine of Western History
Nebraska History
Oklahoma Magazine
Omaha Magazine
Real West
South Dakota History
True West
University of Nebraska Studies in Language, Literature and Criticism
Variety
Women's Rights Law Reporter
Yale Journal of Law & the Humanities

NOTES

INTRODUCTION

1. Elliott West, "Scarlet West: The Oldest Profession in the Trans-Mississippi West," *Montana: The Magazine of Western History*, Spring 1981, 17–18.

2. Therese Oneill, *Unmentionable: The Victorian Lady's Guide to Sex, Marriage, and Manners* (New York, Boston, and London: Little, Brown and Company, 2016), 178–82; Jan MacKell, *Brothels, Bordellos & Bad Girls: Prostitution in Colorado, 1860–1930* (Albuquerque, NM: University of New Mexico Press, 2003), 33–34, 41.

3. Anna Marie Munns, "Money and Ill Fame: Interpreting a Prostitution Hierarchy in Fargo, North Dakota's Historic Red-Light District," North Dakota State University of Agriculture and Applied Science, November 2017, 23.

4. West, "Scarlet West," 18.

5. Rachel Wolters, "Vice and Race: Segregation in Kansas Cattle Towns," Southern Illinois University, Carbondale, May 2013, 23–24.

6. *Pond Creek Tribune* (Oklahoma), December 5, 1893, 2.

7. Josie Washburn and Sharon E. Wood, *The Underworld Sewer: A Prostitute Reflects on Life in the Trade, 1871–1909* (Lincoln and London: University of Nebraska Press, 1997), 7, 9, 15–16, 18.

8. Jay Moynahan, *Forty Fallen Women: Western Doves and Madams, 1885–1920* (Spokane, WA: Chickadee Publishing, 2008), 55; Jan MacKell Collins, *Good Time Girls of California: A Red-Light History of the Golden State* (Lanham, MD: Rowman & Littlefield Publishing Group, 2021), 113, 174; West, "Scarlet West," 26.

9. Ruth Rosen, *The Lost Sisterhood: Prostitution in America, 1900–1918* (Baltimore, MD: The Johns Hopkins University Press, 1982), 146.

10. Ellinwood Underground Tunnel Tour, author visit, September 2015.

11. North Platte Nebraska Public Library, "The Movers and Shakers of Little Chicago," 2008 Cemetery Tour, 15.

12. Ellinwood Underground Tunnel Tour.

13. Society for Historical Archaeology, "A Call to Action: The Past and Future of Historical Archaeology, Conference Abstracts," January 2016, https://sha.org/wp-content/uploads/2015/05/Abstract-Book-Final-10116.pdf, accessed August 2, 2021.

CHAPTER 1

1. Schuyler Jones, ed., *Hunting and Trading on the Great Plains 1859–1875* (Norman, OK: University of Oklahoma Press, 1986), 68.

2. Rachel Wolters, "Vice and Race: Segregation in Kansas Cattle Towns," Southern Illinois University, Carbondale, May 2013, 5–6.

3. Robert Dykstra, *The Cattle Towns: A Social History of the Kansas Cattle Trading Centers Abilene, Ellsworth, Wichita, Dodge City and Caldwell, 1867–1885* (New York: Atheneum, 1970), 260.

4. Dykstra, *The Cattle Towns*, 260–61.

5. Gary L. Cunningham, "Gambling in the Kansas Cattle Towns: A Prominent and Somewhat Honorable Profession." *Kansas History: A Journal of the Central Plains*, Spring 1982, 7.

6. Theophilus Little, "Early Days of Abilene and Dickinson County: Reminiscence of the Long Horn Days of Abilene," in *Pioneer History of Kansas*, edited by Adolph Roenigk (Lincoln, KS: A. Roenigk, 1933), 38.

7. Jessica K. Smith, "Morality and Money: A Look at How the Respectable Community Battled the Sporting Community Over Prostitution in Kansas Cowtowns, 1867–1885," Kansas State University, 2013, 16.

8. Wolters, "Vice and Race," 5–6.

9. Little, "Early Days of Abilene and Dickinson County," 38.

10. Jeremy Agnew, *Brides of the Multitude: Prostitution in the Old West* (Lake City, CO: Western Reflections Publishing Company, 2008), 163–64.

11. Carol Leonard and Isidor Wallimann, "Prostitution and Changing Morality in the Frontier Cattle Towns of Kansas," *Kansas History*, Spring 1979, 42, 44.

12. Smith, "Morality and Money," 53.

13. Leonard and Wallimann, "Prostitution and Changing Morality," 40.

14. Agnew, *Brides of the Multitude*, 165.

15. Rod Cook, *George and Maggie and the Red Light Saloon: Depravation, Debauchery, Violence and Sundry Cussedness in a Kansas Cowtown* (Lincoln, NE: iUniverse, Inc., 2003), 77.

16. *Ellsworth Reporter*, September 4, 1873, 3.

17. George Hart, "Hays City 'Under the Guardian Care' of Wild Bill," *Real West* magazine, April 1971, 27.

18. Joanna L. Stratton, *Pioneer Women: Voices from the Kansas Frontier* (New York: Touchstone Books, 1982), 191–92.

19. "No Man's Land," Oklahoma History Center, www.okhistory.org/publications/enc/entry.pho?entry=NO001, accessed September 3, 2021.

20. *Kansas Farmer and Mail and Breeze*, September 24, 1897, 11.

21. *Kansas Farmer and Mail and Breeze*, September 24, 1897, 11.

22. Kansas Historical Society, Kansas Council of Women Records, https://www.kshs.org/archives/40739, accessed September 1, 2021.

23. Ruth Rosen, *The Lost Sisterhood: Prostitution in America, 1900–1918* (Baltimore and London: The Johns Hopkins University Press, 1982), 146.

24. Joshua Edgar, "Scratching the Itch: The Role of Venereal Disease during the Settling of the American Frontier," 20–22, https://krex.k-state.edu/dspace/bitstream/handle/2097/38166/HIST586_Finalcopy_Revised.pdf?sequence=1&isAllowed=y, accessed September 1, 2021.

25. Edgar, "Scratching the Itch," 18–21.

CHAPTER 2

1. Robert Dykstra, *The Cattle Towns: A Social History of the Kansas Cattle Trading Centers Abilene, Ellsworth, Wichita, Dodge City and Caldwell, 1867–1885* (New York: Atheneum, 1970), 105.

2. Rachel Wolters, "Vice and Race: Segregation in Kansas Cattle Towns," Southern Illinois University, Carbondale, May 2013, 7.

3. Wolters, "Vice and Race," 25.

4. Carol Leonard and Isidor Wallimann, "Prostitution and Changing Morality in the Frontier Cattle Towns of Kansas," *Kansas History*, Spring 1979, 45.

5. Rod Cook, *George and Maggie and the Red Light Saloon: Depravation, Debauchery, Violence and Sundry Cussedness in a Kansas Cowtown* (Lincoln, NE: iUniverse, Inc., 2003), 2.

6. Leonard and Wallimann, "Prostitution and Changing Morality," 45; Jessica K. Smith, "Morality and Money: A Look at How the Respectable Community Battled the Sporting Community Over Prostitution in Kansas Cowtowns, 1867–1885," Kansas State University, 2013, 46, 56; Jan MacKell, *Brothels, Bordellos & Bad Girls: Prostitution in Colorado 1860–1930* (Albuquerque, NM: University of New Mexico Press, 2007), 27.

7. Leonard and Wallimann, "Prostitution and Changing Morality," 38.

8. "Reign of the Rough-Scuff: Law and Lucre in Wichita," HistoryNet, https://www.historynet.com/reign-of-the-rough-scuff-law-and-lucre-in-wichita.htm, accessed September 2, 2021.

9. *Wichita Daily Eagle*, September 20, 1900, 6.

10. *Wichita Daily Eagle*, September 20, 1900, 5.

11. *Wichita Eagle*, May 7, 1907, 6.

12. *Wichita Beacon*, March 28, 1902, 5.

13. *Wichita Eagle*, March 17, 1923, 5.

CHAPTER 3

1. *Junction City Weekly Union*, July 3, 1869, 3.

2. John B. Jeffries, "An Early History of Junction City, Kansas: The First Generation" (Master's Thesis, Oklahoma State University, 1963), 113, https://krex.k-state.edu/dspace/bitstream/handle/2097/25740/LD2668T41963J44.pdf?sequence=1, accessed September 21, 2021; *Junction City Weekly Union*, December 18, 1869, 3.

3. *Junction City Weekly Union*, December 18, 1869, 3.

4. *Junction City Weekly Union*, August 17, 1872, 1:2; for Tom Allen's nickname, see *Leavenworth Times*, April 26, 1885, 5.

5. *Junction City Weekly Union*, August 24, 1972, 1.

6. George W. Martin, ed., *Transactions of the Kansas State Historical Society, 1905–1906*, vol. 9 (Topeka, KS: State Printing Office, 1906), 536–38.

7. *Junction City Weekly Union*, February 26, 1870, 2 and 3.

8. *Junction City Weekly Union*, March 16, 1872, 2.

9. Jeffries, "An Early History of Junction City, Kansas," 115.

10. *Junction City Weekly Union*, July 15, 1876, 3.

11. *Junction City Weekly Union*, September 17, 1881, 5.

12. Martin, *Transactions of the Kansas State Historical Society*, 538.

13. Martin, *Transactions of the Kansas State Historical Society*, 538; *Leavenworth Times*, April 26, 1885, 5.

14. *Junction City Daily Union*, March 30, 1887, 4.

15. United States Department of the Interior National Park Service National Register of Historic Places Registration Form for Junction City Downtown Historic District, 2006, https://npgallery.nps.gov/GetAsset/bcd1b2d0-bde1-43c0-a608-aa1c06150b17, accessed September 21, 2021.

16. United States Department of the Interior, National Park Service, National Register of Historic Places Registration Form for Junction City Downtown Historic District, 2006.

CHAPTER 4

1. Rod Cook, *George and Maggie and the Red Light Saloon: Depravation, Debauchery, Violence and Sundry Cussedness in a Kansas Cowtown* (Lincoln, NE: iUniverse, Inc., 2003), xi.

2. Harry Sinclair Drago, *Notorious Ladies of the Frontier* (New York: Ballantine Books, 1969), 112.

3. Charles F. Colcord, *The Autobiography of Charles Francis Colcord* (Tulsa, OK: C. C. Helmerich, 1970), 46–47.

4. *Wichita Herald*, May 24, 1879, 8.

5. Cook, *George and Maggie*, 6, 15–17.

6. *Caldwell Advance*, May 20, 1880, 3.

7. Cook, *George and Maggie*, 19–20.

8. Cook, *George and Maggie*, 22–23, 35.

9. Jay Moynahan, *Culinary Delights from the Red Lights: Recipes from the Bordellos and Backstreets of the Frontier West* (Spokane, WA: Chickadee Publishing, 1999), n.p.

10. Cook, *George and Maggie*, 25.

11. *Caldwell Commercial*, July 29, 1880, 2.

12. Cook, *George and Maggie*, 33–35.

13. Cook, *George and Maggie*, 64–65, 69.

14. Cook, *George and Maggie*, 70–71.

15. Carol Leonard and Isidor Wallimann, "Prostitution and Changing Morality in the Frontier Cattle Towns of Kansas," *Kansas History*, Spring 1979, 40–41.

16. Cook, *George and Maggie*, 41–44.

17. Cook, *George and Maggie*, 45–49.

18. *Wichita City Eagle*, August 25, 1881, 3.

19. Cook, *George and Maggie*, 49.

20. *Wichita City Eagle*, December 1, 1881, 3.

21. Cook, *George and Maggie*, 49–50; "Fred Kuhlman," Findagrave.com.

22. Cook, *George and Maggie*, 52–56, 70; "Mike Meagher," Cowley County Historical Society Museum, www.cchsm.com/resources/misc/wortman_cc/meagher_mike.html, accessed September 5, 2021.

23. Cook, *George and Maggie*, 56, 65.

24. *Jamestown Weekly Alert* (North Dakota), June 23, 1882, 1.

25. Cook, *George and Maggie*, 65–66.

26. Moynahan, *Culinary Delights from the Red Lights*, n.p.

27. *Wichita Eagle*, December 19, 1884, 1.

28. *Colorado City Iris*, July 13, 1892, 1.

29. *Aspen Daily Leader*, July 13, 1892, 2.

30. *Colorado City Iris*, November 30, 1895, 4.

31. "May Margaret Cavanaugh," Findagrave.com; "Colorado Springs Burial Records for Evergreen Cemetery," Pikes Peak Library Special Collections, Colorado Springs, Colorado.

Chapter 5

1. *Dodge City Times*, July 21, 1877, 4:4.

2. Carol Leonard and Isidor Wallimann, "Prostitution and Changing Morality in the Frontier Cattle Towns of Kansas," *Kansas History*, Spring 1979, 40.

3. Kelley of Beatty and Kelley was James H. "Dog" Kelley, who had come to Fort Dodge as a soldier back in 1872. Following his discharge from the army he settled in Dodge City proper, and would be elected Mayor of Dodge around the same time Fanny was attacked. "James 'Dog' Kelley," *Dodge City Daily Globe*, March 22, 2016, https://www.dodgeglobe.com/article/20160322/NEWS/160329973, accessed December 29, 2020; "James H. Kelley," Military Wikia, military.wikia.org/wiki/James_H._Kelley, accessed September 5, 2021.

4. Jessica K. Smith, "Morality and Money: A Look at How the Respectable Community Battled the Sporting Community Over Prostitution in Kansas Cowtowns, 1867–1885," Kansas State University, 2013, 55.

5. Smith, "Morality and Money," 64.

6. Robert Dykstra, *The Cattle Towns: A Social History of the Kansas Cattle Trading Centers Abilene, Ellsworth, Wichita, Dodge City and Caldwell, 1867–1885* (New York: Atheneum, 1970), 105.

7. Dykstra, *The Cattle Towns*, 265; "James 'Dog' Kelley," *Dodge City Daily Globe*, March 22, 2016, https://www.dodgeglobe.com/article/20160322/NEWS/160329973, accessed December 29, 2020.

8. Leonard and Wallimann, "Prostitution and Changing Morality," 40, 46.

9. Smith, "Morality and Money," 50.

10. Jan MacKell Collins, "Did She or Didn't She? Deadwood's Dora DuFran is Credited with Coining the Word 'Cathouse,'" *True West* magazine, May 27, 2019, https://truewestmagazine.com/dora-dufran/, accessed September 6, 2021.

11. Leonard and Wallimann, "Prostitution and Changing Morality," 38.

12. Leonard and Wallimann, "Prostitution and Changing Morality," 39–40.

13. *Dodge City Globe*, July 30, 1878, 3:3; James C. Malin, "Dodge City Varieties: A Summer Interlude of Entertainment, 1878," *Kansas Historical Quarterly*, Summer 1956, Kansas Historical Society, kshs.or/p/dodge-city-varieties/13130, accessed September 5, 2021.

14. *Topeka State Journal*, October 7, 1878, 4:3.

15. Susan L. Silva and Lee A. Silva, "The Killing of Dora Hand," HistoryNet, https://www.historynet.com/the-killing-of-dora-hand.htm, accessed September 5, 2021.

16. *Dodge City Times*, October 5, 1878, 2:2 and October 12, 1878, 2:2.

17. Dykstra, *The Cattle Towns*, 105–6.

18. Leonard and Wallimann, "Prostitution and Changing Morality," 37, 47.

19. Dykstra, *The Cattle Towns*, 280, 282.

CHAPTER 6

1. E. C. (Ted) Meyers, *Mattie: Wyatt Earp's Secret Second Wife* (Blaine, WA: Hancock House Publishers, 2010), 27.

2. Meyers, *Mattie*, 44.

3. Sherry Monahan, *Mrs. Earp: The Wives and Lovers of the Earp Brothers* (Lanham, MD: TwoDot, A division of Rowman & Littlefield Publishing Group, 2013), 13.

4. Tom Correa, "Wyatt Earp—The Peoria Bummer," *The American Cowboy Chronicles*, August 11, 2016, http://www.americancowboychronicles.com/2016/08/wyatt-earp-peoria-bummer.html, accessed May 15, 2021.

5. Roger Jay, "Wyatt Earp's Lost Year," HistoryNet, https://www.historynet.com/wyatt-earps-lost-year.htm, accessed May 2, 2021.

6. Meyers, *Mattie*, 84, 218–19.

7. Meyers, *Mattie*, 100.

8. Rod Cook, *George and Maggie and the Red Light Saloon: Depravation, Debauchery, Violence and Sundry Cussedness in a Kansas Cowtown* (Lincoln, NE: iUniverse, Inc., 2003), 2.

9. Meyers, *Mattie*, 102–8.

10. Meyers, *Mattie*, 102–8.

11. Chris Enss, *According to Kate: The Legendary Life of Big Nose Kate, Love of Doc Holliday* (Lanham, MD: TwoDot, A division of Rowman & Littlefield Publishing Group, 2019), 23; Meyers, *Mattie*, 100–101.

12. Jan MacKell, *Red Light Women of the Rocky Mountains* (Albuquerque: University of New Mexico Press, 2009), 67.

13. *Atchison Daily Champion*, November 8, 1876, 2:4.

14. *Dodge City Times*, July 7, 1877, 4:2.

15. *Dodge City Globe*, May 14, 1878, 3:3.

16. Monahan, *Mrs. Earp*, 16.

17. Casey Tefertiller, *Wyatt Earp: The Life Behind the Legend* (New York: John Wiley & Sons, 1997), 32.

18. *Dodge City Globe*, September 9, 1879, 3:1.

19. Gary L. Roberts, "Allie's Story: Mrs. Virgil Earp and the 'Tombstone Travesty,'" https://web.archive.org/web/20160307033040/http://home.earthlink.net/~knuthco1/Travesty/AlliesStory1source.htm, accessed September 6, 2021.

20. Chris Enss, *According to Kate: The Legendary Life of Big Nose Kate, Love of Doc Holliday* (Lanham, MD: TwoDot, A division of Rowman & Littlefield Publishing Group, 2019), 71–73.

21. Roberts, "Allie's Story."

22. Ann Kirschner, *Lady at the O.K. Corral: The True Story of Josephine Marcus Earp* (New York: HarperCollins, 2013), 41.

23. Jan MacKell Collins, *Good Time Girls of Arizona and New Mexico: A Red-Light History of the American Southwest* (Lanham, MD: TwoDot, A division of Rowman & Littlefield Publishing Group, 2019, 24.

24. Collins, *Good Time Girls of Arizona and New Mexico*, 23–24.

25. Meyers, *Mattie*, 183–84, 201.

CHAPTER 7

1. Ethan Anderson, "Femme Fatales of the Frontier," *Kansas Memory Blog*, https://www.kansasmemory.org/blog/post/358280567, accessed September 25, 2021.

2. Anderson, "Femme Fatales of the Frontier"; Jay Moynahan, *Forty Fallen Women: Western Doves and Madams, 1885–1920* (Spokane, WA: Chickadee Publishing, 2008), 17.

3. "William 'Billy' Thompson," Findagrave.com.

4. *American Statesman* (Austin, TX), October 28, 1876, 3.

5. *Dodge City Times*, July 17, 1880, 5.

6. *Brenham Weekly Banner*, March 23, 1882, 1.

7. *San Antonio Light* (San Antonio, TX), March 15, 1884, 3.

8. Robertson Family Tree, Ancestry.com; "Mary Elizabeth 'Libby, Squirrel Tooth Alice' Haley Thompson," Findagrave.com.

9. "Mary Elizabeth 'Libby' Haley," Robertson Family Tree, Ancestry.com.

10. *Los Angeles Mirror*, April 14, 1953, 27.

CHAPTER 8

1. Gary Wiles and Delores Brown, *Femme Fatales, Gamblers, Yankees and Rebels in the Goldfields* (Hemet, CA: Birth of America Books, 2005), 68–70.

2. A. F. Buechler and R. J. Barr, eds., *History of Hall County, Nebraska* (Lincoln, NE: Western Publishing and Engraving Company, 1920), 94.

3. Anne P. Diffendal, "Prostitution in Grand Island, Nebraska, 1870–1913," 1–6, *Diffendal* 16, no. 3, https://esirc.emporia.edu/bitstream/handle/123456789/767/Diffendal%20Vol%2016%20Num%203.pdf?sequence=1, accessed July 1, 2021.

4. Diffendal, "Prostitution in Grand Island," 1–6.

5. *Grand Island Evening Times*, June 29, 1894, 3; June 30, 1894, 4; and July 3, 1894, 3.

6. *Grand Island Daily Independent*, July 4, 1894, 3.

7. *Grand Island Evening Times*, July 4, 1894, 3.

8. *Omaha Daily Bee*, July 3, 1900, 7.

9. Diffendal, "Prostitution in Grand Island," 1–6.

10. "Secretary of State Archival Record RG002," Nebraska, 76, https://history .nebraska.gov/sites/history.nebraska.gov/files/doc/Secretary%20of%20State%2C%20 Nebraska%20%5BRG0002%5D.pdf, accessed September 10, 2021.

11. *Red Cloud Chief*, February 17, 1888, 1.

12. *Columbus Journal*, May 9, 1888, 3.

13. Lillian Linder, "Nebraska Place-Names" (Lincoln, NE: *University of Nebraska Studies in Language, Literature and Criticism*, no. 6, 1925), 48.

14. J. R. Johnson, "Covington, Nebraska's Sinful City," *Nebraska History* magazine, vol. 49, 1968, 269.

15. *Stanton Register* (Nebraska), May 27, 1886, 3.

16. Johnson, "Covington, Nebraska's Sinful City," 269.

17. *Custer County Republican* (Broken Bow, NE), May 26, 1886, 1:5.

18. Johnson, "Covington, Nebraska's Sinful City," 271, 274, 277.

19. Johnson, "Covington, Nebraska's Sinful City," 280–81.

20. Betty Loudon, "Pioneer Pharmacist J. Walter Moyer's Notes on Crawford and Fort Robinson in the 1890s," *Nebraska History* magazine, no. 58, 1977, 99–100.

21. Wayne C. Lee, *Wild Towns of Nebraska* (Caldwell, ID: The Caxton Press, 2008), 82–87.

22. "Otoe County, Nebraska Records, 1855–1994," 163, *History Nebraska*, https://history .nebraska.gov/sites/history.nebraska.gov/files/doc/Otoe%20County%20%5BRG210%5 D.pdf, accessed September 12, 2021.

23. *Valentine Democrat*, August 6, 1896, 2:6.

24. Sioux City *Dakota County Record*, January 13, 1900, 4:1.

25. "Richardson County, Nebraska Archives Records, 1855–1979," 496, 498, https:// history.nebraska.gov/sites/history.nebraska.gov/files/doc/Richardson%20County%20 %5BRG245%5D.pdf, accessed September 13, 2021.

26. *Cobbey's Annotated Statutes of Nebraska*, vol. 2 (Beatrice, NE: J. E. Cobbey, 1907 edition), 3329.

27. Peter C. Hennigan, "Property War: Prostitution, Red-Light Districts, and the Transformation of Public Nuisance Law in the Progressive Era," *Yale Journal of Law & the Humanities* 16, no. 1, article 5 (January 2004): 44–45, 168.

28. "US Public Health Service" pamphlet (Washington DC: Government Printing Office, 1921), 13.

29. Louise E, Rickard, "The Politics of Reform in Omaha, 1918–1921," *Nebraska History*, no. 53, 1972, 434, https://history.nebraska.gov/sites/history.nebraska.gov/files/doc/ publications/NH1972ReformOmaha.pdf, accessed October 13, 2021.

CHAPTER 9

1. *Rocky Mountain News*, November 11, 1869, 4.

2. *Rocky Mountain News*, November 30, 1873, 4.

3. *Cheyenne Daily Leader*, October 5, 1876, 2.

4. *Black Hills Weekly Times*, January 27, 1878, 2.

5. *Black Hills Daily Times,* June 13, 1879, 1.

6. Tenth Census of the United States, 1880 (NARA microfilm publication T9, 1,454 rolls). Records of the Bureau of the Census, Record Group 29. National Archives, Washington, DC.

7. *Cheyenne Daily Leader,* February 3, 1882, 5.

8. *Cheyenne Daily Leader,* June 6, 1882, 1.

9. Brian G. Shellum, *Black Officer in a Buffalo Soldier Regiment: The Military Career of Charles Young* (London and Lincoln, NE: University of Nebraska Press, 2010), n.p., https://epdf.pub/black-officer-in-a-buffalo-soldier-regiment-the-military-career-of -charles-young.html, accessed September 12, 2021.

10. Sioux City is in Iowa. South Sioux City is across the Missouri River in Nebraska. The writer in Gothenberg, some 264 miles from Crawford, likely confused Octavia's place with the notorious demimonde of Covington near both locales, or perhaps Crawford, Iowa. The town of Crawford in Iowa is located some eighty miles from Sioux City, but there could be a chance the writer was talking of a second hog ranch Octavia Reeves owned there. *Gothenburg Independent* (Nebraska), January 30, 1886, 2.

11. *Falls City Daily News* (Nebraska), July 1, 1886, 6.

CHAPTER 10

1. "'Queen of the Underworld' Anna Wilson," https://www.scribd.com/document/ 13273842/Queen-of-the-Underworld-Anna-Wilson, accessed January 6, 2022.

2. Lindsey Peterson, "Trolley Takes Omahans on 'Gritty City' Stroll," KVNO News, August 9, 2011, https://www.olliethetrolley.com/trolley-takes-omahans-on-gritty-city -stroll, accessed January 7, 2022.

3. Susanne George Bloomfield, ed., *Impertinences: Selected Writings of Elia Peattie, a Journalist in the Gilded Age* (Lincoln, NE, and London: University of Nebraska Press, 2005), 272.

4. Richard Erdoes, *Saloons of the Old West* (Avenel, NJ: Gramercy Books, a division of Random House Value Publishing, 1979), 196.

5. Therese Oneill, *Unmentionable: The Victorian Lady's Guide to Sex, Marriage, and Manners* (New York, Boston, and London: Little, Brown and Company, 2016), 10–15.

6. "Census Taker's Lament," History Nebraska, https://history.nebraska.gov/publica tions/census-takers-lament, accessed September 13, 2021.

7. Lawrence Harold Larsen, *The Gate City: A History of Omaha* (Lincoln, NE: University of Nebraska Press, 1997), 113.

8. Bloomfield, *Impertinences,* 73, 75.

9. Bloomfield, *Impertinences,* 78.

10. Bloomfield, *Impertinences,* 79, 272n6.

11. Paul Emory Putz, "From the Pulpit to the Press: Frank Crane's Omaha, 1892–1896," *Nebraska History,* no. 96, 2015, 142–44, 147; "Omaha Mayors, from the Beginning to Now," *Omaha World Herald,* September 30, 2019, https://omaha.com/ omaha-mayors-from-the-beginning-to-now/collection_cda2ad65-6d45-5dd6-ad33 -89742001fb01.html#1, accessed September 22, 2021.

12. Leah M. Thomas, "Ada Everleigh (1864–1960)," *Dictionary of Virginia Biography*, Library of Virginia (1998–), 2015, http://www.lva.virginia.gov/public/dvb/bio.asp?b=Everleigh_Ada, accessed September 22, 2021; Terry Beigie, "The Scarlet Sisters: The Story of the Infamous Everleigh Sisters," *Greene County Record* (Virginia), November 5, 2020, https://dailyprogress.com/community/greenenews/lifestyles/the-scarlet-sisters-the-story-of-the-infamous-everleigh-sisters/article_f9d1a664-1f68-11eb-9082-87a834001c8e.html, accessed September 22, 2021; Nina Renata Aron, "Meet the Sisters Who Ran 'the Most Famous and Luxurious House of Prostitution in the Country,'" *Timeline*, April 16, 2017, https://timeline.com/meet-the-sisters-who-ran-the-most-famous-and-luxurious-house-of-prostitution-in-the-country-b2fc0a0d414c, accessed July 1, 2021; Erica Gunderson, "Historical Happy Hour: A Toast to the Everleigh Sisters," WTTW, July 28, 2017, https://news.wttw.com/2017/07/28/historical-happy-hour-toast-everleigh-sisters, accessed July 1, 2021.

13. Cordell, *Oklahoma Herald-Sentinel*, June 2, 1894, 8.

14. *Chicago Chronicle*, April 5, 1896, 1.

15. *Chicago Inter Ocean*, July 21, 1898, 10.

16. Savannah, Georgia, *Morning News*, October 16, 1898, 1.

17. *Omaha Daily Bee*, April 29 1902, 10.

18. "Wicked Omaha," *Omaha Magazine*, April 27, 2017, https://www.omahamagazine.com/2017/04/27/302603/wicked-omaha, accessed May 1, 2021.

19. "C. A. Sorensen and the Downfall of Omaha Crime Boss Tom Dennison," History Nebraska, https://history.nebraska.gov/blog/c-sorensen-and-downfall-omaha-crime-boss-tom-dennison, accessed September 23, 2021; John Kyle Davis, "The Gray Wolf: Tom Dennison of Omaha," *Nebraska History*, Spring 1977, 25–52, https://www.nebraskahistory.org/publish/publicat/history/full-text/1977-1-Tom_Dennison.pdf, accessed September 23, 2021.

20. Josie Washburn and Sharon E. Wood, *The Underworld Sewer: A Prostitute Reflects on Life in the Trade, 1871-1909* (Lincoln and London: University of Nebraska Press, 1997), 45–48.

21. "Dennison's Political Machine," Nebraskastudies.org, https://www.nebraskastudies.org/en/1900-1924/racial-tensions/dennisons-political-machine/, accessed September 23, 2021.

22. Karen Strike, "The Indomitable Goldie Williams: The Life And Times of a Defiant Prostitute (1898)," *Flashbak*, October 8, 2019, flashbak.com/the-indomitable-goldie-williams-the-life-and-times-of-a-defiant-prostitute-1898-419879/.

23. Sheritha Jones, "Back in the Day, February 14, 1934: Notorious Omaha Political Crime Boss Tom Dennison Dies," *Omaha World Herald*, February 14, 2021, https://omaha.com/news/local/history/back-in-the-day-feb-14-1934-notorious-omaha-political-crime-boss-tom-dennison-dies/article_f0ca2d82-64c5-11eb-bbd7-ab9361a65853.html, accessed December 26, 2021.

CHAPTER 11

1. "'Queen of the Underworld' Anna Wilson," https://www.scribd.com/document/13273842/Queen-of-the-Underworld-Anna-Wilson, accessed January 6, 2022.

2. *Omaha Daily Bee*, November 5, 1911, 8.

3. For Dora Topham, see Jan MacKell Collins, *Good Time Girls of Nevada and Utah: A Red-Light History of the American West* (Lanham, MD: Globe Pequot, 2022), 175.

4. "'Queen of the Underworld' Anna Wilson," https://www.scribd.com/document/13273842/Queen-of-the-Underworld-Anna-Wilson, accessed January 6, 2022.

5. *US Federal Population Census, 1880* (NARA microfilm publication Series T9), Records of the Bureau of the Census, Record Group 29. National Archives, Washington, DC.

6. *Omaha Daily Bee*, May 24, 1891, 6, and June 10, 1891, 2.

7. *Omaha Daily Bee*, July 26, 1901, 9.

8. *Omaha Daily Bee*, April 14, 1909, 5.

9. "Anna Wilson," Findagrave.com.

10. *Omaha Daily Bee*, August 3, 1911, 9.

11. *Omaha Daily Bee*, October 29, 1911, 8.

12. "Anna Wilson," Findagrave.com.

13. "'Queen of the Underworld' Anna Wilson."

14. Adam Fletcher Sasse, "A History of Anna Wilson's Mansion in North Omaha," North Omaha History, https://northomahahistory.com/2016/10/06/north-omaha-mansion-13-anna-wilsons-home/, accessed September 24, 2021.

CHAPTER 12

1. "Annie Cook's Poor House," *Seeks Ghosts*, March 25, 2016, https://seeksghosts.blogspot.com/2016/03/annie-cooks-poor-house.html, accessed September 25, 2021.

2. "Annie Cook's Poor House."

3. *North Platte Semi-Weekly Tribune*, August 4, 1911, 1.

4. Nellie Snyder Yost, "Evil Obsession, the Annie Cook Cemetery Tour" brochure, North Platte Library Association, vol. 12, September 2018, 2, https://www.npplfoundation.org/wp-content/uploads/2019/04/ct-2018-life-and-times-of-annie-cook.pdf, accessed September 25, 2021.

5. Walt Sehnert, "Annie Cook and Her Evil Obsession," *McCook Gazette*, April 27, 2009, https://www.mccookgazette.com/story/1534218.html, accessed September 25, 2021.

6. *Hershey Times*, February 7, 1924, 6.

7. *North Platte Daily Telegraph*, March 20, 1924, 1.

8. *North Platte Daily Telegraph*, 4.

9. Yost, "Evil Obsession," 2.

10. *Lincoln County Tribune*, May 27, 1932, 2; *North Platte Daily Transcript*, January 9, 1934, 4.

11. *North Platte Daily Bulletin*, January 30, 1934, 4.

12. Sehnert, "Annie Cook and Her Evil Obsession."

13. *North Platte Daily Telegraph*, May 29, 1934, 1.

14. "Anna Maria 'Annie' Petzke Cook," Findagrave.com.

15. "Elizabeth Louise 'Lizzie' Petske Knox," Findagrave.com.

16. Robert Mitchell, "Cannes: 'Top Gun' Star Kelly McGillis to Play Midwest Crime Queen in 'Annie Cook,'" *Variety*, May 12, 2017, https://variety.com/2017/film/global/cannes-top-gun-kelly-mcgillis-crime-queen-annie-cook-1202424633/, accessed September 25, 2021; "Annie Cook," Imdb.com.

CHAPTER 13

1. Ruby Coleman, *The Wild Years 1868–1951: North Platte and Lincoln County, Nebraska* (North Platte, NE: Ruby Coleman, 2020), 29.

2. "North Platte Commercial Historic District," United States Department of the Interior, National Park Service, National Register of Historic Places Registration Form, https://static1.squarespace.com/static/58b2397a2e69cf75a40cc057/t/5f3ef7639e22f56c0a96d08d/1597962124988/NorthPlatteCommercialHistoricDistrict.pdf, accessed June 10, 2014.

3. Locust Street was later renamed Jeffers Street. Ruby Coleman, *The Wild Years 1868–1951: North Platte and Lincoln County, Nebraska* (North Platte, NE: Ruby Coleman, 2020), 33–34, 37.

4. *North Platte Semi-Weekly Tribune*, December 11, 1912, 4.

5. Coleman, *The Wild Years*, 29–30.

6. *North Platte Semi-Weekly Tribune*, November 21, 1911, 8.

7. *North Platte Telegraph*, January 18, 1912, 3.

8. *North Platte Semi-Weekly Tribune*, March 1, 1912, 5.

9. *O'Neill Frontier*, June 4, 1914, 6.

10. *North Platte Semi-Weekly Tribune*, April 7, 1914, 5.

11. *North Platte Semi-Weekly Tribune*, February 11, 1915, 1.

12. *North Platte Semi-Weekly Tribune*, February 16, 1915, 4, and February 23, 1915, 4.

13. *North Platte Semi-Weekly Tribune*, February 26, 1915, 10.

14. For reference see Jan MacKell Collins, *Good Time Girls of Colorado: A Red-Light History of the Centennial State* (Lanham, MD: Rowman & Littlefield Publishing Group, 2019), 43–44.

15. *North Platte Telegraph-Bulletin*, February 4, 1957, 14.

16. Coleman, *The Wild Years*, 30–32.

17. *North Platte Daily Telegraph*, May 27, 1930, 1.

18. *North Platte Daily Bulletin*, September 10, 1941, 7.

CHAPTER 14

1. Josie Washburn and Sharon E. Wood, *The Underworld Sewer: A Prostitute Reflects on Life in the Trade, 1871–1909* (Lincoln and London: University of Nebraska Press, 1997), vii.

2. Washburn and Wood, *The Underworld Sewer*, 27–28.

3. Washburn and Wood, *The Underworld Sewer*, viii–ix, 28–31.

4. *Lincoln Evening Call*, July 2, 1896, 4.

5. *Lincoln Nebraska State Journal* (Lincoln), August 26, 1900, 7.

6. Washburn and Wood, *The Underworld Sewer*, 31–33.

7. Washburn and Wood, *The Underworld Sewer*, 33–35.

8. Washburn and Wood, *The Underworld Sewer*, 35–36.

9. Washburn and Wood, *The Underworld Sewer*, 5.

10. *Omaha Daily Bee*, June 15, 1890, 4.

11. *Lincoln Evening News*, January 12, 1893, 4.

12. Probate record for Mary Elizabeth Wallace, *Nebraska, Wills and Probate Records, 1806–1989*, Ancestry.com; *Lincoln Evening News*, August 10, 1893, 8, and March 11, 1895, 8.

13. Mollie's Hall may have actually been the name of Madam Molly Hall's place. See A. J. Sawyer, ed., *Lincoln the Capital City and Lancaster County: The Incarceration of the Lincoln City Council* (Chicago: The S. J. Clarke Publishing Co., 1916), 274–93.

14. *Nebraska State Journal* (Lincoln), January 11, 1885, 1.

15. Sawyer, *Lincoln the Capital City and Lancaster County*, 274–93.

16. *McCook Tribune*, October 31, 1890, 10.

17. *Lincoln Star Journal*, October 16, 1900, 1.

18. "Rose Kirkwood Brothel," United States Department of the Interior, National Park Service, National Register of Historic Places Registration Form; "Kirkwood Brothel," City of Lincoln, Nebraska Planning Department, https://app.lincoln.ne.gov/city/plan/long/hp/sites/sitestemplate.htm?site=kirkwood, accessed September 29, 2021.

Chapter 15

1. John W. Morris, *Ghost Towns of Oklahoma* (Norman, OK: University of Oklahoma Press, 1978), 3.

2. Morris, *Ghost Towns of Oklahoma*, 25.

3. "The Santa Fe Trail in Oklahoma," *Legends of America*, https://www.legendsofamerica.com/ok-santafetrail/, accessed October 1, 2021.

4. "Important Oklahoma Land Rush Archive—Prostitutes Saved Dad's Life Opening Day," Worthpoint, https://www.worthpoint.com/worthopedia/important-oklahoma-land-rush-archive-18505186, accessed October 5, 2021.

5. *Kingfisher Free Press*, January 26, 1893, 5.

6. *Guthrie Daily Leader*, August 22, 1893, 2; *Purcell Register*, October 27, 1893, 5; *Enid Daily Enterprise*, November 25, 1893, 1.

7. *Muskogee Phoenix*, January 18, 1894, 5.

8. *Ardmore Chickasaw Chieftain*, July 18, 1895, 3.

9. *Oklahoma State* newspaper (Oklahoma City), March 15, 1894, 8.

10. *Perry Evening Democrat*, March 3, 1894, 3.

11. *Muskogee Phoenix*, March 27, 1895, 3.

12. *Daily Ardmoreite*, April 29, 1896, 1; *Tahlequah Telephone*, April 26, 1895, 2.

13. Sue Woolf Brenner, "Dead Woman's Crossing," *Chronicles of Oklahoma* 60, no. 3 (Fall 1982): 280–91.

14. *Daily Ardmoreite*, February 27, 1910, 3.

15. Thirteenth Census of the United States, 1910 (NARA microfilm publication T624, 1,178 rolls), Records of the Bureau of the Census, Record Group 29, National Archives, Washington, DC.

16. Morris, *Ghost Towns of Oklahoma*, 197.
17. Morris, *Ghost Towns of Oklahoma*, 59–60, 64–65.
18. "Roxana," Exploring Oklahoma History, http://blogoklahoma.us/place.aspx?id=266, accessed October 5, 2021.

Chapter 16
1. *Daily Ardmoreite*, January 2, 1894, 3.
2. Marilyn A. Hudson, "A Sad Tale," *Mystorical*, July 6, 2016, http://mystorical.blogspot.com/2016/07/a-sad-tale.html, accessed October 2, 2021.
3. *Ardmore Chickasaw Chieftain*, August 30, 1894, 3.
4. Maxine Bamburg, "Ardmore," Oklahoma Historical Society, https://www.okhistory.org/publications/enc/entry.php?entry=AR008, accessed October 2, 2021; *Ardmore Chickasaw Chieftain*, July 11, 1895, 3.
5. *Daily Ardmoreite*, June 19, 1899, 3.
6. *Daily Ardmoreite*, November 14, 1899, 3.
7. *Daily Ardmoreite*, October 23, 1902, 2.
8. "National Register Nominations by Property Type Dwellings," Oklahoma Historical Society, https://www.okhistory.org/shpo/docs/swokenergy1900-1930pt2.pdf, accessed October 2, 2021.

Chapter 17
1. Denel Campbell, "Gambling and Prostitution," https://denelecampbell.com/2017/11/01/gambling-and-prostitution/, accessed October 2, 2021.
2. *Oklahoma State Capital*, March 15, 1890, 7.
3. Tanya McCoy and Jeff Provine, *Haunted Guthrie, Oklahoma* (Charleston, SC: The History Press, 2015), 56–57.
4. *Oklahoma State Capital*, March 15, 1890, 7.
5. *Oklahoma State Capital*, July 5, 1890, 9.
6. *Oklahoma State Capital*, October 25, 1890, 5.
7. *Guthrie Daily Leader*, July 28, 1897, 4.
8. *Guthrie Daily Leader*, September 16, 1893, 1, and May 27, 1894, 4; *Guthrie Daily News*, October 17, 1893, 1, and May 4, 1894, 1.
9. *Oklahoma State Capital*, August 5, 1897, 4.
10. "The Blue Bell Saloon," The Historical Marker Database, https://www.hmdb.org/m.asp?m=141776, accessed October 6, 2021.
11. Wander Wisdom, https://wanderwisdom.com/travel-destinations/Oklahomas-Most-Haunted-City-Ghost-Stories-from-Guthrie, accessed October 8, 2021.
12. McCoy and Provine, *Haunted Guthrie, Oklahoma*, 51–55.

Chapter 18
1. Pendleton Woods, *Historic Oklahoma County: An Illustrated History* (San Antonio, TX: Historical Publishing Network, 2007), 15; "Hell's Half Acre," Historical Marker Database, https://www.hmdb.org/m.asp?m=141984, accessed October 4, 2021.

2. Albert Mcrill, "And Satan Came Also," December 11, 2013, *This Land Press*, https://thislandpress.com/2013/12/11/and-satan-came-also/, accessed October 1, 2021.

3. "Hell's Half Acre," Historical Marker Database, https://www.hmdb.org/m.asp?m=141984, accessed October 4, 2021.

4. Mcrill, "And Satan Came Also."

5. *Oklahoma Daily Times Journal*, January 2, 1892, 3.

6. *Daily Oklahoman*, June 15, 1902, 5.

7. Mcrill, "And Satan Came Also."

8. Mcrill, "And Satan Came Also."

9. *Daily Oklahoman*, June 24, 1902, 6.

10. *Oklahoma City Weekly Times-Journal*, June 27, 1902, 6.

11. *Daily Oklahoman*, July 13, 1902, 1.

12. *Oklahoma City Daily Times-Journal*, October 24, 1902, 8.

13. *Weekly Times-Journal*, November 21, 1902, 3.

14. *Daily Oklahoman* (Oklahoma City), May 13, 1913, 5.

15. Oklahoma, US, Wills and Probate Records, 1801–2008, Ancestry.com.

16. *Oklahoma City Times*, May 28, 1913, 3.

17. *Daily Law Journal-Record* (Oklahoma City), July 31, 1913, 4.

18. Mcrill, "And Satan Came Also."

19. *Daily Oklahoman* (Oklahoma City), June 1, 1918, 9.

20. *Oklahoma City Times*, August 27, 1920, 52.

21. Mcrill, "And Satan Came Also."

22. David Ferris, "Big Anne Wynn and Hell's Half Acre," *Edmond Life and Leisure*, https://edmondlifeandleisure.com/big-anne-wynn-and-hells-halfacre-p12171-76.htm, accessed October 4, 2021.

23. Ferris, "Big Anne Wynn and Hell's Half Acre."

24. *Daily Oklahoman* (Oklahoma City), April 21, 1905, 5.

25. *Daily Ardmoreite*, May 8, 1917, 6.

CHAPTER 19

1. Albert Mcrill, "And Satan Came Also," December 11, 2013, *This Land Press*, https://thislandpress.com/2013/12/11/and-satan-came-also/, accessed October 1, 2021.

2. Mcrill, "And Satan Came Also." Notably, there was no "Main Street" in Leadville; the writer was likely talking about the main drag, Harrison Avenue.

3. Jan MacKell Collins, *Good Time Girls of Colorado: A Red-Light History of the Centennial State* (Lanham, MD: TwoDot, A division of Rowman & Littlefield Publishing Group, 2019), 49.

4. *Daily Oklahoman* (Oklahoma City), May 21, 1908, 2.

5. "Hell's Half Acre," Historical Marker Database, https://www.hmdb.org/m.asp?m=141984, accessed October 10, 2021.

6. Joe Wertz, "Hell's Half Acre" (courtesy of the Gazette and Tierco Media), OKC History, http://www.okchistory.com/index.php?option=com_content&view=article&id=245:hells-half-acre&catid=41:people&Itemid=78, accessed October 10, 2021.

7. *Daily Oklahoman* (Oklahoma City), May 21, 1908, 2.

8. Mcrill, "And Satan Came Also."

9. *Daily Republican* (Oklahoma City), February 15, 1896, 1.

10. *Daily Times-Journal* (Oklahoma City), April 2, 1896, 4.

11. David Farris, "Big Anne Wynn and Hell's Half-Acre," https://edmondlifeandleisure
.com/big-anne-wynn-and-hells-halfacre-p12171-76.htm, accessed October 10, 2021.

12. Marilyn A. Hudson, "Who was Annie Wynn?" *Mystorical: Where History Meets
Mystery*, 2015. http://mystorical.blogspot.com/2015/08/who-was-anne-wynn-bailey
-part-2.html, accessed October 3, 2021.

13. *Oklahoma Reports: Cases Determined in the Supreme Court of the State of Oklahoma*,
vol. 15 (Ann Arbor, MI: Harlow Publishing Company, 1906), 153.

14. *Weekly Times-Journal* (Oklahoma City), February 6, 1903, 5.

15. Farris, "Big Anne Wynn and Hell's Half-Acre."

16. *Daily Oklahoman* (Oklahoma City), September 1, 1907, 2; *Daily Oklahoman* (Oklahoma City), September 3, 1907, 19.

17. Wertz, "Hell's Half Acre."

CHAPTER 20

1. "Snippets from *Tulsa Spirit*, #4," Tulsa County Oklahoma, 100, http://www.tulsa
okhistory.com/tulsaspirit/spirit04.html, accessed October 11, 2021.

2. *Tulsa Democrat*, September 20, 1907, 2.

3. *Oklahoma Critic*, January 14, 1908, 1.

4. *Tulsa Daily Democrat*, August 8, 1913, 1.

5. I. Marc Carlson, "The Tulsa Race Massacre," *The Tulsa Race Riot of 1921* (blog),
May 28, 2014, https://tulsaraceriot.wordpress.com/tag/brothel/.

6. Carlson, "The Tulsa Race Massacre."

7. Carlson, "The Tulsa Race Massacre."

8. "1921 Tulsa Race Massacre," Tulsa Historical Society and Museum, https://www
.tulsahistory.org/exhibit/1921-tulsa-race-massacre/#flexible-content, accessed October
12, 2021.

9. *Tulsa Tribune*, April 3, 1926, 1.

10. Clara Nipper, "Sex in the City," *This Land Press*, 2011, https://thislandpress.com/
2011/10/08/sex-in-the-city/, accessed October 2, 2021.

11. "Rideshy and the May Rooms," Tulsa TV Memories, http://tulsatvmemories.com/
mayrooms.html, accessed October 13, 2021.

12. Nipper, "Sex in the City."

13. Nipper, "Sex in the City."

14. Terrell Lester, "Strictly Business: May Rooms Was Best-Run Brothel in Town,"
July 20, 1997, accessed via Tulsa TV Memories, http://tulsatvmemories.com/mayrooms
.html, October 12, 2021.

15. Debbie Jackson, "Throwback Tulsa: Madam of Longtime Tulsa Brothel Was Unre-
pentant to the End," *Tulsa World*, February 5, 2015, https://tulsaworld.com/news/local/
history/throwback-tulsa-madam-of-longtime-tulsa-brothel-was-unrepentant-to-the
-end/article_f2aa1d98-4c7e-52f1-9e0f-d30d6b0d42ee.html, accessed October 1, 2021.

16. Edwyna Synar, "Remember the Ladies: Living a Double Life," *Muskogee Phoenix News*, September 11, 2020, https://www.muskogeephoenix.com/news/remember-the -ladies-living-a-double-life/article_e04f3ded-9d3b-5376-8715-94301df171c5.html, accessed October 2, 2021.

17. *Tulsa Daily Legal News*, February 7, 1958, 6, and February 10, 1958, 6.

18. Nipper, "Sex in the City."

19. Nipper, "Sex in the City."

20. Criminal Docket, US District Court, "The United States vs. Clara Pauline Lambert Palmer," September 1969, https://oknd.uscourts.gov/sites/default/files/oknd/paper_ dockets/69cr0112.pdf, accessed October 13, 2021.

21. Nipper, "Sex in the City."

22. Nipper, "Sex in the City."

23. "Lambert v. State, Oklahoma Court of Appeals," Case Number F-79-09, 1980, Justia US Law, https://law.justia.com/cases/oklahoma/court-of-appeals-criminal/1980/ 5410.html, accessed October 2, 2021.

24. Jackson, "Throwback Tulsa."

25. Jackson, "Throwback Tulsa."

26. Nipper, "Sex in the City."

27. One source says Pauline died at St. John Medical Center in Tulsa, but another claims she died in Henryetta, and was buried in the potter's field before being moved to Tulsa's Rose Hill Cemetery. Jackson, "Throwback Tulsa"; Nipper, "Sex in the City."

28. Nipper, "Sex in the City."

29. Jackson, "Throwback Tulsa."

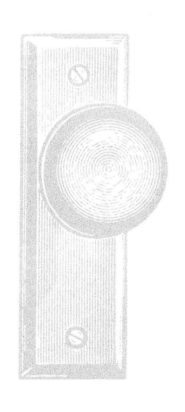

Index

About the Author

Jan MacKell Collins has been a published author, speaker, and presenter since 2003. Her focus is western history, with an emphasis on historical prostitution. Collins has published numerous articles in such magazines as *True West*, *All About History*, and several regional magazines. She currently resides in the east, where she continues researching the history of prostitution.

Ingram Content Group UK Ltd.
Milton Keynes UK
UKHW021300190423
420428UK00031B/220